Real-World SQL-DMO for SQL Server

ALLAN MITCHELL AND MARK ALLISON

apress™

Real-World SQL-DMO for SQL Server
Copyright © 2003 by Allan Mitchell and Mark Allison

ISBN (pbk): 1-59059-040-6

Printed and bound in the United States of America 12345678910

Trademarked names may appear in this book. Rather than use a trademark symbol with every occurrence of a trademarked name, we use the names only in an editorial fashion and to the benefit of the trademark owner, with no intention of infringement of the trademark.

Technical Reviewer: Ron Talmage

Editorial Directors: Dan Appleman, Gary Cornell, Jason Gilmore, Simon Hayes, Karen Watterson, John Zukowski

Managing Editor: Grace Wong

Project Manager and Development Editor: Tracy Brown Collins

Copy Editor: Nicole LeClerc

Compositor: Susan Glinert

Illustrator: Cara Brunk, Blue Mud Productions

Cover Designer: Kurt Krames

Indexer: Valerie Perry

Production Manager: Kari Brooks

Manufacturing Manager: Tom Debolski

Marketing Manager: Stephanie Rodriguez

Distributed to the book trade in the United States by Springer-Verlag New York, Inc., 175 Fifth Avenue, New York, NY, 10010 and outside the United States by Springer-Verlag GmbH & Co. KG, Tiergartenstr. 17, 69112 Heidelberg, Germany. In the United States, phone 1-800-SPRINGER, email orders@springer-ny.com, or visit http://www.springer-ny.com. Outside the United States, fax +49 6221 345229, email orders@springer.de, or visit http://www.springer.de.

For information on translations, please contact Apress directly at 2560 9th Street, Suite 219, Berkeley, CA 94710. Phone 510-549-5930, fax: 510-549-5939, email info@apress.com, or visit http://www.apress.com.

The source code for this book is available to readers at http://www.apress.com in the Downloads section.

*This book is dedicated to Tony Houghton
and Graham Potts, who showed me in those
long early days which end of a PC did what.*
—Allan Mitchell

*This book is dedicated to my wife, Inez, our children,
Lucy and Benedict, and our unborn baby boy,
due October 2002.*
—Mark Allison

Contents at a Glance

Foreword by Gert Drapers xi

Foreword by Sharon Dooley xv

About the Authors xix

About the Technical Reviewer xx

About the Foreword Writers xxi

Acknowledgments xxiii

Introduction xxv

Chapter 1   Getting Started with SQL-DMO 1

Chapter 2   Backup and Restore: A DBA's Bread and Butter 45

Chapter 3   Managing Users of Your Database and Server 99

Chapter 4   Using SQL-DMO with OLE Automation 155

Chapter 5   Jobs, Alerts, and Operators 179

Chapter 6   Viewing and Setting Server-wide Options 247

Chapter 7   Replication and SQL-DMO 281

Chapter 8   QALite 309

Chapter 9   Using SQL-DMO to Script an Entire Server 323

Appendix A   SQL-DMO Object Library Quick Reference 345

Appendix B   Knowledge-Base Articles
             and Other SQL-DMO Resources 371

Index 377

Contents

Foreword by Gert Drapers xi

Foreword by Sharon Dooley xv

About the Authors xix

About the Technical Reviewer xx

About the Foreword Writers xxi

Acknowledgments xxiii

Introduction xxv

Benefits to Programming in SQL-DMO xxv
What This Book Covers xxvi
How This Book Is Organized xxvi
What You Should Know Before Reading This Book xxvii
Additional Resources xxvii

Chapter 1   Getting Started with SQL-DMO 1

What Is SQL-DMO and Where Can I Get It? 2
Creating a Database on a Server 3
Setting Database Options 9
Creating Database Objects 19
Summary 44

Chapter 2   Backup and Restore:
            A DBA's Bread and Butter 45

Types of Backup Available 46
Sample Backup Scenarios and Methods 48
Considerations for Choosing Your Backup Method 50
Using Backup Devices 53
Performing the Backup 56
The 15-Minute Database Checker 93
Summary 97

Chapter 3   Managing Users of Your Database and Server 99

Database Terminology *100*
The Applications *114*
Summary *153*

Chapter 4   Using SQL-DMO with OLE Automation *155*

Using OLE *156*
Summary *178*

Chapter 5   Jobs, Alerts, and Operators *179*

Defining General Concepts *179*
Adding an Operator to SQL Server *181*
Viewing Your Jobs *190*
Adding a Job *214*
Creating an Alert *242*
Summary *246*

Chapter 6   Viewing and Setting Server-wide Options *247*

Viewing Server Options *248*
Extracting Enterprise Management Server Properties *249*
Creating Your Own Enterprise Manager Tabs *270*
Setting Server-wide Options *272*
Summary *280*

Chapter 7   Replication and SQL-DMO *281*

Types of Replication *281*
Installing Merge Replication Using SQL-DMO *284*
Installing Merge Replication Using Enterprise Manager *288*
Generating Replication Scripts Using SQL-DMO *306*
Scripting Replication Using SQL-DMO *308*
Summary *308*

Chapter 8   QALite

Chapter 8   QALite 309

The QALite Application 309
Summary 321

Chapter 9   Using SQL-DMO to Script an Entire Server

Chapter 9   Using SQL-DMO to Script
              an Entire Server 323

What Scripter Does 325
What Scripter Doesn't Do 326
Overview of Scripter's Structure 328
Summary 344

Appendix A SQL-DMO Object Library Quick Reference

Appendix A SQL-DMO Object Library
              Quick Reference 345

SQLServers Collection 345
Databases Collection 347
DatabaseRoles Collection 348
FileGroups Collection 349
DBFiles Collection 350
FullTextCatalogs Collection 351
StoredProcedures Collection 351
Tables Collection 352
Columns Collection 354
Users Collection 355
Views Collection 356
Triggers Collection 357
Jobs Collection 358
JobSchedules Collection 359
JobSteps Collection 360
Operators Collection 361
Logins Collection 361
Replication Object... 365
The SQL-DMO Object Model 367

Appendix B Knowledge-Base Articles and Other SQL-DMO Resources 371

Bugs 371
Fixes 373
Problems 374
Information and How-To's 374
Useful URLs 375

Index 377

Foreword

By Gert Drapers

THE WORLD OF MANAGING DATABASES has changed a lot since the first release of SQL Server in 1988. In the early days, everything was done through a command-line interface using T-SQL. Indeed, some will argue this was the era of "real DBAs." The only tool you got was ISQL, and the language was T-SQL—nothing more, nothing less.

When I received the first version of the Ashton-Tate Microsoft SQL Server PDK for OS/2 in 1988, the tools included were BCP, ISQL, and System Administrator Facility (SAF). SAF, which most of you have probably never seen or used, was basically the character-based predecessor to ISQL/w (which later became SQL Query Analyzer). In those days, managing SQL Server meant that you had to master T-SQL—and this remained true until the first release of SQL Server on Windows NT.

By that time, server development was still done by Sybase and then ported to Windows NT by a small team of people at Microsoft. One of the biggest changes we faced was replacing the Sybase threading library with Windows NT's OS threads. Later, in order to make SQL Server a first-class Windows NT citizen, Event Log, Performance Monitor, and real Windows-based "management" tools were added to the product. SQL Server 4.21a for Windows NT, released in 1994, introduced three new GUI-based management tools, SQL Administrator, SQL Object Manager, and ISQL/w, among other tools. Although it was unknown at the time, this release laid the foundation for a new style of database management (one that IBM and Oracle eventually emulated) and introduced the concept of "point and click" database administration.

The first release of SQL Server on Windows NT was quickly followed by SQL95, better known as SQL Server 6.0, which was released in June 1995. Aside from numerous engine changes, one of the big additions was an enhanced toolset that combined the SQL Administrator and SQL Object Manager functionality into one new tool named SQL Enterprise Manager. Enterprise Manager provided a user-friendly management front end to SQL Server and became the first integrated database management console in the industry.

SQL Enterprise Manager literally redefined the way we managed databases and made the world of SQL Server database management accessible to the non–T-SQL guru. That SQL Enterprise Manager successful was silently confirmed by the competition, who all copied the idea and created their own Enterprise Manager implementations, some of which even showed more than a casual resemblance to the original.

SQL Enterprise Manager, however, was nothing more then a nice shell—all internal functionality was implemented in a layer called SQL-OLE, which today we know as SQL-DMO. The idea was simple: Create an object model that exposes all database management functionality and layer a nice graphical tool on top of it.

The other reason SQL-OLE was created was to abstract our GUI developers from having to learn too much about SQL Server. Finding good GUI developers was already a challenge, but finding good GUI developers who were also experts in SQL Server database management was simply impossible, so we embraced the COM revolution and copied the idea of an application object model like those implemented by Word and Excel. SQL Server was the first Microsoft server product to expose a COM-based management object model, and it immediately became the biggest one as well (which was the part we were never that proud of).

These object models didn't start off as a management-scripting interface, but simply as a UI abstraction layer, and today you can still find traces of that origin in the SQL-OLE and SQL-DMO object models. It's no secret that collections of instantiated objects aren't the most scalable mechanism. Keeping these collections around in memory is a typical example of a client- and UI-focused optimization. Reducing the cost of repainting the UI was favored over lowering the memory footprint. (The fact that you have to Refresh() collections to make changes from other nodes visible is another example that makes this background very clear.) In SQL Server 6.0 and 6.5, this wasn't that much of a problem—script hosts were a rare sighting, and the SQL Server tools all used SQL-OLE as their intermediate layer, so all key functionality was covered and indirectly tested through the UI test automation. Scalability in general was also less of a concern because in those days the number of objects in a database wasn't overwhelming and the memory footprint per object was relatively low (a mere 90 bytes key per stored object [!], the size of a three-part name used to identify the object). Life was good; the object model was providing access to all main functionality in a consistent way and abstracting the user from having to learn T-SQL or DBCC and having to interpret the information hidden in system tables.

However, beginning in November 1996, when Sphinx (the code name for SQL Server 7.0) was moving from the development labs into production, the rules of the game immediately changed. The size of three-part name object identifiers exploded from 90 bytes to 768 bytes due to enlarged size and the switch to Unicode of the SYSNAME type. Still, Sphinx could host significantly more objects than 6.*x* would ever be able to; our SAP test database contained ~15K tables and ~42K objects in total. The introduction of new tools such as Table Designer, Open Table, View Designer, and Query Builder broke the golden rule about using one common abstraction layer, which resulted in an object model that didn't expose all functionality. On top of that, we changed the ProgID, and code that was written for SQL-OLE had to be reworked to function with SQL Server 7.0 SQL-DMO.

The end result was an admittedly slow start for SQL-DMO that was plagued by confusion, lack of direction, and performance and scalability problems. This was the status quo for SQL-DMO when my former team started working on the Shiloh project (SQL Server 2000). We gave ourselves strict boundaries:

- Backward compatibility (i.e., old code had to remain working, resulting in the introduction of the versioned interfaces that expose new functionality)

- Improved scalability

- Reduced memory overhead

And all that without breaking the existing collection model (this change was back-ported to 7.0 SP3 to help customers on the previous release). We also actively started evangelizing SQL-DMO as a management object model.

The end result isn't perfect, but within the boundaries defined, it gets the job done. There are, however, some "quirks" that you have to be aware of, which is why this book plays a crucial role in finishing my last Shiloh objective: evangelizing the use of SQL-DMO. This book shows you how to use SQL-DMO in a practical fashion by providing practical and useful working examples. Many of the questions I used to answer on the SQL Server newsgroups are explained in this book much more clearly than I did in my newsgroup postings. It provides the crucial background information to help readers make the right design decisions and touches on the most important classes of SQL-DMO. As I said in the beginning, SQL-DMO is a *huge* object model, and nobody will be able to describe every gory detail in a single book.

So what's next in database management, perhaps in the Yukon timeframe? We learned a lot from developing and using SQL-DMO and observing how customer usage evolved over time, and we'll surely be weaving features from .NET and Web Services into the next incarnations of SQL-DMO. We're also continuing to work with standards bodies to provide an open and interoperable database management model. Not all initiatives survive: In 1994, there was RFC 1697 (aka the database MIB that never gained strong adoption), and in early 2002, the Desktop Management Taskforce (DMTF) jump-started a working group to develop a CIM-based Database Management Standard. As always, the road to open standards is an important but long process, with no guarantee of adoption or success. In the meantime, SQL-DMO and this book provide the foundation for managing your SQL Server environment.

Gert E.R. Drapers
Architect, Transaction Services (former product unit manager of the SQL Server Management Tools team)
Microsoft Corporation
Redmond, Washington
August 26, 2002

Foreword

by Sharon Dooley

LIKE GERT, I BEGAN my love affair with SQL Server early on and began using it when Sybase, Microsoft, and Ashton-Tate released the first version for OS/2. In those days, the tools *were* BCP and ISQL. If you wanted to do anything that couldn't be done with pure Transact-SQL or bcp (such as develop a user interface), you wrote a C program. I was then a modest C programmer with no particular love of the language, but I also had SQL experience going back to a relational query tool written to query a CODASYL database. I also had a few years of Oracle's PL/SQL under my belt, but it wasn't long before T-SQL became the focal point of my professional life. I confess to being a complete T-SQL bigot. To this day, I resist graphical tools and firmly believe that "real DBAs write T-SQL."

If you've read this far, you're probably asking, "why on earth did they ask *her* to write a foreword?" Well, there are two reasons that I was delighted to be asked to do this:

1. I have a real awareness of the power of SQL-DMO, and

2. I have both a great fondness and a great respect for Mark Allison and Allan Mitchell.

Along with many of you, I discovered the object model when SQL Server 6.0 was released. It was clear that it was the answer to some very vexing problems, such as trying to find a facility for a client to configure various aspects of SQL Server without having to maintain T-SQL scripts or wade through Enterprise Manager. Nobody but me seemed very interested in it. I devoted an entire chapter on the Distributed Management Framework (DMF) in my book, *Professional Microsoft SQL Server 6.5 Admin*, and included a brief chapter on DMF in my SQL Server 6.0 and 6.5 Admin classes for Learning Tree International (http://www.learningtree.com). Aside from the occasional student who perked up when he or she saw this, most of them dozed. In retrospect, it probably wasn't the best chapter to teach as the grand finale, just before the students filled out their evaluations!

Apparently, most of the world shared my students' indifference to the object model. Microsoft went to significant efforts to ensure that all existing applications would run on SQL Server 7 when it was released. I think Microsoft's success in this area was phenomenal—no other company could completely replace the insides of a product and preserve existing code. But Microsoft's research showed that there was little use of this object layer, then called SQL OLE, in the real world, and it didn't bother to maintain backward compatibility in that area. The only complaints I ever heard about this was that one couldn't manage SQL Server 6.5 from the SQL Server 7 Enterprise Manager. Nobody complained that his or her existing SQL-DMO applications didn't work.

The new SQL-DMO for SQL Server 7 was much improved, but still people didn't seem interested. I could see a whole lot of value in it (though I abandoned trying to teach it to my DBA students). When I wrote my SQL 7 book, *SQL Server 7 Server Essential Reference* (still available, folks!), I showed readers how to do everything with T-SQL and Enterprise Manager. I also included—mostly in reference format, about two steps up from Books Online—brief descriptions of how to do everything with SQL-DMO, because I thought it was important. Some people let me know that they liked this, but SQL-DMO still didn't get much press.

Even after the release of SQL 2000, my occasional "Gentle Introduction to SQL-DMO" presentations at various conferences drew small, more-or-less interested crowds. My presentations on topics such as backup and recovery, in contrast, drew large, intensely interested crowds.

Among the few people I knew who were actually—and productively—using SQL-DMO were Mark Allison and Allan Mitchell. We met, as is so common these days, electronically. We were all participants on a list server run by the famous http://www.SWYNK.com. (These days, we have moved to http://www.SSSWUG.org.) I had the pleasure of meeting Mark face to face at the PASS (Professional Association for SQL Server, www.sqlpass.org) conference in London in March 2000. I finally met Allan as well when I was stranded in London after the September 11 terrorist attacks in the U.S. last year. We had all been planning to meet up at the PASS conference in Orlando, along with a lot of other folks from the SWYNK lists. There had been numerous discussions of "beer in Allan's room," and other plans being made. Of course, the world changed and the PASS conference was postponed. Feeling somewhat lost and not able to go home, I sent them a message with "no conference beer?" as the title. We got together for a delightful evening, and I finally had a face to put with Allan's name as well.

I've known about this book almost from its inception. I knew they were the right people to do this book, and I was sure it would be good. Now that I've seen it, I *know* that it's good.

What I like best about this book isn't simply that Allan and Mark tell you how to develop applications with SQL-DMO, but they also tell you what you need to think about. This book provides a comprehensive treatment of the "why" behind various administrative tasks, as well as SQL-DMO code that you can virtually use as a cookbook for your own applications.

Like Gert, I think SQL-DMO has great power. I see it being extremely useful for Web-based administrative interfaces to SQL Server. Enterprise Manager has become a reasonably capable tool (remember, I don't like GUIs), but it's still a thick client. I hope that this book will finally bring SQL-DMO to the masses, and that SQL-DMO will start getting the respect that it deserves.

Sharon Dooley
SQL Server Mentor and MVP
Philadelphia, Pennsylvania
September 1, 2002

About the Authors

ALLAN MITCHELL is currently working as a lead data architect for a multinational media company in the United Kingdom. He provides developer and user support over all the company's SQL Servers, and he designs data solutions as well. He is an MCSE and an MCDBA, and in 2002 he was awarded the title of MVP by Microsoft. His interests include mountain biking and rugby. You can find Allan on the Microsoft public newsgroups and on the SSWUG list answering questions on a variety of topics. Allan is co-founder of Allison Mitchell Database

Consultants Ltd, a successful database-consulting firm based in southeast England.

MARK ALLISON is a freelance database consultant working for various blue-chip organizations in London. Mark likes to work both as a development DBA/database architect and as a production DBA in order to keep his feet on the ground. Mark is also co-founder of Allison Mitchell Database Consultants Ltd, a successful database-consulting firm based in southeast England. Mark is a SQL Server MCP and was awarded the title of MVP by Microsoft in 2002.

About the Technical Reviewer

RON TALMAGE heads Prospice, LLC, a database-consulting firm based in Seattle. He is a SQL Server MVP, the president of the Pacific Northwest SQL Server Users Group, and the co-editor of *PASSnews*. He writes for *SQL Server Professional*, *SQL Server Magazine*, and *CoDe Magazine*. You can contact Ron at rtalmage@prospice.com.

About the Foreword Writers

GERT DRAPERS is the former product unit manager of the SQL Server Management Tools team and group manager/architect of the SQL Server Data Transformation Services (DTS) development team. Gert started working on SQL Server in 1988 while working for Ashton-Tate. He joined Microsoft in 1991, where he held various development positions within the developer relation group and Microsoft consulting services before joining the SQL Server development team in 1996.

Currently, Gert is an architect in the XML Web Services team inside the .NET developer division, responsible for transaction services. Gert is also a co-founder of http://SQLDev.Net.

SHARON DOOLEY has been working with databases since before the authors of this book (as well as many of its potential readers) were born. Her experience with SQL Server began with version 1, and she was named a Microsoft SQL Server MVP in 2001. Ms. Dooley operates a small consulting business out of her Philadelphia house with the able assistance of her three feline associates: Tigger, Patchwork, and Druid. She specializes in database design and performance tuning. Sharon is also SQL Server

Curriculum Manager for Learning Tree International, and is the author of its SQL Server 6.5 administration, SQL 7 administration, and SQL Server 2000 administration courses and, most recently, its course on developing high-performance Microsoft SQL Server databases course. She also teaches all of the courses in

Learning Tree's SQL Server curriculum. She was the lead author of *Professional Microsoft SQL Server 6.5 Database Administration* (Wrox) and the sole author of *SQL Server 7 Essential Reference* (New Riders). Sharon is a frequent presenter at SQL Server conferences and an active PASS volunteer. Ms. Dooley graduated from the University of Pennsylvania with a degree in Computer and Information Sciences, magna cum laude. In her spare time, she enjoys gardening, being bossed around by the cats, cooking for a homeless shelter, and serving as the chair of the Festivals and Seasons committee at her church.

Acknowledgments

THE GREATEST OF THANKS must go to the people that you as the readers will never see as being part of this book. The editorial team at Apress (Karen Watterson, Tracy Brown Collins, Sofia Marchant, and Nicole LeClerc) were fantastic, and their patience in reassembling my version of English into one that is used by the rest of the English-speaking world was nothing short of amazing. Technical Editor Ron Talmage was tireless in his technical critique and was always there to put us right about the finer points. I'd also like to thank Kari Brooks for managing this book through the production process. Altogether, a great team, and we hope that you the reader will see this when you read our book.

—Allan Mitchell

I would like to thank, as Allan has mentioned, the editorial and production teams at Apress. Their tireless, hard work—often seven days a week—was an inspiration to both of us. I would also like to thank Jeremy Van Dijk for his Visual Basic help. Jeremy provided many hours of help voluntarily, without any expectation of reward, via e-mail.

My wife has been unbelievably patient and supportive throughout the writing of this book, especially because we have two toddlers and a baby due imminently. This book wouldn't have my name on it if it weren't for her. Last, but not least, I would like to thank MVP Sharon Dooley for her help and guidance during my early years using SQL Server. Sharon is a beacon of light in the SQL Server industry and is a huge influence in the online communities, especially the SQL Server Worldwide Users Group (http://www.sswug.org).

—Mark Allison

Introduction

WITH THE RELEASE OF SQL Server 2000, Microsoft has created a true enterprise database solution. It currently holds top spot in the TPC-C and TPC-W benchmarks, according to the Transaction Processing Performance Council (http://www.tpc.org). With its ease of use and scalability, we see SQL Server being deployed in more and more businesses. SQL Distributed Management Object (SQL-DMO) is one of the technologies that SQL Server is built on, and with it you can start to make the sexier features of SQL Server work for you how you want them to. In this book we are going to show you the reader how to harness the power of SQL-DMO and use it your advantage. Once you've used it to create your own applications, you'll wonder how you ever got by without it.

Benefits to Programming in SQL-DMO

So why would you want to program in SQL-DMO? That's is a very good question. SQL Server database administrators (DBAs) already have Enterprise Manager, so why should they build an application that does the same thing? The best answer is that with SQL-DMO, you can do all you can with Enterprise Manager and more. Using SQL-DMO, you can take a portion of Enterprise Manager and build an application around it. This helps you find what you're looking for more quickly without having to remember that, for example, "Jobs" is under "SQL Server Agent" which is under "Management." (Been there, done that!)

But to only use SQL-DMO in this way would be selling it short. If you limit yourself to using SQL-DMO to show you a tree of all databases on a server, then you'll miss a lot of its functionality—and, yes, even its beauty.

With Enterprise Manager, it can be difficult to get to the objects you want to manage quickly. This is accentuated if you're managing a large number of servers. Throughout this book, we'll build scaled-down versions of Enterprise Manager views so we can show you how to cut down on all that clicking and get to where you need to be faster.

SQL-DMO can be used for Administrative tasks that simply aren't possible with Transact SQL (T-SQL) commands (or at least not without jumping through a lot of hoops first). In Enterprise Manager they're possible, but we very rarely have enough time on our hands to implement the method. With SQL-DMO, a few lines of script, and the SQL Server Agent, you can automate the functionality you get from Enterprise Manager and more.

SQL-Namespace (SQL-NS) and SQL-DMO are in some ways closely related but are actually very different. SQL-NS is the graphical part of SQL Server Enterprise Manager. Like SQL-DMO, SQL-NS is a set of COM interfaces, but it sits on top of the SQL-DMO layer. It's also, in our opinions, slightly less intuitive to work with than SQL-DMO.

What This Book Covers

In this book, we're going to take you through a series of tasks that can be accomplished using the SQL-DMO object library. We'll show you real-world implementations using SQL-DMO and provide you with ideas to help you go out there and create your own tools (if anyone becomes the next Bill Gates through this, please remember us).

We'll take you through some basics in Chapter 1, showing you how to traverse objects we generally associate with databases, i.e., tables, stored procedures, and users. We'll show you how to build such objects, too. We'll then start to look underneath the hood of SQL Server and really show you how SQL-DMO can benefit your business.

All of our code has been tested against both SQL Server 7 and 2000. If there's a difference in the implementation, we highlight it and tell you the alternative method. And where there's an alternative in T-SQL, we highlight this and point you to the Enterprise Manager method.

We promise you plenty of code samples and pictures to help illustrate points throughout the book, although not so many that it looks as though we spent most of our time capturing screenshots.

How This Book Is Organized

We'll concentrate in the main chapters on administration of SQL Server. In the appendixes, we'll give you excellent sources of reference including the object model and knowledge base articles related to SQL-DMO. Here's how the book is structured:

Chapter 1: A Gentle Introduction
Chapter 2: Backup and Restore
Chapter 3: Permissions and Users
Chapter 4: OLE Automation
Chapter 5: Jobs and Alerts
Chapter 6: Server Options
Chapter 7: Replication
Chapter 8: Lite QA (freeware)

Chapter 9: Scripter
Appendix A: SQL-DMO Object Library Quick Reference
Appendix B: Knowledge-Base Articles and Other SQL-DMO Resources

What You Should Know Before Reading This Book

To get the most from this book, you should be comfortable with the following:

- SQL Server databases and database objects

- Traversing the objects in Enterprise Manager

- Getting information from Books Online (BOL)

- Basic programming skills—in this book, the tools of choice are VB (we used VB6 SP5) and VBScript

- Coding using T-SQL

Although this book focuses on a programming library, it's not just a book for programmers. After all, we're both SQL Server DBAs and we use SQL-DMO virtually every day through applications that we've written to help us do some of the things that Microsoft didn't give us a tool for.

Additional Resources

Several worthwhile SQL-DMO resources are available to you. We subscribe to Microsoft TechNet and would urge all database administrators to do the same. The equivalent material for developers can be found in the MSDN library. Additionally, Microsoft SQL Server's BooksOnline (BOL) is a wealth of information, but one that's sadly overlooked on a lot of occasions. There are Resource Kits available for both SQL Server7 and 2000, and these contain wonderful documentation that you can even put in your PDA—so there's no excuse for not carrying it around with you. The object model can be seen in BOL and also we've conveniently provided it for you in Appendix A—as can most of the methods and properties you may need. If they aren't in there, we tend to use the Object browser in VB. TechNet, as mentioned earlier, is a superb resource and one that is especially useful for special features and "gotchas."

Welcome to the real world usage of SQL-DMO!

CHAPTER 1

Getting Started with SQL-DMO

THIS IS WHERE it all begins. Learning a new programming language can be an arduous task, but luckily SQL Distributed Management Objects (SQL-DMO) is not too difficult. In this chapter, you'll skim the surface and start to use SQL-DMO to create objects familiar to anyone using a database. You'll also tweak those objects to behave in the way you want them to. We give you a gentle introduction to using SQL-DMO to manipulate Microsoft SQL Server objects and data, and a glimpse of the possibilities that exist within the SQL-DMO object library (which you'll explore further in the chapters that follow).

You may be wondering why, if you have Enterprise Manager and Query Analyzer, you would need to build extra tools using SQL-DMO. Simply put, Enterprise Manager and Query Analyzer, good as they are, don't give you everything you need. If you implement the Microsoft Data Engine (MSDE) version of Microsoft SQL Server, which is the freely distributable, scaled-down version of SQL Server, you won't get any front-end tools, so you'll have to build your own toolkit anyway. SQL-DMO also provides a very easy way of giving users with certain administrative responsibilities a front end that allows them to perform certain tasks and nothing more. For example, you may want to restrict the databases a user can see on a server. This isn't possible with Enterprise Manager, because if a user is granted access to a server, then that user can see all the databases on that server. With SQL-DMO, however, restricting the databases a user can view is very easy to do.

In this chapter, we present a logical walk-through of creating a database with some objects inside it. We discuss how to create a database, where to place database files, how to size a database, and how to set database-related options. The examples we present in this chapter can be done using Transact-SQL (T-SQL, Microsoft's interpretation of the Structured Query Language).

Throughout this chapter (and indeed throughout the book) we show you how easy it is to code in SQL-DMO whatever tasks you used to use SQL Server's Enterprise Manager to do. Wherever possible, we provide the equivalent T-SQL statements and screen shots to help show the results of our statements. We then discuss how to create database objects, such as tables, stored procedures, and views.

We begin with an overview of what SQL-DMO is and where you can get it. We then move on to cover the following topics:

- Creating a database on a server

- Setting database options

- Creating database objects

What Is SQL-DMO and Where Can I Get It?

SQL-DMO is an object library that can be called through any application that supports the Component Object Model (COM) or object linking and embedding (OLE). When you use Enterprise Manager, you are using SQL-DMO. Microsoft has built a graphical user interface (GUI) over the top of it, but all that does is issue commands through DMO. A lot of the errors you'll see in pop-up boxes and the error logs are SQL-DMO errors. This means that almost anything you see in Enterprise Manager you can re-create in your favorite programming language.

This book is concerned with manipulating SQL Server versions 7.0 and 2000, as they are the most common implementations of the product in the workplace at the time of print. SQL-DMO is implemented through Sqldmo.dll, which is installed as part of SQL Server. You can freely redistribute this dynamic link library (DLL) to your development machines and you're also free to connect to your SQL Servers with it providing you have the appropriate licensing in place. The other files you'll need are as follows:

- Sqldmo.rll

- Sqlresld.dll

- Sqlsvc.dll

- Sqlsvc.rll

- Sqlwoa.dll (put in your $(WinSysPath) directory)

- Sqlwid.dll

- W95scm.dll

Once sqldmo.dll has been registered, you have access to all the objects and collections in your SQL Servers (again, permissions allowing). You can register these DLLs in a couple of ways, but we use the following steps:

1. Click the Start button and go to Run.

2. In the dialog box that opens, type **REGSVR32**. Open up Windows Explorer and find the DLLs on your system.

3. Drag the DLL file you want to register into the Run dialog box and place it after the entry you just typed. Windows will insert the file path for you.

4. Press Enter and you will be greeted by a message telling you the completion outcome.

With the registration complete, let's move on to creating the actual database.

....

SQL Server Books Online

SQL Server Books Online is a superb reference for nearly everything concerned with SQL Server. SQL-DMO is no exception to this. If you do a search in the index on SQL-DMO, SQL Server Books Online returns a wide range of information that you can then go on to refine. The times we most often use it are when we know the parent object of the property we're searching on and the function of the property we want. The only thing we've forgotten is the name of the property (isn't that always the case?). A quick search in SQL Server Books Online tells us what we need to know.

....

Creating a Database on a Server

A simple definition of a *database* is a collection of objects that holds and manages your data. With the following code, you're going to create the shell of your database. Later, you'll add some objects to it and prepare it to receive your data. A database consists of two or more files—never less. These files are the *data file* and the *transaction log*.

NOTE   One of the most common questions on newsgroups is "Can I get rid of the log file?" The answer is quite simply "No." Why not? SQL Server uses the transaction log as a kind of consistency checker. It knows what's committed and what isn't in the case of a database failure. You can minimize the number of items logged, but you can't do away with logging altogether. We discuss logging further in Chapter 2.

Here's the syntax for the CREATE DATABASE command in T-SQL, which comes straight from SQL Server Books Online:

```
CREATE DATABASE database_name

[ ON [PRIMARY]
        [ <filespec> [,...n] ]
        [, <filegroup> [,...n] ]
]
[ LOG ON { <filespec> [,...n]} ]
[ FOR LOAD | FOR ATTACH ]
<filespec> ::=
  ( [ NAME = logical_file_name, ]
  FILENAME = 'os_file_name'  [, SIZE = size]
  [, MAXSIZE = { max_size | UNLIMITED } ]
  [, FILEGROWTH = growth_increment] ) [,...n]
<filegroup> ::=
FILEGROUP filegroup_name <filespec> [,...n]
FILEGROUP filegroup_name <filespec>[,….n]
```

Now let's examine a practical implementation of the CREATE DATABASE command. In this example, you're only using the default file group PRIMARY—you aren't creating your own:

```
CREATE DATABASE MyDMODatabase
ON PRIMARY
( NAME = DMODB_dat,
  FILENAME = 'c:\mssql7\data\MyDMODatabaseFile1.mdf',
  SIZE = 100,
  MAXSIZE = UNLIMITED,
  FILEGROWTH = 10% ),
( NAME = DMODB_dat2,
  FILENAME = 'c:\mssql7\data\MyDMODatabaseFile2.ndf',
  SIZE = 100,
```

```
  MAXSIZE = 500,
  FILEGROWTH = 10% )
LOG ON
( NAME = 'MyDMODatabase_log',
  FILENAME = 'c:\mssql7\data\MyDMODatabaselog.ldf',
  SIZE = 25MB,
  MAXSIZE = UNLIMITED,
  FILEGROWTH = 5MB )
GO
```

The only thing left to do is show you how to do the exact same thing in SQL-DMO. We'll explain a few things as you go along.

Declaring Your Variables

Before you jump into coding, you need to declare some variables to hold the objects you'll be manipulating. As you can see, the object types give away their usage. First, you declare your variables.

SQL-DMO

```
Dim objServer As SQL-DMO.SQLServer
Dim objDatabase As SQL-DMO.database
Dim objLogFile As SQL-DMO.LogFile
Dim objDBDevice As SQL-DMO.DBFile
Dim objDBDevice2 As SQL-DMO.DBFile
```

Logging On to Your Server

Next, you need to log on to your server. In the following code example, we've chosen to log in with our NT account. You can easily change this to use a SQL Server Authenticated login by changing the code to the following:

```
objServer.Connect "AM5", "SQL Login Name", "Password for that account"

Set objServer = New SQL-DMO.SQLServer
objServer.LoginSecure = True
objServer.Connect "AM5"
```

You have to then prepare your variables to receive the objects you're going to assign them, as follows:

```
Set objDatabase = New SQL-DMO.database
Set objLogFile = New SQL-DMO.LogFile
Set objDBDevice = New SQL-DMO.DBFile
Set objDBDevice2 = New SQL-DMO.DBFile
```

Next, name the database MyDMODatabase:

```
objDatabase.Name = "MyDMODatabase"
```

Creating Your Log Files and Data Files

Now you get to the meat of what it is you're trying to do (i.e., create your first database using SQL-DMO). Transaction logs, the files that hold the transactions (among other things in SQL Server), and data files, the files that hold the data in SQL Server, have elements in common that will become evident when you create the objects in this section.

NOTE In the code we haven't specified a value for maximum size in one of the data files and the log file. This is because we don't want to restrict the growth of these files, and by not specifying a value here we're asking SQL Server to let them grow as and when they need to, and to whatever size they need (disk space allowing).

In the following code, you're going to define the properties of your log and data files.

```
objLogFile.Name = "MyDMODatabase_log"
objLogFile.PhysicalName = "c:\mssql7\data\MyDMODatabaselog.ldf"
objLogFile.Size = 25
objLogFile.FileGrowth = 5
objLogFile.FileGrowthType = SQL-DMOGrowth_MB
```

Now you create your data files as follows:

```
objDBDevice.Name = "DMODB_dat"
objDBDevice.PhysicalName = "c:\mssql7\data\MyDMODatabaseFile1.mdf"
objDBDevice.Size = 100
objDBDevice.FileGrowth = 10
objDBDevice.FileGrowthType = SQL-DMOGrowth_Percent


objDBDevice2.Name = "DMODB_dat2"
objDBDevice2.PhysicalName = "c:\mssql7\data\MyDMODatabaseFile2.ndf"
objDBDevice2.Size = 100
objDBDevice2.FileGrowth = 10
objDBDevice2.FileGrowthType = SQL-DMOGrowth_Percent
objDBDevice2.MaximumSize = 500
```

Adding Your Data File(s) and Log File(s) to the Database Object

After you have sized your data file(s) and log file(s), you need to add them to your new database object. The data file will be added to the DBFiles collection of the FileGroup object in your database. When you create a database, there's always a default file group called Primary. The Primary file group will house your system tables and common database objects. You can then create more file groups and add them to your database. Once you've done that, you can begin to create objects and assign them to this new file group.

Assigning objects to the new file group can be especially useful in areas where performance on very large tables is an issue. In such a case, you create a new file group on a separate high-speed disk and create the table on it, or you'll need to back up a very large database and the window that you have to do it in won't allow you to do a full or incremental backup overnight. We discuss this issue more and show you how to add file groups to your database in Chapter 2.

Adding a File Group

The Primary file group is the default that you get when you first install SQL Server. You can think of a *file group* as a logical grouping of physical files that your logical objects (i.e., tables) sit on. You can easily add a file group to a database and then add files to that new file group in exactly the same way as shown here:

```
objDatabase.FileGroups("Primary").DBFiles.Add objDBDevice
objDatabase.FileGroups("Primary").DBFiles.Add objDBDevice2
objDatabase.TransactionLog.LogFiles.Add objLogFile
```

The only thing left to do now is add the new Database object to the Databases collection on your server:

```
objServer.Databases.Add objDatabase
```

Figure 1-1 shows the locations of the database's data files.

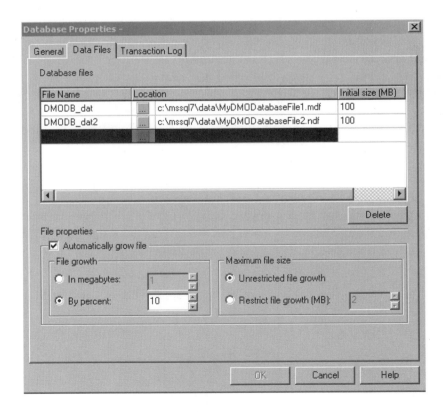

Figure 1-1. The new database (data files)

Figure 1-2 shows you where your transaction log for the database is located on the physical disk.

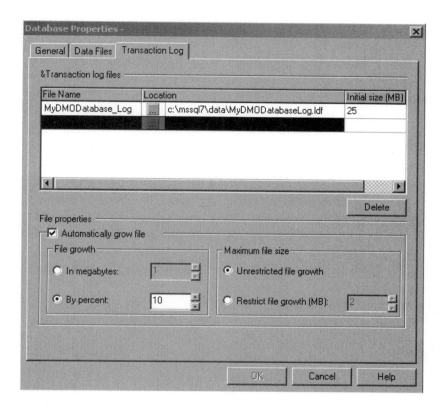

Figure 1-2. *The new database (log file)*

 NOTE   One thing to note here is that in order to create a database, you'll need to be specifically granted the CREATE DATABASE permission in the master database, or you'll need to be a member of the sysadmin or dbcreator role.

Setting Database Options

Once you have your database on the server, you may need to change some of the options associated with it. In this section, we discuss how to set your database options.

All databases by default inherit the properties of the Model database, so the options set there will be the default options of your new database. An example of this is the autoclose option. This option is set to true for the Desktop Edition of Microsoft SQL Server. It's used because on a desktop server you'll typically have fewer resources available to your PC, and the amount of traffic in your databases should be less than on your production servers. By closing the databases down when the last user exits, you free up resources on your PC to use somewhere else.

On a production system, however, this is a bad thing, because there's a lot of overhead in closing the database files down and then reopening them. In such cases, databases with a lot of transactions happening will go up and down like a yo-yo and the server will see a marked drop in performance. Desktop servers aren't supposed to be used as production servers, so the chances of them being used less often is very high. Because you don't want to tie up the resources, set this option to true. In general, a database in production is used much more frequently than one that isn't in production. We say this with some reservation, as we've seen production databases that are accessed once a week by a single person who only comes in from maternity leave every now and then. Having the database start up every time somebody uses it would be a real performance drag.

There are five types of options available to a database. These, in no particular order, are as follows:

- *State options:* Is the database single user, online, or offline?

- *Recovery options:* What are your recoverability options?

- *SQL options:* What are the ANSI settings? How will the database deal with numeric overflows?

- *Auto options:* Will the database automatically close down? Will it automatically shrink itself?

- *Cursor options:* What is the default scope of the cursor? Will your cursors close automatically if you don't close them manually?

In the sections that follow, we'll take you through each of these types of options. We'll show you how to check for one or more of the options and also how to set the options based on what you want to do.

State Options

Say you need to make your database read-only for some reason. A common reason for making the database read-only is that the database is purely a reporting tool and you won't ever need to update it (e.g., a database containing last year's football league tables and match results). To save you from the embarrassment of someone (perhaps a database administrator [DBA]) deleting something, you can set the READ ONLY option to true. Because you can only ever SELECT from this database, you won't have to worry about getting locked out from the tables because SQL Server only allows shared locks on your data. This means that all pages in your indexes are full with no redundant spare space. This in turn means that SQL Server has to traverse fewer pages to find the information it needs.

The following code shows how to check if the database is already READ ONLY. If it is, you walk away; otherwise, you check the option to make it so.

T-SQL

```
IF(select databaseproperty('MyDMODatabase','IsReadOnly')) = 0
BEGIN
        EXEC sp_DBOPTION 'NetworkUsers','read only',TRUE
END
```

Figure 1-3 shows the database's Options tab in Enterprise Manager (version 2000).

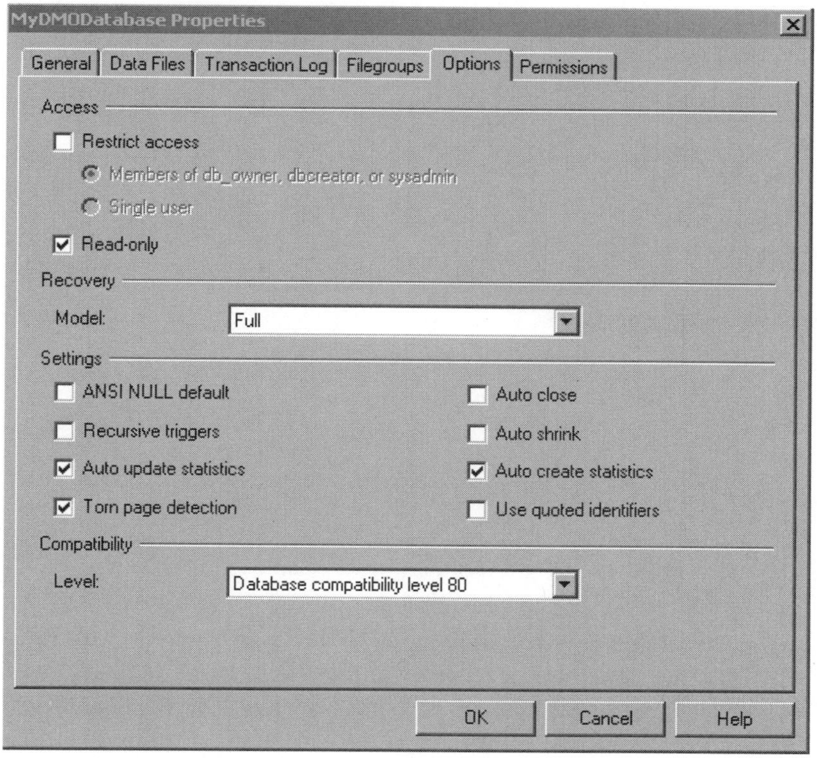

Figure 1-3. The Options tab in Enterprise Manager

Let's now move on to setting database options using SQL-DMO.

SQL-DMO

```
Dim objServer As SQL-DMO.SQLServer
Dim objDatabase As SQL-DMO.database
Dim oDBOption As SQL-DMO.DBOption

Set objServer = New SQL-DMO.SQLServer
objServer.LoginSecure = True
objServer.Connect "AM5"

If objServer.Databases("MyDMODatabase").DBOption.ReadOnly <> True Then
    objServer.Databases("MyDMODatabase").DBOption.ReadOnly = True
End If
```

All that you've done here is logged on to your server (in this case, AM5), gone to the Databases collection, and specified the MyDMODatabase database. You then looked at the DBOption collection of that Database object and found the ReadOnly property, which you set to true. This is really straightforward and involves very little coding. Figure 1-4 shows the effect in Enterprise Manager of setting the database to Read-Only.

Figure 1-4. The result of executing the state options code

Recovery Options

Recovery options govern how much of your data you'll be able to recover should a disaster strike. The options are slightly different between SQL Server 7.0 and SQL Server 2000. Version 7.0 has the options SELECT INTO/BULK COPY and TRUNCATE LOG ON CHKPT, whereas 2000 has the recovery modes FULL, BULK LOGGED, and SIMPLE. (You can also use the SQL Server 7.0 options in SQL Server 2000, but those are supplied for backward compatibility only.) We'll go into the ramifications of setting and not setting each of these options in Chapter 2.

T-SQL (Version 7.0)

```
EXEC sp_DBOption 'MyDMODatabase','trunc.',True
EXEC sp_DBOption 'MyDMODatabase','Select',True
```

T-SQL (Version 2000)

```
ALTER DATABASE MyDMODatabase SET RECOVERY SIMPLE
ALTER DATABASE MyDMODatabase SET RECOVERY BULK_LOGGED
ALTER DATABASE MyDMODatabase SET RECOVERY FULL
```

Figure 1-5 shows the database's Options tab in Enterprise Manager (version 7.0).

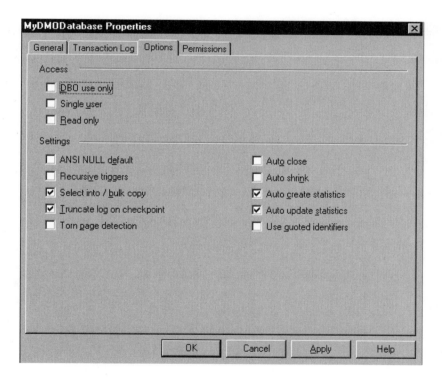

Figure 1-5. The database's Options tab in Enterprise Manager version 7.0

Figure 1-6 shows where in Enterprise Manager (version 2000) you set the recovery mode.

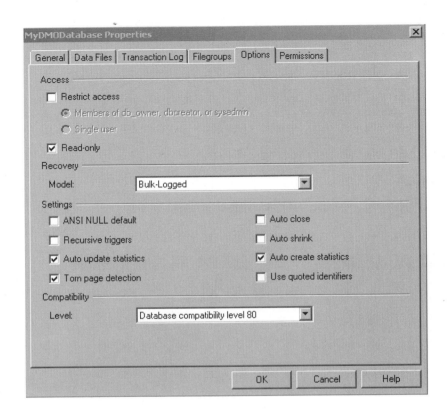

Figure 1-6. The database's Options tab in Enterprise Manager version 2000

The way you set the recovery mode using SQL-DMO is slightly different between the two versions of SQL Server. Version 7.0 doesn't have recovery options, so you need to do a bit more coding than you do in version 2000.

SQL-DMO (Version 7.0)

```
Dim objServer As SQL-DMO.SQLServer
Dim objDatabase As SQL-DMO.database



Set objServer = New SQL-DMO.SQLServer
objServer.LoginSecure = True
objServer.Connect "AM5"
```

```
If objServer.Databases("MyDMODatabase"). _DBOption.TruncateLogOnCheckpoint <> _
True Then
    objServer.Databases("MyDMODatabase").DBOption.TruncateLogOnCheckpoint = True
End If

If objServer.Databases("MyDMODatabase").DBOption.SelectIntoBulkCopy <> True Then
    objServer.Databases("MyDMODatabase").DBOption.SelectIntoBulkCopy = True
End If
```

SQL-DMO (Version 2000)

```
Dim objServer As SQL-DMO.SQLServer
Dim objDatabase As SQL-DMO.database

Dim oDBOption2 As SQLDMO.DBOption2


Set objServer = New SQL-DMO.SQLServer
objServer.LoginSecure = True
objServer.Connect "AM5"

Set oDBOption2 = objServer.Databases("MyDMODatabase").DBOption
```

Recovery models are a feature of SQL Server 2000:

```
oDBOption2.RecoveryModel = ( choice of SQLDMORECOVERY_BulkLogged
                                        SQLDMORECOVERY_Full
                                        SQLDMORECOVERY_Simple)
```

Here's the SQL Server 7.0 equivalent. SQL Server 7.0 doesn't have the DBOption2 object, so you need to use the DBOption object instead. However, the part that you're interested in changes like this:

```
oDBOption.SelectIntoBullkCopy = True
oDBOption.TruncateLogOnCheckpoint = True
```

Having the SelectIntoBulkCopy property set to true is the equivalent of the BulkLogged 2000 property. Having the TruncateLogOnCheckpoint property set to true is the equivalent of the Simple Recovery model in 2000. Finally, by having neither set to true is the equivalent of the Full Recovery model in 2000.

SQL Options

SQL options are settings for your database. Depending on your needs, you'll set different SQL options to different values, and you may never use some of them at all. We're going to use READ ONLY to illustrate the use of one of these options. By default, this value is set to OFF. Before you all shout "Why would I want a database to be read-only?", let us explain.

When SQL Server is working away normally, it has to take out what are known as *locks*. These locks are there to make sure, for example, that when you read a line once in a transaction and then later read it again in the same transaction, it hasn't disappeared. READ ONLY is good when you have a reporting database. You don't want users to change anything, so you don't let them or the administrator do so. This also has the nice side effect of placing less workload on SQL Server, as it doesn't have to think so much about how it's managing the data. In this state, SQL Server just hands the data out on an as-needed basis.

If you want to set the option to ON, you can use the following piece of T-SQL code.

T-SQL

```
IF (SELECT DATABASEPROPERTY('MyDMODatabase','IsReadOnly')) = 0

    BEGIN
        EXEC sp_DBOption 'MyDMODatabase','Read Only',TRUE
    END
```

SQL-DMO

```
Dim objServer As SQLDMO.SQLServer
Dim objDatabase As SQLDMO.database


Set objServer = New SQLDMO.SQLServer
objServer.LoginSecure = True
objServer.Connect "AM5"

If objServer.Databases("MyDMODatabase").DBOption.ReadOnly <> True Then
    objServer.Databases("MyDMODatabase").DBOption.readOnly = True
End If
```

TIP When we first started to look at using SQL-DMO, we struggled to find the object library, or at least it was difficult to find in any depth. We decided to cheat. If you know roughly what it is you want to do in SQL-DMO but you're struggling with the syntax, this method may help you find what you're looking for. Open up Microsoft Visual Basic or any of the other Microsoft tools (even Access). Go to the References section of your project and choose the SQL-DMO library. In the object browser (accessed by pressing F2) you'll be able to search on partial strings of what you're looking for. Wonderful.

Auto Options

Auto options are database settings that happen automatically in SQL Server. They have their good points and their bad points. In most cases, you'll want to review which auto options are set and whether they're appropriate. Let's say you have a test SQL Server upon which you've installed SQL Server Desktop Edition. You're going to be simulating a lot of users connecting and disconnecting. You know that by default the option to AUTO_CLOSE the database is set to true in this edition of SQL Server. It will produce a lot of overhead if you leave it like this, so for this exercise you'll want to change the default.

T-SQL

```
IF (DATABASEPROPERTY ('MyDMODatabase','IsAutoClose')) = 1

    Begin
        EXEC sp_DBOption 'MyDMODatabase','autoclose',FALSE
    End
```

Figure 1-7 shows where you can set your auto options (version 2000).

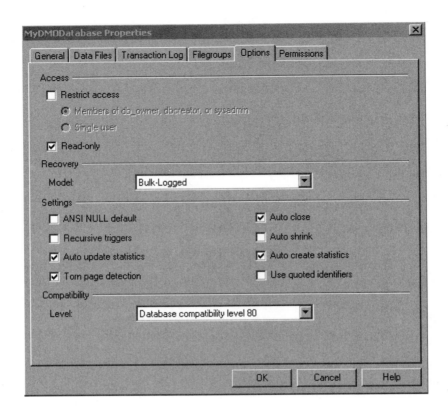

Figure 1-7. The Auto close option in Enterprise Manager

Using SQL-DMO, here is how you set the AutoClose option to Off.

SQL-DMO

```
Dim objServer As SQLDMO.SQLServer
Dim objDatabase As SQLDMO.database


Set objServer = New SQLDMO.SQLServer
objServer.LoginSecure = True
objServer.Connect "AM5"

If objServer.Databases("MyDMODatabase").DBOption.AutoClose <> False Then
    objServer.Databases("MyDMODatabase").DBOption.AutoClose = False
End If
```

Cursor Options

Cursor options are settings that determine how your database will handle cursors. If you open a cursor and forget to close it, by default SQL Server won't close it for you. The American National Standards Institute (ANSI) states that when a connection closes or a transaction finishes, the cursor should close automatically. To comply with this ruling, you'll need to set the CURSOR_CLOSE_ON_COMMIT option to true. There is no way in Enterprise Manager to set this option. If you want to set this option on a per-setting basis as opposed to changing the default database way of handling it, you could issue CURSOR_CLOSE_ON_COMMIT ON | OFF to the connection. Here, you'll change the default database option, though.

T-SQL

```
IF    (
SELECT DATABASEPROPERTY('MyDMODatabase','IsCloseCursorsOnCommitEnabled')
    ) = 0
    BEGIN
    EXEC sp_DBOption 'MyDMODatabase',' cursor close on commit',TRUE
END
```

SQL-DMO

```
Dim objServer As SQLDMO.SQLServer
Dim objDatabase As SQLDMO.database


Set objServer = New SQLDMO.SQLServer
objServer.LoginSecure = True
objServer.Connect "AM5"

If objServer.Databases("MyDMODatabase").DBOption.CursorCloseOnCommit
<> True Then
    objServer.Databases("MyDMODatabase").DBOption.CursorCloseOnCommit
= True
End If
```

Creating Database Objects

A database without objects isn't very effective, so in this section we're going to show you how to create some tables, stored procedures, and views. We'll also show you how to create links called *foreign keys* between those tables. In the table you're going to add a default constraint, whether the column is a primary key or not, if the column will accept NULLs. Finally, you'll add a trigger to the table.

To aid our demonstration, we've put together a small application that will help you visualize what you're creating. After going through the application, we'll show you how to do some of the things we haven't included in this quick application in case you have need for them. Figure 1-8 shows the first screen of our application.

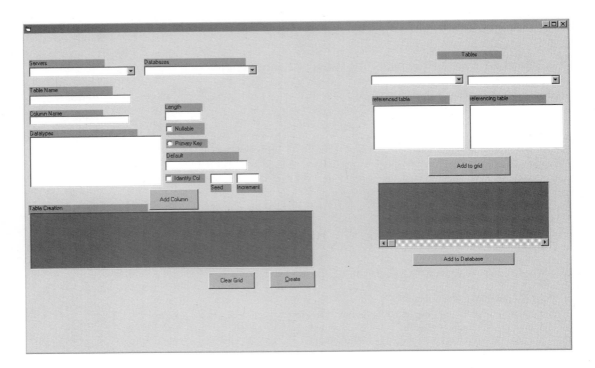

Figure 1-8. Object creation application

The best way to show you how we built the application is to go through it and point out the relevant parts. None of this is particularly complicated and we believe it to be very intuitive.

On the form is a Servers drop-down combo box, which lists all the registered servers. Next to the Servers combo box is a Databases combo box, which lists the databases on the server you select. Below the combo boxes are text boxes that are ready to take the name of the table you want to create and the columns you want to add to that table, and other controls for the details of those columns. At the bottom of the screen you can see a flex grid that shows you the table being built as you go along. The controls on the right side of the form are for creating the relationship between the tables, which we'll go through later. In the next section, you're concerned with only those items on the left side of the screen.

How the Sample Application Works

The way the application works is this: You select a server and then a database on that server. You enter the name of a table in the Table Name text box and then you enter a column name in the Column Name text box. You select a datatype for the new column, and if it's a character field, you can enter a length for it. You also have options to assign defaults to the column and indicate whether the column will accept NULLs or not.

Figure 1-9 shows the design of your new table and Table 1-1 helps you to visualize it.

Table 1-1 shows the grid columns and their meaning. The first column in the grid indicates whether the column is a primary key column, the second column contains the name of the column, the third column holds the datatype, the fourth column contains the length (if any), the fifth column indicates whether the column will accept NULL values or not, the sixth column shows any default constraint on the column, and finally, the seventh tells us if the column is an identity column, and the eighth and ninth columns show the increment and seed for the column identity property.

Table 1-1. Grid Columns and Their Meanings

Column	Meaning
1	Primary key
2	Column name
3	Datatype
4	Column length (character fields only)
5	Nullability
6	Default value
7	Identity field
8	Seed
9	Increment

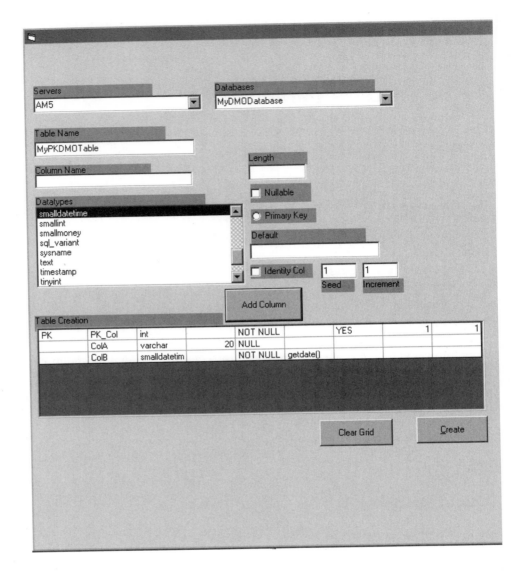

Figure 1-9. Table creation

Creating the Physical Table

Once you've built your table definition, click the Create button to create the actual physical table. If you wanted to do the same in T-SQL, you would need to execute the following code.

T-SQL

```
CREATE TABLE MyPKDMOTable (
PK_Col int NOT NULL IDENTITY(1,1) PRIMARY KEY,
ColA varchar(20) NULL,
ColB smalldatetime NOT NULL DEFAULT GETDATE()
    )
```

Figure 1-10 shows the result of either of these statements in Enterprise Manager.

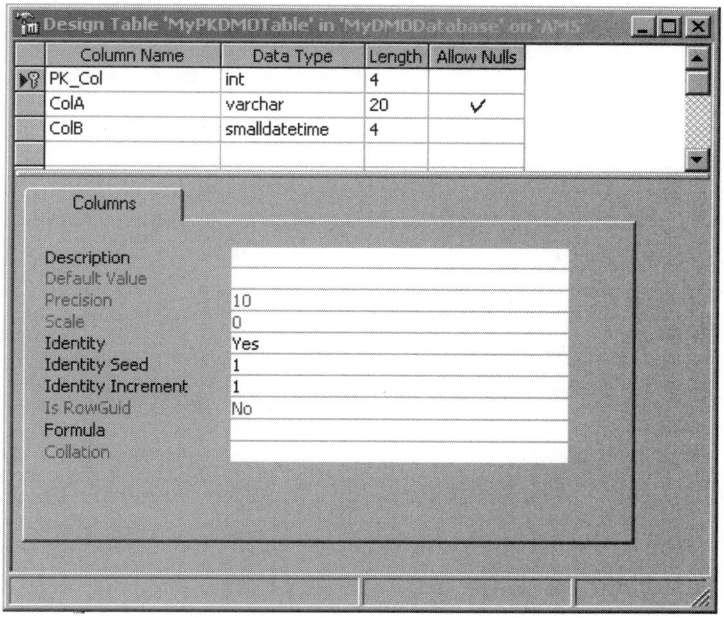

Figure 1-10. Enterprise Manager result

Now that you've seen what the application does, let's take a look under the covers and see how we made it possible.

Populating the Server Drop-Down Box

The first thing we needed to do was fill our drop-down boxes with the names of our servers. Once we chose a server, we filled in the names of the databases on that server. There is no way in T-SQL to do this, because we're doing this on the front end.

```
Private Sub listServers()

Dim oServer As SQLDMO.SQLServer
Dim oApp As New SQLDMO.Application
Dim oServerGroup As SQLDMO.ServerGroup
Dim oRegisteredServer As SQLDMO.RegisteredServer

cboServers.Clear

 Set oServer = New SQLDMO.SQLServer
For Each oRegisteredServer In oApp.ServerGroups(1).RegisteredServers
     cboServers.AddItem oRegisteredServer.Name
Next oRegisteredServer
 End Sub
```

There is more than one way to grab the names of all your SQL Servers using SQL-DMO. The way we use here is the RegisteredServers collection of the ServerGroup object. If a server isn't registered on our PC, then as far as we're concerned it does not exist. We loop through each registered server and output its name to the cboServer drop-down box. The other method is the ListAvailableSQLServers method of the Application object. The reason we don't use this method is that if we're on a different network segment to some of our SQL Servers, because this method uses a broadcast to discover the SQL Servers it does not pass through the routers. We would therefore end up with an incomplete list of servers. *Server groups* are the groupings of SQL Servers you see in Enterprise Manager. The default is SQL Server Group, but you could easily create server groups for Development, UAT, and Production, for example. Figure 1-11 shows the Server Group tree in Enterprise Manager.

Figure 1-11. Server groups

Populating the List of Databases

The next thing we needed to do was populate cboDatabases with the list of databases for the server we chose. The following code shows how to populate the drop-down box in the database:

```
Private Sub ListDataBases(servername As String)
Dim dmoSrv As SQLDMO.SQLServer
Dim dmoDB As SQLDMO.database

Set dmoSrv = New SQLDMO.SQLServer
cboDatabases.Clear
dmoSrv.LoginSecure = True
dmoSrv.Connect servername

For Each dmoDB In dmoSrv.Databases
    cboDatabases.AddItem dmoDB.Name
Next dmoDB
End Sub
```

Logging In Using Windows Authentication

In order to find out what databases were on the server, we needed to log into it. In this example, we again logged in using Windows authentication. Having logged in, we looped through the Databases collection of the server and output the name of the server to the cboDatabases drop-down box.

Once we chose our database, we then needed to populate our lstDatatypes list box with the names of the possible datatypes in our database. Datatypes exist in two forms: System and UserDefined.

Populating Our List of Available Datatypes

```
Private Sub ListDataTypes(servername As String, DatabaseName As String)
Dim dt As SQLDMO.SystemDatatype
Dim udt As SQLDMO.UserDefinedDatatype
Dim dmoSrv As SQLDMO.SQLServer
lstDatatypes.Clear

Set dmoSrv = New SQLDMO.SQLServer

dmoSrv.LoginSecure = True
dmoSrv.Connect servername

For Each dt In dmoSrv.Databases(DatabaseName).SystemDatatypes
    lstDatatypes.AddItem dt.Name
Next dt
```

```
For Each udt In dmoSrv.Databases(DatabaseName).UserDefinedDatatypes

    lstDatatypes.AddItem udt.Name
Next udt
```

```
End Sub
```

Here we looped through the Datatypes and UserDefinedDatatypes collections of the Server object and output them to our lstDatatypes list box.

Creating a New Datatype

Earlier we mentioned that the application wouldn't let you create a new datatype, but we would show you separately how to do it. Well, that time is now and here it is. The following code shows how to create your own datatype:

```
Private Sub AddDataType(servername As String, DatabaseName As String)

Dim udt As SQLDMO.UserDefinedDatatype
Dim dmoSrv As SQLDMO.SQLServer

Set dmoSrv = New SQLDMO.SQLServer
Set udt = New SQLDMO.UserDefinedDatatype

dmoSrv.LoginSecure = True
dmoSrv.Connect servername


udt.Name = "MyDataType"
udt.BaseType = "varchar"
udt.Length = 20

dmoSrv.Databases(DatabaseName).UserDefinedDatatypes.Add udt

End Sub
```

A UserDefinedDatatype needs to be mapped to a base datatype. In this case, "varchcar" has a name, "MyDataType," and if it's a character datatype, it needs a length of 20. UserDefinedDatatypes are not new datatypes. The most common use we see for them is when a developer/DBA wants to present a datatype with a specific meaning. An example might be that instead of defining a Telephone Number attribute with a datatype of varchar(20), we might create a UDDT and call it tel_no. We then add that UserDefinedDatatype object to the UserDefinedDatatypes collection of the Database object. The result of this is shown in Figure 1-12.

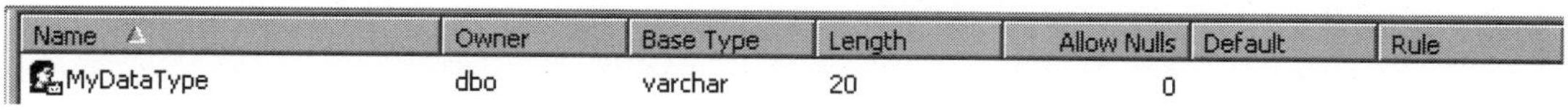

Name △	Owner	Base Type	Length	Allow Nulls	Default	Rule
MyDataType	dbo	varchar	20		0	

Figure 1-12. New datatype created

Creating Triggers for a Table

Because the application doesn't create triggers, we'll very quickly show you how to create one for a table. A trigger can fire on any of these actions on your table: INSERT, UPDATE, and DELETE. SQL Server 7.0 has only one type of trigger, which is referred to as an AFTER trigger. It works in this way: You perform your action against the table that the trigger is defined on, and this fires the trigger. The trigger then performs whatever it is that you've specified in the code. SQL Server 2000 has another type of trigger known as an INSTEAD OF trigger. This trigger is often referred to incorrectly as a BEFORE trigger, which gives the impression that the trigger code will execute before the action that you want to perform on the trigger table, and then do the action that you requested (i.e., INSERT, UPDATE, or DELETE). What actually happens is that your request fires the trigger and the code in the trigger executes *instead* of your request. This is best illustrated by an example.

Say you have a table where an INSTEAD OF trigger is defined and is set to fire on INSERT into the table. Before you do the actual insert, you want to check that you won't violate any constraints. You set the trigger code to look for the errors. If everything is OK, then you must reissue the INSERT command to actually do the INSERT. No INSERT happens until you reissue the command in the trigger.

The following listings show how to create a trigger for your table.

T-SQL (Version 7.0)

```
CREATE TRIGGER My_Insert_Trigger ON MyPKDMOTable
FOR INSERT AS
SELECT * FROM INSERTED
```

SQL-DMO

```
Private Sub CreateATrigger(Servername As String,
DatabaseName As String, TableName As String,
TriggerName As String)
Dim oSrv As SQLDMO.SQLServer
Dim oTrigger As SQLDMO.Trigger

Set oSrv = New SQLDMO.SQLServer
Set oTrigger = New SQLDMO.Trigger

oSrv.LoginSecure = True
oSrv.Connect Servername

oTrigger.Name = TriggerName
oTrigger.Text = "CREATE TRIGGER " & TriggerName & "
ON " & TableName & " for insert as select * from INSERTED"

oSrv.Databases(DatabaseName).Tables(TableName).Triggers.Add oTrigger

End Sub
```

Here are a couple of points to note about creating triggers:

- The Text and Name properties of the Trigger object are required.

- Even though you give the process the name of the trigger using the Name property, you still need to fully specify the CREATE TRIGGER syntax in the Text property, which seems like a duplication of effort to us.

T-SQL (version 2000)

```
CREATE TRIGGER tr_MyDMOTrigger ON MyPKDMOTable
INSTEAD OF INSERT
AS
select colA from Inserted
```

SQL-DMO

```
Private Sub CreateInsteadOfTrigger(ServerName As String,
DatabaseName As String, TableName As String,
TriggerName As String)
Dim oSrv As SQLDMO.SQLServer
Dim oTrigger As SQLDMO.Trigger

Set oSrv = New SQLDMO.SQLServer
Set oTrigger = New SQLDMO.Trigger

oSrv.LoginSecure = True
oSrv.Connect ServerName

oTrigger.Name = TriggerName
oTrigger.Text = "CREATE TRIGGER " & TriggerName & "
ON " & TableName & " INSTEAD OF insert as select *
from INSERTED"


oSrv.Databases(DatabaseName).Tables(TableName).Triggers.Add oTrigger


End Sub
```

NOTE   The only difference between our creation of a trigger in version 2000 and the way we would create one in SQL Server 7.0 is the use of INSTEAD OF. SQL Server Books Online states that to add a trigger to the Triggers collection of a table, you need to issue a BeginAlter command to the table beforehand and a DoAlter command to the table object after you've finished. It's our experience that this isn't the case, as you can see here.

Exploring the Underlying Code

Now you've come to the meat of the code, the part that actually tells your SQL Server to add the table you want to create to its list of tables and create it exactly how you want.

```
Private Sub AddTableToDatabase(Servername As String,
DatabaseName As String, TableName As String)
```

Declare your variables up front:

```
Dim i As Integer
Dim oSrv As SQLDMO.SQLServer
Dim oTable As SQLDMO.table
Dim ocol As SQLDMO.Column
Dim colname As String
Dim datatype As String
Dim collength As Integer
Dim objPK As SQLDMO.Key
```

You define a Key object that you'll use to hold the definition of any primary key column you create in your table:

```
Set objPK = New SQLDMO.Key
```

```
Set oSrv = New SQLDMO.SQLServer
```

Next, log in to your server:

```
oSrv.LoginSecure = True
oSrv.Connect Servername
```

You define a Table object to hold the definition of your new table. The Name property is passed as an argument to the procedure:

```
Set oTable = New SQLDMO.table
oTable.Name = TableName
```

You're now going to loop through every row within the flex grid, picking up the cell values and turning them into valid SQL values:

```
For i = 0 To TableBuilderGrid.Rows - 1
```

You need to initialize a New column every time you go to a new row in the grid, as you essentially want this to be a new column in your table:

```
Set ocol = New SQLDMO.Column
```

The TextMatrix property of the grid gives you the details in the cell found at the position of the parameters you supply (i.e., *(row,column)*). If on a row in the third column you find a character datatype, then you need to make sure that you also specify a length for it.

```
    If TableBuilderGrid.TextMatrix(i, 2) = "char"
Or TableBuilderGrid.TextMatrix(i, 2) = "varchar" Or
TableBuilderGrid.TextMatrix(i, 2) = "nvarchar" Or
TableBuilderGrid.TextMatrix(i, 2) = "nchar" Then
```

The second column in the grid is the name of your new column:

```
        ocol.Name = TableBuilderGrid.TextMatrix(i, 1)
```

The third column in the grid is the datatype of your new column:

```
        ocol.datatype = TableBuilderGrid.TextMatrix(i, 2)
```

The fourth column in the grid is the length of your new column:

```
        ocol.Length = CStr(TableBuilderGrid.TextMatrix(i, 3))
```

If you want the column to accept NULL values, use the following code:

```
        If TableBuilderGrid.TextMatrix(i, 4) = "NOT NULL" Then
            ocol.AllowNulls = False
        Else
            ocol.AllowNulls = True
        End If
    Else
```

If the column is not a character field, use this code:

```
        ocol.Name = TableBuilderGrid.TextMatrix(i, 1)
        ocol.datatype = TableBuilderGrid.TextMatrix(i, 2)
            If TableBuilderGrid.TextMatrix(i, 4) = "NOT NULL" Then
                ocol.AllowNulls = False
            Else
                ocol.AllowNulls = True
            End If
    End If
```

You need to check whether the column you're about to add has an Identity property associated with it, and if so, what the seed and increment values are:

```
If TableBuilderGrid.TextMatrix(i, 6) = "YES" Then
        ocol.Identity = True
        ocol.IdentitySeed = TableBuilderGrid.TextMatrix(i, 7)
        ocol.IdentityIncrement = TableBuilderGrid.TextMatrix(i, 8)
    End If
```

Add the column to the table and continue until you get to the end of the grid:

```
oTable.Columns.Add ocol
```

```
Next i
```

Add the table to your database:

```
oSrv.Databases(DatabaseName).Tables.Add oTable
```

Now for primary keys and defaults. The following code is for primary keys. A primary key can consist of more than one column, so you loop through looking for the columns you've defined as being the primary key.

```
Set objPK = New SQLDMO.Key
```

Loop through the table looking for a value of PK in the first column of the grid, as shown here:

```
For i = 0 To TableBuilderGrid.Rows - 1
    If TableBuilderGrid.TextMatrix(i, 0) = "PK" Then
```

Add the name of that column, which you find in the second column of the grid, to the list of columns in the grid.

```
        objPK.KeyColumns.Add TableBuilderGrid.TextMatrix(i, 1)
    End If
Next I
```

If you've looped through the grid and find that the number of columns in your key is greater than 0, you'll want to create a key:

```
If objPK.KeyColumns.Count > 0 Then
```

Assign a name to the key as follows:

```
objPK.Name = "My_PK_" & CStr(Minute(Now())) & "_" & CStr(Second(Now()))
```

Assign a FillFactor (how full the data pages will be) to the key and also tell it what type of key you want to create:

```
objPK.FillFactor = 85
objPK.Type = SQLDMOKey_Primary
```

Finally, add your new key to the Keys collection of your new table:

```
oSrv.Databases(DatabaseName).Tables(TableName).Keys.Add objPK
```

```
End If
```

Now the time has come to add your default constraint.

```
For i = 0 To TableBuilderGrid.Rows - 1
```

Give the constraint a name just in case you find a column that wants a constraint:

```
    objDefault.Name = "DEFAULT_" & TableBuilderGrid.TextMatrix(i, 1)
```

The sixth cell in the grid indicates if the column has a default constraint. Here you check to see if that cell has a value in it. If it does, you take the appropriate action.

```
    If TableBuilderGrid.TextMatrix(i, 5) <> "" Then
```

To add a default constraint, you need to alter the table as follows:

```
    oSrv.Databases(DatabaseName).Tables(TableName).BeginAlter
```

There are two ways to add a Default to a column: as an object and as a constraint. Here you use a constraint, as this is the way that Microsoft wants you to go, and Default objects are provided for backward compatibility. You add the default constraint to the column by specifying the value you found in the fifth cell as the text of the constraint.

```
oSrv.Databases(DatabaseName).Tables(TableName).
Columns(TableBuilderGrid.TextMatrix(i, 1)).
DRIDefault.Text = "'" & TableBuilderGrid.TextMatrix(i, 5) & "'"
```

Although it isn't easily visible in the code, the single quotes are sandwiched between double quotes.

You now commit those changes to the table:

```
oSrv.Databases(DatabaseName).Tables(TableName).DoAlter
    End If
    Next i


TableBuilderGrid.Rows = 0


End Sub
```

Adding Relationships to Your Tables

Now you'll move on to creating a relationship between two tables in your database. This involves moving over to the right side of the form. The way this side works is that you select a server and database as before. The two drop-down boxes on the right side of the form underneath the Tables label will be populated with the names of all the tables in the database. Once you select a table, the list boxes underneath the Tables label will be populated with the columns in those tables. You select your columns and add them to the grid underneath—again, for visibility—and then you add the relationship to your tables. Sounds simple? Well, it's not too difficult, and once we show you how to do it, this will quickly become apparent. Figure 1-13 shows how to create a relationship between tables and columns in your application.

You first of all have to create a second table in your database to be able to refer to the table you've just created.

T-SQL

```
CREATE TABLE [dbo].[MyReferencingTable] (

[ref_Col] [int] NULL,
[colA] [int] NOT NULL
)
```

You then create the relationship at the table level.

```
ALTER TABLE [dbo].[MyReferencingTable]  WITH
CHECK  ADD CONSTRAINT
[FKEY_MYPKDMOTable_MyReferencingTable]
FOREIGN KEY ([ref_Col]) REFERENCES
MYPKDMOTable ([PK_Col])
```

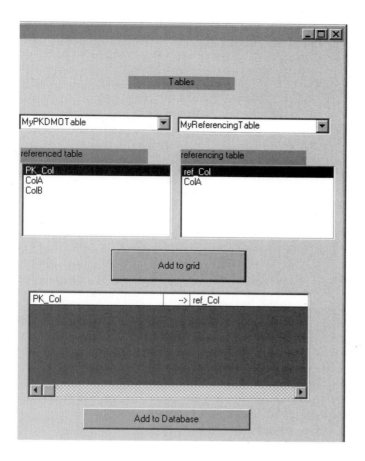

Figure 1-13. Creating a relationship using the application

Earlier we showed you how to create drop-down boxes for the servers and databases. Now you need to know how to loop through the Tables and Columns collections. See the following code.

SQL-DMO

```
Private Sub ListTables(Servername As String, DatabaseName As String)

Dim oSrv As SQLDMO.SQLServer
Dim oTable As SQLDMO.table

Set oSrv = New SQLDMO.SQLServer
cbotables.Clear
oSrv.LoginSecure = True
oSrv.Connect Servername
```

Here you loop through the Tables collection of your database. You only want to include user tables, so you exclude the system objects. You then add the name of the table to the Tables drop-down box.

```
For Each oTable In oSrv.Databases(DatabaseName).Tables
    If oTable.SystemObject = False Then
        cbotables.AddItem oTable.Name
    End If
Next oTable
End Sub
```

Then you insert columns:

```
Private Sub Listcols(Servername As String, DatabaseName As String,
TableName As String)
Dim oSrv As SQLDMO.SQLServer
Dim ocol As SQLDMO.Column

Set oSrv = New SQLDMO.SQLServer
lstcol1.Clear
oSrv.LoginSecure = True
oSrv.Connect Servername
```

Next, all you do is loop through the Columns collection of your table and output the name to your list box of columns:

```
For Each ocol In oSrv.Databases(DatabaseName).Tables(TableName).Columns
    lstcol1.AddItem ocol.Name
Next ocol
End Sub
```

Now you move to the actual code that allows you to create the relationship between the two tables:

```
Private Sub AddRelationshipToTable(Servername As String,
DatabaseName As String, reffingTable As String, reffedTable As String)

Dim oServer As SQLDMO.SQLServer
Dim oKey As SQLDMO.Key
Dim i As Integer

Set oServer = New SQLDMO.SQLServer

oServer.LoginSecure = True
oServer.Connect Servername
```

Relgrid is the name of the relationship-visualizing grid. You check to see whether it contains any data, and if it does, you create a new key and make it a foreign key. The next thing to do is assign it a name.

```
If relgrid.Rows > 0 Then
    Set oKey = New SQLDMO.Key
        oKey.Type = SQLDMOKey_Foreign
        oKey.Name = "FKEY_" & reffedTable & "_" & reffingTable
```

You only need to set the referenced table name, as you'll be adding the key to the referencing table.

```
        oKey.ReferencedTable = reffedTable
```

Now you loop through the grid, picking up the columns that need to be linked between the two tables.

```
        For i = 0 To relgrid.Rows - 1
            oKey.KeyColumns.Add relgrid.TextMatrix(i, 2)
            oKey.ReferencedColumns.Add relgrid.TextMatrix(i, 0)
        Next I
```

You then add that key to the Keys collection of the referencing table.

```
        oServer.Databases(DatabaseName).Tables(reffingTable).Keys.Add oKey
End If

End Sub
```

The resulting relationship is shown in Figure 1-14.

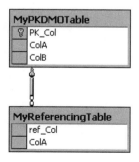

Figure 1-14. The relationship created

Creating a View

Views are portals to the underlying base tables. In SQL Server 2000 they became even more powerful, in that version 2000 has *indexed views*. These views enable SQL Server to hold the data in the view and can speed up queries dramatically. In the following code section, we'll show you how to create both variations: the indexed view and the nonindexed view. Views in general serve a couple of purposes:

- They hide the complexity of the T-SQL statements underneath.

- They can be used to enforce security. For example, you may only want general users to see employee names and addresses, but not salary details, whereas users in the finance department would require access to that information. Using views is a great way of enforcing this.

On your MYPKDMOTable you may want to restrict users' view of the table to only columns ColA and ColB, so you need to create a view over the top of it.

T-SQL (Version 7.0)

```
CREATE VIEW myDMOView
AS
SELECT ColA , ColB FROM MYPKDMOTable
```

SQL-DMO (Version 7.0)

```
Private Sub CreateAView(ServerName As String,
DatabaseName As String, ViewName As String)
Dim oSrv As SQLDMO.SQLServer
Dim oView As SQLDMO.View

Set oSrv = New SQLDMO.SQLServer

oSrv.LoginSecure = True
oSrv.Connect ServerName

Set oView = New SQLDMO.View
```

This is the definition of the view:

```
oView.Name = ViewName
oView.Text = "CREATE VIEW " & ViewName & "
AS SELECT ColA , ColB FROM MYPKDMOTable"
```

Add the view to the Views collection of your database with the following code:

```
oSrv.Databases(DatabaseName).Views.Add oView
End Sub
```

Again, you can see here as you did with the creation of the trigger on your table that you need to specify the name of the view in the Name and Text properties of the View object.

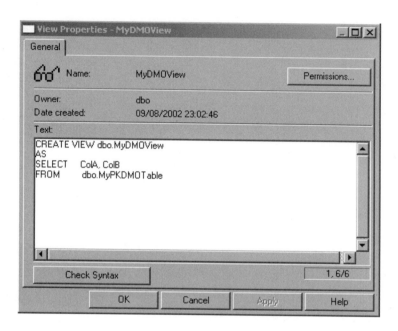

Figure 1-15. Result of view creation

Now you come to the more difficult of the views to create: the indexed view.

T-SQL (Version 2000)

```
CREATE VIEW dbo.vw_MyDMOView
WITH SCHEMABINDING
AS
SELECT ColA , ColB FROM MYPKDMOTable


CREATE UNIQUE CLUSTERED INDEX idx_vw_index
ON dbo. vw_MyDMOView (colA)
```

SQL-DMO (Version 2000)

```
Private Sub CreateIndexedView(ServerName As String,
DatabaseName As String, ViewName As String,
 indexname As String)
Dim oSrv As SQLDMO.SQLServer
Dim oView As SQLDMO.View2
Dim idx As SQLDMO.Index


Set oSrv = New SQLDMO.SQLServer

oSrv.LoginSecure = True
oSrv.Connect ServerName
```

The first change is that because an indexed view is only available in SQL Server 2000, you must declare it as a View2 object:

```
Set oView = New SQLDMO.View2

oSrv.QuotedIdentifier = True
oView.AnsiNullsStatus = True

oView.Name = ViewName
```

The view must be bound to the schema of the underlying tables as follows:

```
oView.Text = "CREATE VIEW " & ViewName & " WITH SCHEMABINDING AS
SELECT ColA , ColB FROM dbo.MYPKDMOTable"

Set idx = New SQLDMO.Index
```

The first index you place on a view must be clustered and unique:

```
idx.Name = indexname
idx.Type = SQLDMOIndex_Unique + SQLDMOIndex_Clustered
idx.IndexedColumns = "colA"
```

Add the view to the Views collection of the database:

```
oSrv.Databases(DatabaseName).Views.Add oView
```

Then add the index to the view:

```
oView.Indexes.Add idx
End Sub
```

Once you've run the code, you'll see the results shown in Figure 1-16 from Enterprise Manager.

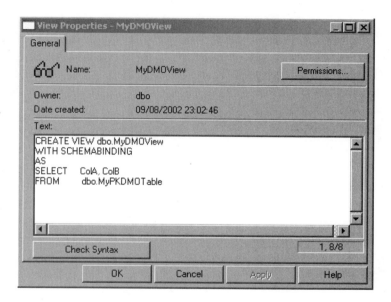

Figure 1-16. Creation of an indexed view

Note that the only visible difference between an indexed view and a nonindexed view in the CREATE VIEW statement is the inclusion of the WITH SCHEMABINDING clause. The index created on the view can clearly be seen in Figure 1-17.

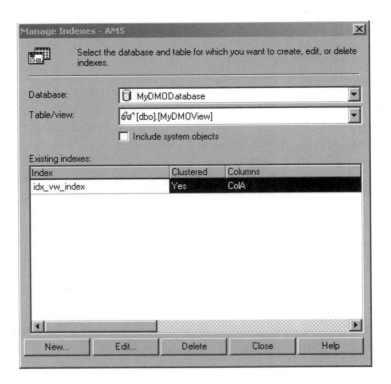

Figure 1-17. Index on the indexed view

CAUTION To create an indexed view, you must follow a stringent series of rules. These rules are fully explained in SQL Server Books Online under "Creating an Indexed View."

Creating a Stored Procedure

Stored procedures are used to batch together T-SQL statements and provide often-complex calculations. You use them to provide a consistent interface to the users, as all the logic can be built into them and the user merely calls them. An example may be that you specify a value as parameter to the stored procedure and you want all records from your table in which a column matches that value. The reason you may choose this option over a simple SELECT statement with a WHERE clause is that stored procedures cache an execution plan on the server and this can have the effect of increasing performance.

T-SQL

```
CREATE PROCEDURE MyDMOProcedure  @Param1 varchar(20)
AS
SELECT * FROM MyPKDMOTable WHERE colA = @Param1
GO
```

SQL-DMO

```
Private Sub CreateStoredProc(ProcName As String, ServerName As String,
DatabaseName As String)

Dim oSrv As SQLDMO.SQLServer
Dim oProc As SQLDMO.StoredProcedure

Set oSrv = New SQLDMO.SQLServer

oSrv.LoginSecure = True
oSrv.Connect ServerName

Set oProc = New SQLDMO.StoredProcedure

oProc.Name = ProcName
```

Here you're creating a standard procedure, but be aware that you could also specify Extended, Macro, and Replication Filter:

```
oProc.Type = SQLDMOProc_Standard
```

Here's the actual declaration for the stored procedure:

```
oProc.Text = "create procedure " & ProcName & " @Param1 varchar(20) AS SELECT *
FROM MyPKDMOTable Where colA = @Param1"


oSrv.Databases(DatabaseName).StoredProcedures.Add oProc
End Sub
```

Figure 1-18 shows the result of using either of these statements.

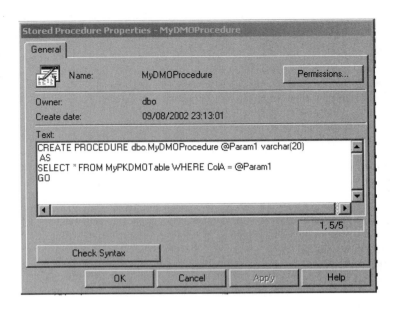

Figure 1-18. Creation of a stored procedure

Summary

We hope this chapter has given you a glimpse of the power of SQL-DMO as a programming object library. In this chapter, you covered a fair amount of ground. You created your first database using SQL-DMO, added some database objects, and set a few options. In the following chapters, you're going to build on these foundations and start to create some really useful, and often very simple, applications using them.

CHAPTER 2

Backup and Restore: A DBA's Bread and Butter

ONE OF A DATABASE ADMINISTRATOR'S (DBA's) primary jobs is backing up a database so that should the need arise it can be restored. This chapter deals with how to do that using SQL-DMO by building a sample application.

In our opinion, one of the most important tasks we perform as DBAs is creating a backup plan for our servers and databases. The type of plan we implement depends on the type of environment we're looking at.

When we arrive at a new client's site, the first thing we like to do is find out what we back up, what we don't back up, and why and where. Even if we never use the backups, it's always good to have them, just in case. We've lost count of the number of times we've been asked by developers to restore a database because they forgot to limit a DELETE statement by using a WHERE clause, and instead of deleting 11 rows they ended up removing 11,000.

DBAs aren't exempt from these sorts of issues, either. We recently had a junior administrator ask us if we could restore a database because he managed to drop half the tables in the database before realizing his mistake. Natural disasters are another reason to keep backups. We recently had to restore a few database servers because when we arrived at the client's site, we found the server room doing an impression of Jacques Cousteau—not a pretty sight, we assure you.

In this chapter we'll show you some of the various backup methods available and how you can implement them using SQL-DMO. We provide quite a bit of explanation at first, as we think it's important that you understand a little about how backups work and how to use them. It's also important to look into any options set on the database that may influence your backup strategy. We then move on to cover restoring your backup. We find this an often-overlooked point— after all, what's the point in creating backups if none of them is any good?

To illustrate the concepts we describe, we're going to take you through a couple of our applications. They're very simple, but they provide practical examples of what we're writing about. The first application will do the backups and the second application will do the restore. Finally, you'll look at doing some log shipping. *Log shipping* is a way of maintaining a copy of your database(s) on another server. Having this kind of fallback can reduce the time it takes you to recover from a disaster.

NOTE If you're using SQL Server 2000 Enterprise Edition, you can configure log shipping in your Database Maintenance Plan Wizard. If you don't use this version of SQL Server, there is a log shipping tool in the SQL Server Resource Kit in ToolsAndSamples\SimpleLogShipper.

We begin with a discussion of the available backup methods, and then we discuss

- Applying sample backup methods

- Choosing your backup method

- Using backup devices

- Performing the backup

- Using the 15-minute database checker application

Types of Backup Available

There are four types of backups available to you: full, differential, file group, and transaction log. We describe each backup type in more detail in the following sections.

Full Backup

In a *full backup*, SQL Server does exactly as the backup's name suggests: It backs up the entire database. Every single database page is taken to the media of your choice, be it file or tape. Users can still be logged in at the time of the backup, but they can't be performing any of the following:

- DBCC SHRINKDATABASE

- DBCC CHECKALLOC

- SELECT INTO

- BCP

If users are active in the database during the backup, it makes sense that there will be transactions in the database that the backup has missed. It is for this reason that at the end of the backup, SQL Server backs up the transaction log to capture these new transactions.

Differential Backup

When a full backup occurs, SQL Server marks all the data pages as having been backed up. When you use your database again, and maybe insert some new data or update a row in a table, SQL Server marks that extent as changed. *Differential backups* hunt through your database and only backup those extents (8 pages of data) that have been tagged as modified.

Differential backups, however, won't reset the marker to indicate that it has been backed up. A differential backup is cumulative, meaning that it will include all database changes made since the last full backup. If you perform a differential backup today and one tomorrow, then the backup tomorrow will contain all of the changes in today's backup as well. This method is faster than the others because it only backs up new data in the database.

NOTE Your mileage may vary with this method, especially in SQL Server 7.0. The number of changes isn't necessarily indicative of the time that a differential takes to happen. Backup file size is also something that varies greatly. We've spoken to people who have a database of 10GB with 32GB differential backup files.

File Group Backup

This is possibly the most difficult type of backup from a management perspective. The way a file group backup works is this: In a database you can have many file groups, which can contain many physical files. You can place objects in your database into certain file groups. You choose this method if, for example, you have a table that has 40 million rows and it is constantly being queried. To get the most from the table, you decide to place it in a file group on the fastest hard disk drive you have or a fast redundant array of independent disks (RAID) 10 array. When this table is queried, you can get to your data more quickly. Another use is when you have a very large database (VLDB) and the amount of time it takes to back up the whole thing is greater than the window of opportunity you have. If you split up the database into different file groups, you can back them up one at a time, and when they're all backed up, you have a full database backup equivalent.

Transaction Log Backup

The transaction log maintains a history of the activity in your database. When you insert a row into a table in your database, you aren't actually writing it to disk but to the log. At specified periods, called *checkpoints,* SQL Server will write out your INSERT statement to the disk. As we hope you can see, the log is a very important file. A *transaction log backup* will back up all transactions that have happened in your database since the last full, differential, or transaction log backup. The way in which the log behaves is dependent on some of the options set in your database, which we explain later in the section "Considerations for Choosing Your Backup Method."

Sample Backup Scenarios and Methods

As we mentioned earlier in the chapter, how you back up your databases is dependent on many factors. In a test environment, you may only need to do a full backup once a week and no more. In a production environment, however, you'll most probably need to be able to recover your database to the time as near as possible to a disaster. You can use a combination of the types of backups we described in the previous section to achieve your aims. In this section, we describe two methods of backing up your database.

Method 1

This first method is the simplest backup strategy. Every day at a predetermined hour you do a full backup of your database. You don't do anything else to it at all. This unfortunately gives you 24 hours of exposure (*exposure* being the amount of data you could lose). If you lost the server or database in the middle of the day, then you could only recover to the backup taken the night before. (Yes, if you got to the log file you would be able to recover more, but we're presuming here that you only have your backups to go on.)

This type of plan may be suitable in a test environment where being up-to-date is not essential, or where you can recover any lost data through scripts. In order to recover this database, you would just need to restore it from the previous night's backup and carry on. This method is very quick to set up, but it's only suitable in a few cases. Figure 2-1 shows a possible backup scenario using only full backups.

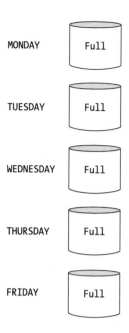

MONDAY Full

TUESDAY Full

WEDNESDAY Full

THURSDAY Full

FRIDAY Full

Figure 2-1. Scenario using only full backups

Method 2

The second method is a more detailed plan that should enable you to recover the database to the second of a disaster. For example, say on a Sunday night you do a full backup of your database. Then Monday through Friday you do hourly transaction log backups during business hours. Each weekday night you do differential backups of the database as well. Then you have a database failure on Thursday at 3:30 P.M. and you manage to back up the current transaction log of the database. To restore this database to its previous state, you would need to do the following:

1. Restore the full backup from Sunday.

2. Restore the differential backup from Wednesday night.

3. Restore the transaction log backups that occurred between start of business on Thursday and 3:00 P.M.

4. Restore the final transaction log backup that you managed to rescue from the database.

As you can see, this method is certainly involved, but it does allow you to recover more data than the first method. In fact, if you're able to get to the current transaction log, then you may be able to recover the database without losing any data at all. Figure 2-2 shows a possible backup scenario using a combination of full, differential, and transaction log backups.

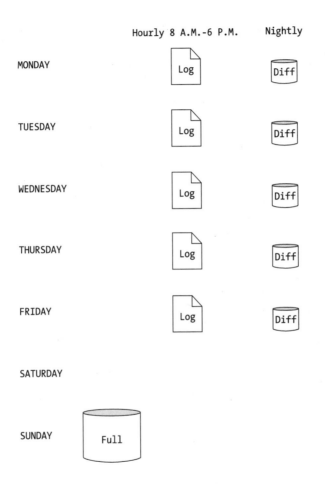

Figure 2-2. Scenario using full, differential, and transaction log backups

Considerations for Choosing Your Backup Method

Remember earlier when we said there were certain database settings that would affect your ability to do some types of backup? Well, here they are. In the sections that follow, the database settings are broken down into the different options for both SQL Server 7.0 and SQL Server 2000.

NOTE We explain how to set these options using T-SQL, SQL-DMO, and Enterprise Manager in Chapter 1.

SQL Server 7.0

In SQL Server 7.0 you have to do a bit more work than you do in SQL Server 2000, as version 2000 sets the version 7.0 options under the covers when you choose your recovery model.

Truncate Log on Checkpoint

This option is very easy to remember. It wrecks your chances of doing transaction log backups. This means that the only backups you can perform with this option set are full and differential. This might not be a problem for you, but we only recommend using this option in development and test environments.

The way the option works is this: When SQL Server has written out your data to disk from the log at preset intervals, it will come along and clean up after itself. It doesn't back up the log—it just gets rid of any transactions that have been marked as completed. If you try to back up the log when this option is set, you'll get an error. It effectively creates holes in the life of a database. You have nothing to put back into your database because SQL Server has removed the entries from the log.

NOTE Lots of people ask if they can just get rid of the transaction log because they don't need it. The answer to this is no. SQL Server needs the transaction log to ensure database consistency. If you get rid of the transaction log and your database has the option Truncate Log on Checkpoint set, then you can't do file group backups, because these backups rely on the transaction log to make them consistent.

Select Into/Bulk Copy

The Select Into/Bulk Copy option enables you to perform actions such as SELECT INTO, BCP, or WRITETEXT in your database. These types of actions are often referred to as *nonlogged*, but this is actually a bit of a misnomer as they're logged but only minimally. Once you perform one of these actions, you invalidate point-in-time recovery of your database. *Point-in-time recovery* is where you can stop a restore of a database at a given time, which is preferably just before the action occurred that caused you to do the restore.

An example of this would be when you have a table with records in it that you want to replicate, perhaps just in case the following operation goes wrong. You could CREATE the table and then do an INSERT INTO to get the records in, but instead you decide to use SELECT INTO, as that will create the table for you as well. SQL Server will then create your new table and pump the records in. It will log the fact that it allocated extents to the table, but it won't log every insertion. This is where gaps in recovery may appear.

 CAUTION   Using SELECT INTO on a large table isn't a good idea. It will lock up tempdb for the duration of the statement; therefore, it has the potential to stop others from working. If you can create the table first and then do an INSERT statement, you'll stop this from happening.

SQL Server 2000

SQL Server 2000 does things a little differently from SQL Server 7.0. You can still use the options described previously, but they're provided for backward compatibility and should only be used as such. In version 2000, you have recovery options, of which there are three.

The Simple Recovery Option

You would use this option when you have no use for the transaction log whatsoever and you want to make sure that it doesn't get too large. As with the Truncate Log on Checkpoint option in SQL Server 7.0, the Simple Recovery option allows you to only use full and differential backups. If your database is set to Simple, then you can't do file group backups, as these backups rely on the transaction log to make them consistent.

The Bulk-Logged Recovery Option

Here is where the differences between the SQL Server 7.0 and SQL Server 2000 options really start to become evident. With this model you can perform your minimally logged operation as you can with the Select Into/Bulk Copy option of SQL Server 7.0. The transaction log will log the fact that a nonlogged operation has occurred, and pages within the database will be marked as having been subjected to minimally logged operations. When you come to back up your database, the log file itself will still be small, but in addition to backing itself up it will also back up those extents that have been modified by the minimally logged operation.

The Full Recovery Option

The Full Recovery option allows you to have the least data loss of the three options. If you've been making transaction log backups, then you have the ability to restore to a point in time. Although this may sound like the best option, there's a penalty to pay. Because everything but the kitchen sink is logged, this option can result in the size of the transaction log being huge. This means, of course, that it will take a longer time to back up as well. You can still perform your minimally logged operations when the database is using the Full Recovery mode.

Using Backup Devices

There are two ways of telling SQL Server where to send your backups. The first is by typing in the file path to the location where you want SQL Server to send your backups every time you issue the BACKUP DATABASE command. The second is by creating a backup device that points to the location where you want SQL Server to send your backups and then using the name of the backup device each time you do a backup. The only difference between the two methods that you'll probably notice is that the second method involves less typing.

Another neat thing about using a backup device is that in Enterprise Manager you can easily see, using the GUI, the contents of the backup device. We'll show you shortly how you can create your own view of the contents of your backup device, and we'll also show you the code that Enterprise Manager is issuing under the covers. Let's see, then, how to add a backup device to your server using three methods: T-SQL, SQL-DMO, and Enterprise Manager.

T-SQL

```
sp_addumpdevice [ @devtype = ] 'device_type' ,
    [ @logicalname = ] 'logical_name' ,
    [ @physicalname = ] 'physical_name'
    [ , { [ @cntrltype = ] controller_type
            | [ @devstatus = ] 'device_status'
        }
    ]
Example
EXEC sp_addumpdevice 'disk','My_Backup_Device','f:\DBBackups\MyBackups.bak'
```

SQL-DMO

In Enterprise Manager, you'll find the option to add a device under the Management folder. Then click the Backup icon. Figure 2-3 shows the prompt in SQL Server when you create a new backup device.

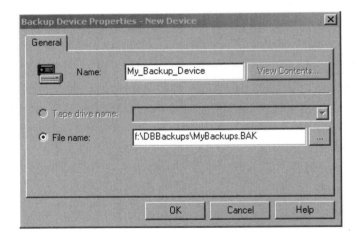

Figure 2-3. Adding a backup device in Enterprise Manager

The following code creates a SQLServer object and a BackupDevice object:

```
Private Sub cmdCreate_Click()
```

```
Dim oServer As SQLDMO.SQLServer
Dim oDevice As SQLDMO.BackupDevice

Set oServer = New SQLDMO.SQLServer

Connect to the SQL Server
oServer.LoginSecure = True
oServer.Connect "AM2"

Set oDevice = New SQLDMO.BackupDevice
```

The following code sets the properties of the backup device. First, you set the Name property of the device:

```
oDevice.Name = "My_Backup_Device"
```

You want to create a device that points to location on the physical hard disk, so you specify the options here to do that:

```
oDevice.Type = SQLDMODevice_DiskDump
oDevice.PhysicalLocation = "f:\DBBackups\MyBackups.bak"
```

Once you've set all the properties of the device, the last thing you need to do is add the Device object to the Devices collection of the server:

```
oServer.BackupDevices.Add oDevice

oServer.DisConnect
Set oServer = Nothing

End Sub
```

The result of these three methods is shown in Figure 2-4.

Name ▲	Physical Location	Device Type
My_Backup_Device	f:\DBBackups\MyBackups.BAK	Disk Backup

Figure 2-4. Creation of the device is confirmed.

TIP SQL Server Books Online provides a list of the other options for the device type and controller type.

Performing the Backup

Now you come to the meat of the chapter, where you'll actually perform your backup. In this section, we show you how to do a full, a differential, and a transaction log backup. We also show you some of the options available to you when you do a backup. The following code shows how to do the backup for the database. The two code listings that follow are taken directly from SQL Server Books Online.

T-SQL

```
BACKUP DATABASE
{ database_name | @database_name_var }
TO < backup_device > [ ,...n ]
[ WITH
    [ BLOCKSIZE = { blocksize | @blocksize_variable } ]
    [ [ , ] DESCRIPTION = { 'text' | @text_variable } ]
    [ [ , ] DIFFERENTIAL ]
    [ [ , ] EXPIREDATE = { date | @date_var }
        | RETAINDAYS = { days | @days_var } ]
    [ [ , ] PASSWORD =
 { password | @password_variable } ]
    [ [ , ] FORMAT | NOFORMAT ]
    [ [ , ] { INIT | NOINIT } ]
    [ [ , ] MEDIADESCRIPTION = { 'text' | @text_variable } ]
    [ [ , ] MEDIANAME =
{ media_name | @media_name_variable } ]
    [ [ , ] MEDIAPASSWORD =
 { mediapassword | @mediapassword_variable } ]
    [ [ , ] NAME =
{ backup_set_name | @backup_set_name_var } ]
    [ [ , ] { NOSKIP | SKIP } ]
    [ [ , ] { NOREWIND | REWIND } ]
    [ [ , ] { NOUNLOAD | UNLOAD } ]
    [ [ , ] RESTART ]
    [ [ , ] STATS [ = percentage ] ]
]
```

Here's the code for backing up the log:

```
BACKUP LOG { database_name | @database_name_var }
{
    TO < backup_device > [ ,...n ]
    [ WITH
        [ BLOCKSIZE =
 { blocksize | @blocksize_variable } ]
        [ [ , ] DESCRIPTION = { 'text' | @text_variable } ]
        [ [ ,] EXPIREDATE = { date | @date_var }
            | RETAINDAYS = { days | @days_var } ]
        [ [ , ] PASSWORD =
 { password | @password_variable } ]
        [ [ , ] FORMAT | NOFORMAT ]
        [ [ , ] { INIT | NOINIT } ]
        [ [ , ] MEDIADESCRIPTION =
 { 'text' | @text_variable } ]
        [ [ , ] MEDIANAME =
 { media_name | @media_name_variable } ]
        [ [ , ] MEDIAPASSWORD =
 { mediapassword | @mediapassword_variable } ]
        [ [ , ] NAME =
 { backup_set_name | @backup_set_name_var } ]
        [ [ , ] NO_TRUNCATE ]
        [ [ , ] { NORECOVERY | STANDBY = undo_file_name } ]
        [ [ , ] { NOREWIND | REWIND } ]
        [ [ , ] { NOSKIP | SKIP } ]
        [ [ , ] { NOUNLOAD | UNLOAD } ]
        [ [ , ] RESTART ]
        [ [ , ] STATS [ = percentage ] ]
    ]
}
```

As you can see, you have a lot of options available to you when you back up a database or log, and you may never use most of them. In our examples, we're concerned with the ones you'll use most, but for completeness, we think it's worthwhile to provide a short description of each option:

- *DATABASE_NAME:* This is simply the name of the database you want to back up.

- *BACKUP_DEVICE:* This is where you want to put the backup. It can be either a physical path or one of the backup devices you created earlier.

- *BLOCKSIZE:* This is the physical size of blocks in bytes. According to SQL Server Books Online, this isn't necessary, as SQL Server will choose the most appropriate size for you.

- *DESCRIPTION:* This is a label for your backup. You may want to include a short description of why you made the backup.

- *DIFFERENTIAL:* This option indicates if this backup is differential.

- *EXPIREDATE:* This option gives a date for when the backup can be overwritten.

- *RETAINDAYS:* This option is like EXPIREDATE, except it indicates how many days the backup is kept before you're able to overwrite it.

- *PASSWORD:* You can password-protect your backup, and you must supply the password in order to restore from it.

- *FORMAT/NO FORMAT:* This option indicates whether or not the media header should be written on all backup devices.

- *INIT/NOINIT:* This option indicates whether or not to clear down the contents of your backup device.

- *MEDIADESCRIPTION:* This option gives you a chance to describe the media as something useful.

- *MEDIANAME:* This option gives you a chance to give the media a name.

- *MEDIAPASSWORD:* If you specify a password for the media, then before you're able to create a backup on it, you must supply that password.

- *NAME:* This is the name of the backup set.

- *NOSKIP/SKIP:* If you've set your backups to have expiration dates, then using NOSKIP will force SQL Server to check that before trying to overwrite it. The SKIP option will bypass checking and overwrite as necessary.

- *NOREWIND/REWIND:* This option indicates to SQL Server whether or not to rewind and release the tape.

- *NOUNLOAD/UNLOAD:* This option indicates to SQL Server whether or not to rewind and unload the tape. SQL Server Books Online says this is only for tape devices, although later you'll see Enterprise Manager using it against disk devices once you get some backups onto your device.

- *RESTART:* This option does exactly what its name indicates: It restarts an interrupted backup at the point of interruption.

- *STATS = [percentage]:* This option indicates to SQL Server to let you know when each percentage of the backup has completed. If you don't specify this option, the default is 10 percent. You only use this on large backups because it means you have something to look at as the backup is happening.

For the following examples you'll back up the same database to the same backup device that you created earlier, but you'll use different options in each so you can see the results of the options.

Backing Up MyDMODatabase

Here you'll back up the database MyDMODatabase and label the backup as having been done using T-SQL. The backup here is a full backup.

T-SQL

```
BACKUP DATABASE MyDMODatabase
TO My_Backup_Device
WITH
     NAME = 'Done using T-SQL'
```

After you do the backup, check its integrity with the following code:

```
RESTORE VERIFYONLY FROM My_Backup_Device
```

If you had more than one backup on the same device, you would need to specify a file number, as in the following code:

```
RESTORE VERIFYONLY FROM My_Backup_Device WITH FILE = 1
```

In Enterprise Manager, there are a number of ways to get your database backed up. We've chosen to show three here for brevity:

- Right-click the database, and then choose All Tasks and Backup Database.

- Choose the Tools menu and then select Backup Database.

- Select the wand from the toolbar, choose Maintenance, and then select Backup Wizard.

Which method you choose to use is immaterial—you end up looking at the same screen eventually—but we rarely use wizards. Figure 2-5 shows the screen that greets you if you choose the Tools menu and then select Backup Database. As you can see from the options selected in the figure, we're doing a differential backup of the MyDMODatabase. We're calling it "Done Using EM" and appending it to the backup device we created earlier.

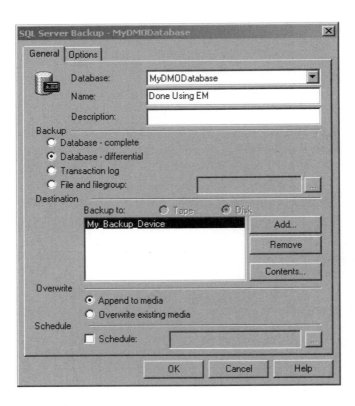

Figure 2-5. Enterprise Manager backup database

Backing Up MyDMODatabase Using the Application

You'll be backing up MyDMODatabase to your backup device using a differential backup and setting the time that SQL Server keeps this backup without allowing it to be overwritten for 2 days. We've provided a GUI along with it to show the ease with which you can do it (see Figure 2-6).

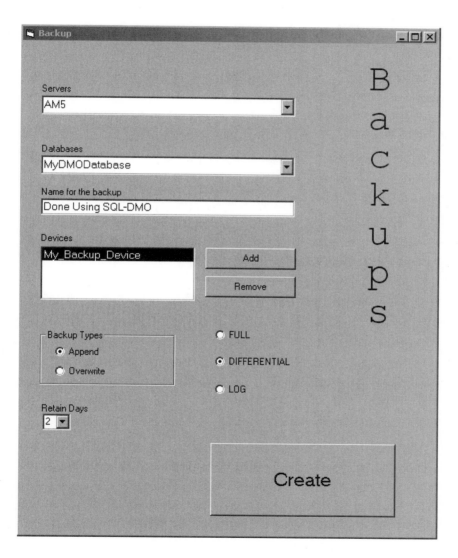

Figure 2-6. The backup application

This simple application takes very little time to create. It does more or less exactly what the GUI in Enterprise Manager does. Now we'll go through the mechanics of what's happening behind the scenes and show you a few things about what Microsoft is doing in Enterprise Manager under the covers.

```
Public oServer As SQLDMO.SQLServer
Public oDevice As SQLDMO.BackupDevice
Public oDatabase As SQLDMO.Database
Public oBackup As SQLDMO.Backup
Public oRegisteredServer As SQLDMO.RegisteredServer
Public oApp As SQLDMO.Application
Public oRestore as SQLDMO.Restore
Public oGroup as SQLDMO.ServerGroup
```

The following procedure will populate the Servers combo box with a list of registered servers:

```
Private Sub ShowServers()

Set oApp = New sqldmo.Application
Set oRegisteredServer = New sqldmo.RegisteredServer

cboServers.Clear
```

Grouping Your Servers

You may group your servers in Enterprise Manager to define their roles in your business or indicate where they're located in the country. First, you need to loop through the ServerGroups collection, looking for the names of your server groups:

```
For Each oGroup In oApp.ServerGroups
```

Groups contain your registered servers, so you need to loop through your groups looking for any to add. To do this, you'll need to loop through the RegisteredServers collection.

```
For Each oRegisteredServer In oApp.ServerGroups(oGroup.Name).RegisteredServers
    cboServers.AddItem oRegisteredServer.Name
Next oRegisteredServer

Next oGroup
```

```
Set oGroup = Nothing
Set oRegisteredServer = Nothing
Set oApp = Nothing

End Sub


Private Sub ShowDatabases(servername As String)
```

> **NOTE** There's another way to look for all your SQL Servers: You can use the ListAvailableSQLServers method of the Application object. The reason we don't use this method here is because although it will find your SQL Servers, it will only do so if you're on the same network segment as the SQL Servers. This is because the ListAvailableSQLServers method uses a broadcast to locate the SQL Servers and this broadcast won't travel through routers. We've met some people on newsgroups that have also had this problem.

Outputting Database Names to the Combo Box

When you select the server that contains the database you want to back up, you need to populate the Databases combo box with a list of available databases on that server. Here you just loop through the Databases collection of the connected SQLServer object and output the database names to the combo box.

```
Set oServer = New SQLDMO.SQLServer

oServer.LoginSecure = True
oServer.Connect servername

cboDatabases.Clear

For Each oDatabase In oServer.Databases
    cboDatabases.AddItem oDatabase.Name
Next oDatabase
```

```
oServer.DisConnect
Set oServer = Nothing
Set oDatabase = Nothing


End Sub

Private Sub ShowBackupDevices(servername As String)
```

For this procedure, you want to list the available predefined backup devices on your server. All you do is loop through the BackupDevices collection of the server.

```
Set oServer = New SQLDMO.SQLServer

oServer.LoginSecure = True
oServer.Connect servername

lstdevices.Clear

For Each oDevice In oServer.BackupDevices
    lstdevices.AddItem oDevice.Name
Next oDevice

oServer.DisConnect
Set oServer = Nothing
Set oDevice = Nothing

End Sub
```

Prompting the Actual Backup

The following procedure will actually do the backup and will be called by the Create button on the form. The procedure takes a number of parameters. The first two, servername and DatabaseName, are obvious. The third, Location, is where you want to send the backup. The fourth, DeviceYN, indicates whether the location you've chosen is a predefined backup device or one that you've added because maybe this is an ad hoc backup. The fifth parameter, BackupType, will tell you whether you're doing a full, differential, or transaction log backup. Next, RetainDays, is how long you want to keep the backup before you're able to overwrite it. Then you tell the backup if you should initialize the device first with InitFirst. Finally, BackupName is the name of the backup.

```
Private Sub BackupTheDatabase(servername As String,
 DatabaseName As String, Location As String,
DeviceYN As Integer, BackupType
As SQLDMO_BACKUP_TYPE, RetainDays As Integer,
 InitFirst As Boolean, BackupName As String)

On Error GoTo Err_handler

Set oServer = New SQLDMO.SQLServer
```

During testing we came across an interesting anomaly. If you try to back up a database in Enterprise Manager and you don't supply a backup name, SQL Server will tell you that you need one, as shown in Figure 2-7.

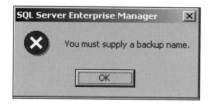

Figure 2-7. Message box requesting a backup name

 NOTE The error also happens if you try to back up the database using SQL-DMO using your application. This seems fair, as all Enterprise Manager does is issue SQL-DMO anyway. The problem is when you try to back up the database using T-SQL. You don't need to supply a name, and SQL Server has no problem with that. If you read the header from your backup, you'll see that the name of the backup set is "NULL," which indicates that no value is passed.

Initializing the Backup

You initialize your backup and restore objects with the following code:

```
Set oBackup = New SQLDMO.Backup
Set oRestore = New SQLDMO.Restore
```

Then you log on to the server on which you want to do a backup:

```
oServer.LoginSecure = True
oServer.Connect servername
```

You now pass your values to the backup object. What type of backup is it?

```
oBackup.Action = BackupType
```

What's the name of the backup?

```
oBackup.BackupSetName = BackupName
```

Which database are you backing up?

```
oBackup.Database = DatabaseName
```

How long are you keeping the backup?

```
oBackup.RetainDays = RetainDays
```

Are you initializing the media first?

```
oBackup.Initialize = InitFirst
```

Here's where you indicate whether or not the location you're sending the backup to is a predefined device or a location you added. Note the different properties of the Backup object you use. You also set the Restore object's place to look for files.

```
If DeviceYN = 1 Then
    oBackup.Devices = Location
    oRestore.Devices = Location
Else
    oBackup.Files = Location
    oRestore.Files = Location
End If
```

Here's the actual backup:

```
oBackup.SQLBackup oServer
```

This is the check of the backup to ensure it's structurally sound. After all, what's the point in a backup that's rubbish?

```
oRestore.SQLVerify oServer

MsgBox "The database Backup Succeeded", vbOKOnly, "Backup Completed"

oServer.DisConnect
Set oServer = Nothing
Exit Sub


Err_handler:
```

The following error number indicates a corrupted backup:

```
If Err.Number = -2147218262 Then
MsgBox "The backup you have just " & _
"performed would appear to be " & _
corrupted", vbCritical, "Backup problem"
Else
    MsgBox "The database Backup " & _
Failed" & vbCrLf & Err.Description, vbOKOnly, _
"Backup Completed"
End If

oServer.DisConnect
Set oServer = Nothing
Exit Sub

End Sub

Private Sub cboServers_Click()
ShowDatabases cboServers.Text
ShowBackupDevices cboServers.Text
End Sub
```

Here's where you add new locations for your backups:

```
Private Sub cmdAdd_Click()
Dim strNewLocation As String

strNewLocation = InputBox("Enter A New Location", "New Backup Location")
```

```
If strNewLocation <> "" Then
    lstdevices.AddItem strNewLocation
End If


End Sub


Private Sub cmdCreate_Click()

Dim servername As String
Dim BackupType As SQLDMO_BACKUP_TYPE
Dim Init As Boolean
Dim DeviceCounter As Integer
Dim BackupName As String

Init = False
```

You need to set the backup type that you're going to be using:

```
If optFull.Value = True Then
    BackupType = SQLDMOBackup_Database
ElseIf OptDiff.Value = True Then
    BackupType = SQLDMOBackup_Differential
ElseIf OptLog.Value = True Then
    BackupType = SQLDMOBackup_Log
End If
```

NOTE As with Enterprise Manager, when you back up the log you get no options for it. The default behavior of SQL Server when backing up the log is to back it up and remove completed transactions from it.

Here you indicate if you want to initialize the device:

```
If OptOverwrite.Value = True Then
    Init = True
End If
```

If you've chosen a server, a database, and somewhere to send it to, you can proceed.

```
If (cboServers.Text <> "" Or cboDatabases.Text <> ""
Or lstdevices.ListIndex <> -1) Then

        Set oServer = New SQLDMO.SQLServer
Set oBackup = New SQLDMO.Backup
```

Finally, log on to the server:

```
oServer.LoginSecure = True
oServer.Connect cboServers.Text
```

Locating the Backup to Restore

Here's where you find out if the location for the backup is in the BackupDevices collection. You do this by looking for a match between the names in the list box on the form and the names of your BackupDevices. If you get a hit, you set DeviceCounter = 1, which indicates "Yes."

```
        For Each oDevice In oServer.BackupDevices
            If oDevice.Name = lstdevices.Text Then
                DeviceCounter = 1
            End If
        Next oDevice
```

Because you need to supply the backup with a name, and you may have forgotten to put anything in the Name box, you supply a default in the form of *<database name>_yyyymmddhhmmss>*.

```
        If txtName = "" Then
            BackupName = _
cboDatabases.Text & "_" & Format(Now(), _
"yyyymmdd") & Format(Now(),"hhmmss")
        Else
            BackupName = txtName.Text
        End If
```

Here you call the backup procedure with the relevant parameters:

```
BackupTheDatabase cboServers.Text, cboDatabases.Text,
 lstdevices.Text, DeviceCounter, BackupType, cboRetain.Text,
 Init, BackupName


End If


End Sub
```

Remove devices from the Devices list box (don't remove them from the server, though):

```
Private Sub cmdremove_Click()
If lstdevices.ListIndex <> -1 Then
    lstdevices.RemoveItem lstdevices.ListIndex
End If
End Sub

Private Sub Form_Load()
cboRetain.ListIndex = 0
ShowServers
optAppend.Value = True
optFull.Value = True
End Sub
```

NOTE When you open up Enterprise Manager and select your database, SQL Server remembers where you last sent it to for backing up. We've chosen not to do this here, but Enterprise Manager uses the following code to do it:

```
use msdb
select
distinct f.device_type, f.physical_device_name, f.logical_device_name,
 b.database_name
from
backupmediafamily f, backupset b  where
 b.database_name = N'MyDMODatabase'
 and
b.backup_finish_date = (select MAX(backup_finish_date)
 from backupmediafamily
INNER JOIN backupset ON
backupmediafamily.media_set_id=backupset.media_set_id
```

```
where backupset.database_name = N'MyDMODatabase'
and (backupmediafamily.device_type=2 or
backupmediafamily.device_type=102))
 and b.media_set_id = f.media_set_id
```

Backing Up the Log

Periodically, you may need to back up the log of your database. Using Enterprise Manager and your SQL-DMO application, you can find everything in the same place and you just specify a log backup. In T-SQL, however, you need to use slightly different syntax. Most of the options are the same, but a few need explanation. Here's the code, which is taken from SQL Server Books Online.

T-SQL

```
BACKUP LOG { database_name | @database_name_var }
{
    TO < backup_device > [ ,...n ]
    [ WITH
        [ BLOCKSIZE =
 { blocksize | @blocksize_variable } ]
        [ [ , ] DESCRIPTION =
{ 'text' | @text_variable } ]
        [ [ ,] EXPIREDATE =
{ date | @date_var }
            | RETAINDAYS = { days | @days_var } ]
        [ [ , ] PASSWORD =
{ password | @password_variable } ]
        [ [ , ] FORMAT | NOFORMAT ]
        [ [ , ] { INIT | NOINIT } ]
        [ [ , ] MEDIADESCRIPTION = { 'text' | @text_variable } ]
        [ [ , ] MEDIANAME =
 { media_name | @media_name_variable } ]
        [ [ , ] MEDIAPASSWORD =
{ mediapassword | @mediapassword_variable } ]
        [ [ , ] NAME =
{ backup_set_name | @backup_set_name_var } ]
        [ [ , ] NO_TRUNCATE ]
        [ [ , ] { NORECOVERY | STANDBY = undo_file_name } ]
        [ [ , ] { NOREWIND | REWIND } ]
        [ [ , ] { NOSKIP | SKIP } ]
```

```
            [ [ , ] { NOUNLOAD | UNLOAD } ]
            [ [ , ] RESTART ]
            [ [ , ] STATS [ = percentage ] ]
        ]
    }
```

We would like to explain the TRUNCATE options:

- *NO_TRUNCATE:* This option indicates that the log should be backed up, but committed transactions shouldn't be removed from it. The SQL-DMO constant for this is

    ```
    SQLDMOBACKUP_Log_NoTruncate
    ```

- *NO_LOG:* This option tells SQL Server to get rid of the committed transactions in the log and to not bother about backing them up to a physical file or tape. You don't need to specify a backup device or location for the option, as the log doesn't get backed up. This creates a hole in your recovery options because you're missing some transactions. It's advisable to follow this type of log backup with a full database backup to restore your ability to recover from a disaster. The SQL-DMO constant for this is

    ```
    SQLDMOBACKUP_Log_NoLog
    ```

- *TRUNCATE_ONLY:* This option is the same as NO_LOG. The SQL-DMO constant for this is

    ```
    SQLDMOBACKUP_Log_TruncateOnly
    ```

Restoring the Database

The primary reason you create a backup is that in the event of a disaster you can have a good go at re-creating your environments with as little loss of data as possible. The following code listings show how to restore a database and log. The code is taken from SQL Server Books Online.

T-SQL

```
RESTORE DATABASE { database_name | @database_name_var }
[ FROM < backup_device > [ ,...n ] ]
[ WITH
    [ RESTRICTED_USER ]
    [ [ , ] FILE = { file_number | @file_number } ]
```

```
      [ [ , ] PASSWORD =
 { password | @password_variable } ]
      [ [ , ] MEDIANAME = { media_name | @media_name_variable } ]
      [ [ , ] MEDIAPASSWORD =
 { mediapassword | @mediapassword_variable } ]
      [ [ , ] MOVE 'logical_file_name'
TO 'operating_system_file_name' ]
             [ ,...n ]
      [ [ , ] KEEP_REPLICATION ]
      [ [ , ] { NORECOVERY | RECOVERY | STANDBY = undo_file_name } ]
      [ [ , ] { NOREWIND | REWIND } ]
      [ [ , ] { NOUNLOAD | UNLOAD } ]
      [ [ , ] REPLACE ]
      [ [ , ] RESTART ]
      [ [ , ] STATS [ = percentage ] ]
]
```

The following code shows how to restore a log:

```
RESTORE LOG { database_name | @database_name_var }
[ FROM < backup_device > [ ,...n ] ]
[ WITH
    [ RESTRICTED_USER ]
    [ [ , ] FILE = { file_number | @file_number } ]
    [ [ , ] PASSWORD = { password | @password_variable } ]
    [ [ , ] MOVE 'logical_file_name' TO 'operating_system_file_name' ]
           [ ,...n ]
    [ [ , ] MEDIANAME = { media_name | @media_name_variable } ]
    [ [ , ] MEDIAPASSWORD = { mediapassword | @mediapassword_variable } ]
    [ [ , ] KEEP_REPLICATION ]
    [ [ , ] { NORECOVERY | RECOVERY | STANDBY = undo_file_name } ]
    [ [ , ] { NOREWIND | REWIND } ]
    [ [ , ] { NOUNLOAD | UNLOAD } ]
    [ [ , ] RESTART ]
    [ [ , ] STATS [= percentage ] ]
    [ [ , ] STOPAT = { date_time | @date_time_var }
        | [ , ] STOPATMARK = 'mark_name' [ AFTER datetime ]
        | [ , ] STOPBEFOREMARK = 'mark_name' [ AFTER datetime ]
    ]
]
```

The syntax for restoring a database and restoring a log is rather similar, but once again we'll explain those options that are perhaps not obvious.

- *FILE:* If you back up to a device on a number of occasions, then you'll need to specify this option. File numbers increment in multiples of one and are allocated on writing to the device. This will enable you to specify the particular backup on the device you require.

- *MOVE:* This option is used when you want or need to place the physical files in a different place than where they were backed up from. For example, say you have a database that has both its data file and log file on the F drive. You want to restore that database to another server, but that server only has a C drive and a D drive. Because the database knows where it previously lived on the disks, it defaults to that location. In this example, you don't have an F drive, so you need to tell SQL Server to move the files.

- *NORECOVERY/RECOVERY/STANDBY:* If you specify RECOVERY, then you'll bring the database up and make it available to users. You won't be able to apply further backups. If you use NORECOVERY, then you can apply more backups to the database, but the database is unavailable. Finally, if you choose STANDBY, then you're able to apply more backups to the database and you also make the database READ-ONLY. With this option, you also need to specify an undo file so you can roll back any transactions.

- *REPLACE:* You use this option if you have an existing database and you want to apply the backup of a different database to it. You force the restore over the top.

- *STOPAT:* This option allows you to specify exactly when you want to restore, down to the thousandth of a second. For example, a user may have dropped all the tables in the database at 2:30 P.M., so you would need to restore to just before that point in the log.

- *STOPATMARK/STOPBEFOREMARK:* SQL Server 2000 allows you to mark the log, and you can then use that mark as a reference point for your restores. For example, say you successfully do a load of a database and you mark the log. You carry on and manage to mess things up later on. You can choose to restore to your previous mark.

Implementing the Restore

In the next example you'll restore a database from a full database backup and a transaction log backup. The database backup will be on a backup device, and the transaction log backup will be on a physical file.

```
RESTORE DATABASE MyDatabase FROM MyBackupDevice
WITH FILE = 1, NORECOVERY

RESTORE LOG MyDatabase FROM
disk = 'C:\Logfilebackups\LogFordatabase.bak'
WITH RECOVERY
```

If you want to look at the details of a backup before you go and restore it, the following three commands won't actually restore the database but will just tell you about the backup:

```
RESTORE FILELISTONLY FROM ….
RESTORE LABELONLY FROM ….
RESTORE HEADERONLY FROM ….
```

Figure 2-8 shows the Restore database screen in Enterprise Manager. Here you decide which database to restore and also where you restore the database from.

You can access the screen in Figure 2-8 in a number of ways. We include only two here for brevity.

- Right-click the database itself or the Databases folder and choose All Tasks followed by Restore Database.

- From the Tools menu, choose Restore Database.

On this screen, you specify the database you want to restore, which can be either an existing database or a new one. You also indicate what type of backup it is and where you want to get the backup from. Figure 2-9 shows the options available for placing the restored files and what state to leave the database in.

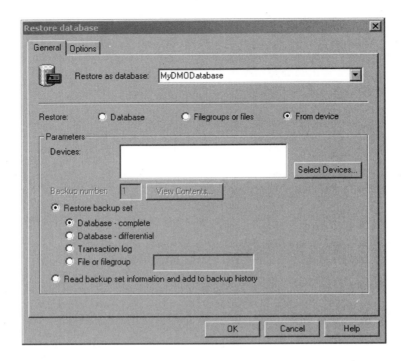

Figure 2-8. The Restore database screen in Enterprise Manager

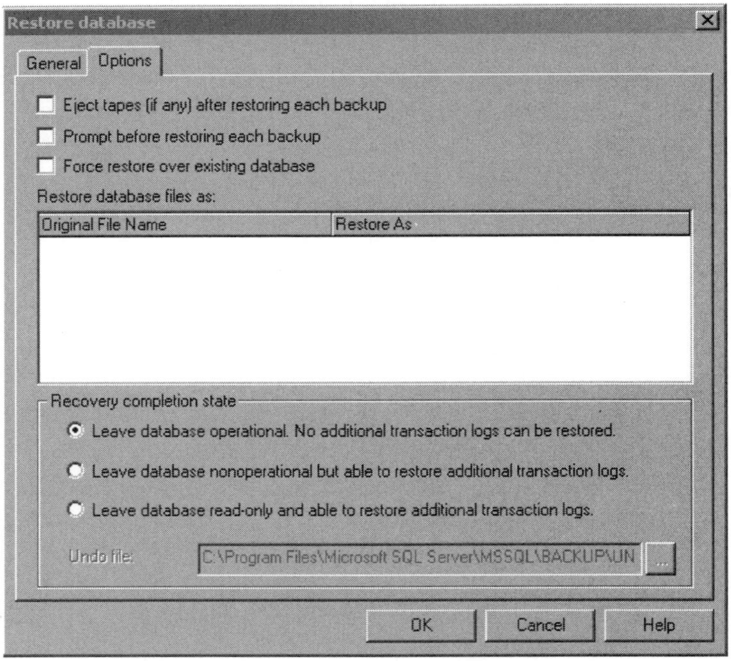

Figure 2-9. The Options tab in the Restore database screen in Enterprise Manager

From the Restore database Options tab, you can choose to move the physical files to a different location (remember the MOVE option in T-SQL). You can also specify the recovery state of your database (RECOVERY, NORECOVERY, or STANDBY). Enterprise Manager is quite easy to get along with.

> **NOTE**   Enterprise Manager isn't particularly good at refreshing, and here's an example of how you can get caught out with it. Say you choose to restore a particular database. The "Restore as database" box on the first screen of Enterprise Manager contains the database name. You then choose to restore from a device with multiple backups on it. Backup number 1 is the default choice, so you see the logical names and physical names of the backup on the Options tab. If the backup is of a different database, then you have incorrectly named files. This is problematic when the database from which the backup was taken is on the same server. And, if you choose to use a different FILE number on the device, Enterprise Manager doesn't update the view of the logical and physical files. Now you're left with a database with one name, logical and physical files from a different database, and a FILE number on the backup device from a completely different backup.

Restoring Using SQL-DMO

To illustrate how you can do restores in SQL-DMO, we've built a very small application that does most of what Enterprise Manager does. (It actually does refreshing better than Enterprise Manager.) We've added a tab for you to look at the data definition language (DDL) you're creating so it can serve as a learning tool for what you need to do in T-SQL as well. Figure 2-10 shows our application prompting for a database to restore.

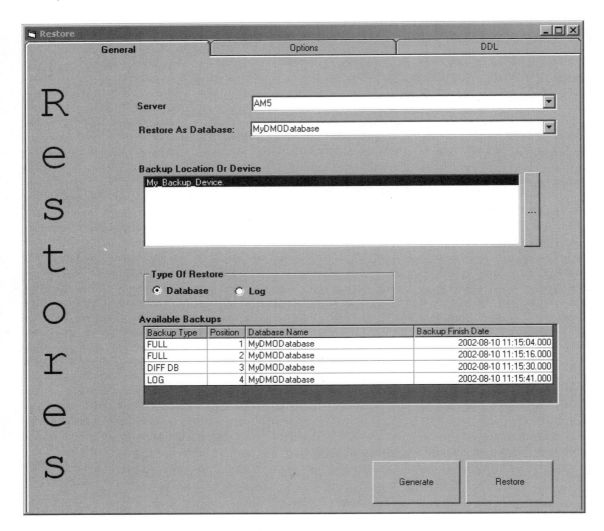

Figure 2-10. The first screen of our application

The first screen is where you choose the server, database, and backup device that you want to restore from. You can, if there are multiple backups on the device (as there are in Figure 2-10), choose which backup device you want to restore from. Figure 2-11 shows our application asking where we want to move a file.

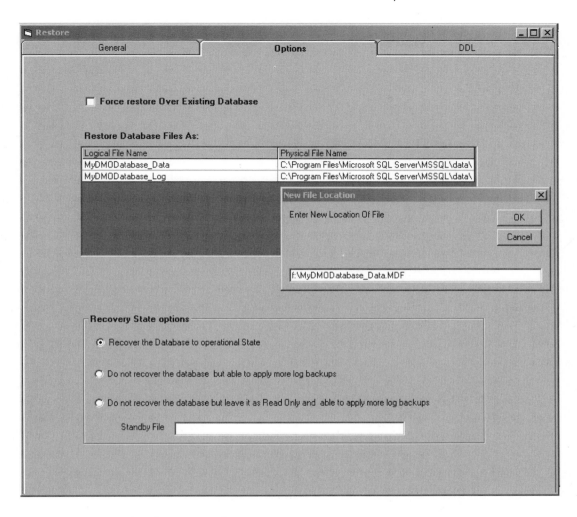

Figure 2-11. Prompting for a restore location

The second screen is where you indicate when you restore the files whether you want to keep them in the same physical location or move them. (In Figure 2-11, you can see that we've chosen to move the file. We made the other screen pop up by clicking the Physical File Name we wanted to change.) The second screen is also the place you determine what condition you want the database left in after the restore.

The DDL screen (see Figure 2-12) generates a T-SQL statement to show you what it is you'll be executing against SQL Server. This can be an excellent learning tool for people who are more comfortable with the GUI but who are looking to learn the T-SQL equivalent.

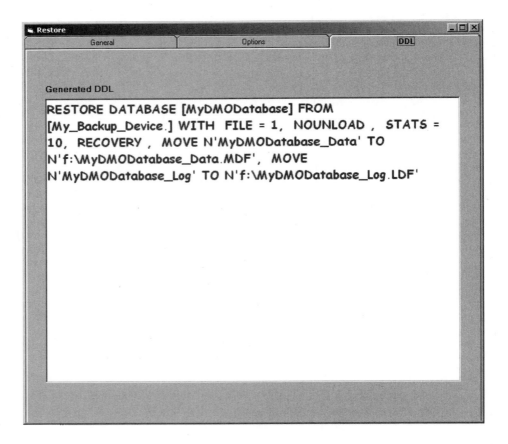

Figure 2-12. The DDL screen

A lot of the code for the application follows. We've chosen not to go through every single line of code. Rather, we explain those code lines that are pertinent and that we think are useful.

Specifying the Backup Origin

Once you've chosen your server and database for the restore, you need to specify where the backup will be coming from (i.e., its origin). In our application, that origin can be one of two places: a predefined backup or a physical file. If you click the ellipses to the right of the Backup Location or Device list box, you're taken to the screen shown in Figure 2-13. This screen allows you to select the location.

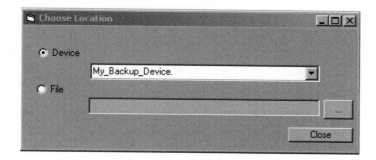

Figure 2-13. Selecting the location of the backup

To populate the combo box with the list of backup devices available, you simply loop through the backup devices of the server. The following code goes through the backup devices defined on the server and adds them to the combo box display in the application:

```
Private Sub ShowBackupDevices(servername As String)

Set oServer = New SQLDMO.SQLServer
oServer.LoginSecure = True
oServer.Connect servername

cboDevices.Clear

For Each oDevice In oServer.BackupDevices
    cboDevices.AddItem oDevice.Name
Next oDevice

oServer.DisConnect
Set oServer = Nothing
Set oDevice = Nothing

End Sub
```

You can choose either a device or a file. Once you've chosen a device or a file, your choice is entered in the list box showing backup devices back on the first screen. You need to have a look at what backups, if any, exist on this device, so you need to execute the equivalent of RESTORE HEADERONLY for the device you select.

```
Private Sub ShowContentsOfBackup(servername As String, devicename As String)

Dim oHeader As SQLDMO.QueryResults
Dim DeviceCounter As Integer
Dim i As Integer
Dim Backup_type As String
DeviceCounter = 0
msf_Available.Rows = 1

Set oServer = New SQLDMO.SQLServer
Set oRestore = New SQLDMO.Restore


oServer.LoginSecure = True
oServer.Connect servername
```

Looping Through the Devices

You'll need to check if the name you passed is a device or an ad hoc file, as this will influence which property of the Device object you supply. Here you check whether there is a device in the Devices collection with the same name as the text you chose in the list box. If there is, you set DeviceCounter = 1 to indicate that.

```
For Each oDevice In oServer.BackupDevices
    If oDevice.Name = devicename Then
        DeviceCounter = 1
    End If
Next oDevice
```

Once you find the device with the same name, you want to know what type of device it is.

```
If DeviceCounter = 0 Then
    oRestore.Files = devicename
Else
    oRestore.Devices = devicename
End If
```

Here's where you read the contents of the backup header into a QueryResults object ready for processing. A QueryResults object is very much like a table with rows and columns, so you just go through it processing the rows and columns.

This is the RESTORE HEADERONLY part. It takes a connected SQLServer object as an argument.

```
Set oHeader = oRestore.ReadBackupHeader(oServer)

For i = 1 To oHeader.Rows
```

Part of the results of ReadBackupHeader is the type of backup. Unfortunately, this is returned to you as an integer. You convert the unintelligible integer value for the backup type into something you can read and comprehend without opening a reference book. These are all the possible values you could ever have. What Microsoft has done with the number 3, we don't know.

Iterating Through the Possible Backup Types

```
Select Case oHeader.GetColumnString(i, 3)
    Case 1
    Backup_type = "FULL"
    Case 2
    Backup_type = "LOG"
    Case 4
    Backup_type = "FILE"
    Case 5
    Backup_type = "DIFF DB"
    Case 6
    Backup_type = "DIFF FILE"
End Select
```

Next, add your required column and row values to the flex grid, which shows you the contents of the backup device you specified. Here we chose to only process certain values from the results, as we wanted to imitate Enterprise Manager. The GetColumnString method of the QueryResults object takes two arguments: row and column, in that order.

```
    msf_Available.AddItem Backup_type & vbTab &
oHeader.GetColumnString(i, 6) & vbTab &
oHeader.GetColumnString(i, 10) & vbTab &
oHeader.GetColumnString(i, 19)
Next i
```

```
oServer.DisConnect
Set oServer = Nothing
Set oRestore = Nothing


End Sub
```

Choosing the Backup to Restore

The next thing you need to do once you click the grid with your list of possible backups is have it populate the grid on the Options tab with the logical and physical names of the particular backup you selected. This section contains the calling procedure followed by the actual workhorse.

Because a single backup device may have multiple backups on it, you need to specify which one you're talking about. The way you managed to pass the FileNumber was to capture where you clicked the other grid and read off the FileNumber column for that particular row.

```
Private Sub msf_Available_Click()

If msf_Available.Row <> 0 Then
ShowMeFileDetails cboServers.Text, _
lstdevices.Text, _
 msf_Available.TextMatrix(msf_Available.Row, 1)
End If
End Sub




Private Sub ShowMeFileDetails(servername As String,
 devicename As String, filenumber As Integer)


Dim oFileResults As SQLDMO.QueryResults

Dim DeviceCounter As Integer
Dim i As Integer

DeviceCounter = 0

msf_FileList.Rows = 1
```

```
Set oServer = New SQLDMO.SQLServer
Set oRestore = New SQLDMO.Restore


oServer.LoginSecure = True
oServer.Connect servername
```

Again, as before, you need to process the device name in the Devices list:

```
For Each oDevice In oServer.BackupDevices
    If oDevice.Name = devicename Then
        DeviceCounter = 1
    End If
Next oDevice


If DeviceCounter = 0 Then
    oRestore.Files = devicename
Else
    oRestore.Devices = devicename
End If

oRestore.filenumber = filenumber
```

Configuring the Restore

Up until now, the code has been exactly the same as when you wanted to populate the other grid with details of your backup headers, but this is the part that you do the equivalent of RESTORE FILELISTONLY. It returns the result as a QueryResults object and takes a connected SQLServer object as an argument.

```
Set oFileResults = oRestore.ReadFileList(oServer)

For i = 1 To oFileResults.Rows
```

Add your required column and row values to the flex grid, which shows you the file details of the backup device you specified. You only want two of the returned column values: the logical and physical names of the backup you specified.

```
    msf_FileList.AddItem
 oFileResults.GetColumnString(i, 1) &
vbTab & oFileResults.GetColumnString(i, 2)
Next i

End Sub
```

On the Options tab, you have the ability to change the physical location of files once they're restored. The way you do that in the application is to click the location you want to change and enter into the prompt the new location (you can see this in Figure 2-11). This action is the equivalent of the WITH MOVE option in T-SQL. Here's the very simple code that does this:

```
Private Sub msf_FileList_Click()
Dim strNewFile As String
```

Only if you click the column with the physical location should you be prompted. If you don't enter anything, then you want to leave the value as is.

```
If msf_FileList.Col = 1 Then
    strNewFile = _
InputBox("Enter New Location Of File", _
"New File Location", msf_FileList.Text)
        If strNewFile = "" Or msf_FileList.Col <> 1 Then
            msf_FileList.Text = msf_FileList.Text
        Else
            msf_FileList.Text = strNewFile
        End If
End If

End Sub
```

All the other options are specific to your restore and will only be relevant once you tell the application to do the restore itself, so let's now look at the procedure that calls the actual restore procedure. We've used this to do the checking:

```
Private Sub cmdRDDL_Click(Index As Integer)
```

On the form you've created a control array of the button that will generate the DDL only, and the one that will generate DDL and do the restore. The reason for this is that it means you can reuse the same code.

```
If cboServers.Text <> "" And cboDatabases.Text <> ""
And lstdevices.Text <> "" And msf_Available.Rows > 1
Then
```

You need to log onto your SQL Server:

```
Set oServer = New SQLDMO.SQLServer
Set oRestore = New SQLDMO.Restore

oServer.LoginSecure = True
oServer.Connect cboServers.Text
```

```
Dim iLeftInState As Integer
Dim iDBRestore As Integer
Dim iForce As Integer
Dim ideviceYN As Integer
Dim iMoveFiles As Integer
Dim iBackupType As Integer
Dim strMoveFiles As String
Dim qry_Comparison As SQLDMO.QueryResults
Dim i As Integer

iForce = 0
ideviceYN = 0
iBackupType = 1
strMoveFiles = ""
iMoveFiles = 0
```

Here you check to see if you've opted to force your restore over the top of an existing database (the REPLACE option in T-SQL):

```
Select Case chkForce.Value

Case vbChecked
iForce = 1
End Select
```

You need to check your devices again because later you're going to need to do some comparisons with the ReadFileList of the Restore object:

```
For Each oDevice In oServer.BackupDevices
    If oDevice.Name = lstdevices.Text Then
        ideviceYN = 1
    End If
Next oDevice
```

Choosing the Restore Type

What type of restore do you want to do? Your options are a database backup and a log backup, and they're set by the option buttons on the first screen of the application.

```
Select Case optDatabase.Value

Case False
iBackupType = 0
End Select
```

How do you want to leave the database? You set this on the Options tab of the application.

The following code shows how to recover the database after a restore:

```
If optrecover.Value = True Then
    iLeftInState = 1
```

This code will leave the database nonoperational but in a state in which you can apply more log backups afterward.

```
ElseIf optNonop.Value = True Then
    iLeftInState = 2
```

This option will leave the database in a read-only state, which is good for reporting. You can also restore more backups to the database.

```
ElseIf optStandby = True Then
    iLeftInState = 3
End If
```

If you choose to leave the database in a standby state, then make sure you have an undo file ready.

```
If iLeftInState = 3 And txtStandby = "" Then
    MsgBox "You have chosen to place the database in standby."
& vbCrLf & "You need to specify an undo file",
 vbInformation, "Missing Undo File"
    Exit Sub
End If
```

Now for the tricky part. You need to compare the values for the placement of the files in the grid with those that you know are in the backup set for the backup you've chosen row for row. If you find any values that are different, then this will need to be your move string for the restore.

```
If ideviceYN = 1 Then
    oRestore.Devices = lstdevices.Text
Else
    oRestore.Files = lstdevices.Text
End If
```

```
oRestore.filenumber = msf_Available.TextMatrix(msf_Available.Row, 1)
```

Here you're doing the equivalent of RESTORE FILELISTONLY. The results are read into a QueryResults object.

```
Set qry_Comparison = oRestore.ReadFileList(oServer)
```

This is the comparison. If you find a difference, you add the logical name and the new physical name from the grid to your string, which will tell SQL Server to move the files. You need to wrap the logical name and physical name in square brackets to cater for spaces in either name. SQL Server, like a lot of other products, can find it difficult to work with spaces, so wrapping in square brackets smoothes things over (don't worry—they don't come out in your code).

```
For i = 1 To qry_Comparison.Rows
    If msf_FileList.TextMatrix(i, 1) <> qry_Comparison.GetColumnString(i, 2) Then
        strMoveFiles = _
strMoveFiles & "[" & msf_FileList.TextMatrix(i, 0) & _
 "],[" & msf_FileList.TextMatrix(i, 1) & "],"
    End If
Next i
```

If you found any files that need moving, then after you've built up this string you're going to have an extra comma at the end of the string, so here you trim that off and set an indicator that you'll later use to indicate that you have files that need moving.

```
If Len(strMoveFiles) > 0 Then
    strMoveFiles = Mid(strMoveFiles, 1, Len(strMoveFiles) - 1)
    iMoveFiles = 1
End If
```

Here all you do is check whether the button you clicked was the Generate DDL only or the Restore button. Based on that, you execute the procedure that does what you've been building up to.

```
Select Case Index
```

The following code only generates the DDL:

```
Case 0
GenerateDDLAndRestore "", cboDatabases.Text,
iForce, lstdevices.Text, ideviceYN, iBackupType,
 oRestore.filenumber, iLeftInState, iMoveFiles, strMoveFiles, txtStandby.Text
```

The following code will generate some DDL statements and actually do the restore:

```
Case 1
GenerateDDLAndRestore "", cboDatabases.Text,
 iForce, lstdevices.Text, ideviceYN, iBackupType,
 oRestore.filenumber, iLeftInState, iMoveFiles,
strMoveFiles, txtStandby.Text
GenerateDDLAndRestore cboServers.Text,
 cboDatabases.Text, iForce, lstdevices.Text,
 ideviceYN, iBackupType, oRestore.filenumber,
 iLeftInState, iMoveFiles, strMoveFiles,
 txtStandby.Text


End Select

End If
End Sub
```

There remains only one piece of code to go through: the actual restore procedure.

```
Private Sub GenerateDDLAndRestore(servername
As String, DatabaseName As String, Force
 As Integer, location As String, deviceYN As Integer,
 DBRestore As Integer, filenumber As Integer,
 LeftInState As Integer, MoveFiles As Integer,
 movestring As String, standbyfilesloc As String)

On Error GoTo err_handler

Set oRestore = New SQLDMO.Restore
```

You now check with the following code to see if you're using a device or a file:

```
If deviceYN = 1 Then
    oRestore.Devices = location
Else
    oRestore.Files = location
End If
```

Here you indicate whether or not you force this backup over the top of the existing database:

```
If Force = 1 Then
    oRestore.ReplaceDatabase = True
End If
```

Here you indicate what type of backup you're doing:

```
If DBRestore = 1 Then
    oRestore.Action = SQLDMORestore_Database
Else
    oRestore.Action = SQLDMORestore_Log
End If
```

Are you moving the files at all? If the answer is yes (MoveFiles = 1), then you need to supply a string in the form of *logical file name, physical file name* for each file you're moving (remember the comparison you did between the results of the ReadFileList and the values in the grid in the previous procedure)—that is, Logical_file_1, c:\MyData\physical_file _1, logical_file_2, c:\MyData\physical_file _2.

```
If MoveFiles = 1 Then
    oRestore.RelocateFiles = movestring
End If
```

In the following code you indicate which database you want to restore:

```
oRestore.Database = DatabaseName
```

Here you set the recovery option:

```
Select Case LeftInState
```

If you specify the following option you recover the database:

```
Case 1
oRestore.LastRestore = True
```

Specifying the following option leaves the database nonoperational:

```
Case 2
oRestore.LastRestore = False
```

Finally, choosing this option leaves the database in Standby mode:

```
Case 3
oRestore.LastRestore = False
oRestore.StandbyFiles = standbyfilesloc

End Select
oRestore.filenumber = filenumber
```

Because you want to reuse this procedure for DDL only or DDL and actual restore, you include the following clause here. If no servername is passed, you only need to generate the DDL.

```
If servername <> "" Then
    Set oServer = New SQLDMO.SQLServer
    oServer.LoginSecure = True
    oServer.Connect servername
```

Here's the actual restore statement that takes an argument of a connected SQLServer object:

```
    oRestore.SQLRestore oServer
End If
```

This is the statement that will generate your T-SQL on the third tab of the application:

```
txtDDL.Text = oRestore.GenerateSQL

Exit Sub

err_handler:
MsgBox "The restore has failed because... " & vbCrLf & Err.Description
Exit Sub

End Sub
```

The 15-Minute Database Checker

When we're out and about at client sites, we often find that databases are created on servers and no one will bother to tell us. Without fail, you can guarantee that when something goes wrong with the database and the client needs it restored, then ours will be the first door they come knocking on. Even if we didn't know anything about the database, it's still rather embarrassing to find that we can't recover the client's data. This is the reason we built this little application. We have made it a rule that if nobody tells us they've built a database server, and hence we haven't registered it in our Enterprise Manager console, then as far as we're concerned it doesn't exist. Fortunately, people do provide us with this information for the most part.

Imagine this scenario: You have a server that has a series of databases that are reliant upon a full database backup being done on a night and a differential backup being done every day at 2-hour intervals between 8:00 A.M. and 8:00 P.M. The full backups are done and scheduled through maintenance plans, but unfortunately you can't do the same with a differential backup. This means you need to write your own procedure, but you want to just let it run and capture any databases on the server, and back it up when the time comes. The procedure to do so may look like this:

```
DECLARE @DBName sysname
DECLARE @EXECString varchar(255)
DECLARE cur_Differentials CURSOR FAST_FORWARD
FOR
select
        Name from master..sysdatabases where name not in ('master','model','tempdb')

OPEN cur_Differentials

FETCH NEXT FROM cur_Differentials INTO @DBName
```

```
WHILE (@@FETCH_STATUS<>-1)
BEGIN

set @EXECString =  _
'BACKUP DATABASE
[' + @DBName + '] to DISK = ''\\NetworkServer\diffBackups\Server1\' +
[' + @DBName + '].DIFF'' WITH INIT,differential'
EXEC(@EXECString)


FETCH NEXT FROM cur_Differentials INTO @DBName
End

Close cur_Differentials
DEALLOCATE cur_Differentials
```

If you were to create a database during the working day, then at the next interval you would attempt to back up that database using a differential backup. Shortly after that, you would get a message telling you that the differential backup job had failed because of the new database.

This application will search through all databases on all your registered servers and look at when they were created. If it finds one that was created in the past 15 minutes, then it will back it up to a default location, *\\MyNetworkServer\FullBackupShare\<Server_Name>\<Database_Name>_<yyyymmdd>.bak*.

The following code shows how to call the procedure:

```
Option Explicit
Sub main()
ListNewDatabases 15
End Sub
```

The following code shows the procedure:

```
Private Sub ListNewDatabases(MinsAgo As Integer)
Dim oServer As SQLDMO.SQLServer
Dim oBackup As SQLDMO.Backup
Dim oDatabase As SQLDMO.Database
Dim OutputString As String
Dim oRserver As SQLDMO.RegisteredServer

On Error GoTo err_handler
```

```
Set oServer = New SQLDMO.SQLServer
Set oBackup = New SQLDMO.Backup

For Each oRserver In SQLDMO.ServerGroups(1).RegisteredServers

    oServer.LoginSecure = True
    oServer.Connect oRserver.name
```

The procedure is self-explanatory so far. Here's where you check each database, and if it isn't Master, Model, msdb, or tempdb, then you log that fact and back it up:

```
    For Each oDatabase In oServer.Databases
        If oDatabase.Name <> "master" and
oDatabase.name <> "tempdb"  and
oDatabase.Name <> "model" and oDatabase.Name <> 'msdb'
Then
```

In the following code you check for any newly created databases:

```
If DateDiff("n", Left(oDatabase.CreateDate, 19),
 Format(Now(), "dd-mm-yyyy hh:mm:ss")) <= MinsAgo Then
    OutputString = OutputString & "Database " &
oDatabase.Name & " on " & oServer.Name &
 " was created on " & Left(oDatabase.CreateDate, 19)
& " by " & oDatabase.Owner & vbCrLf &
 "The database was backed Up to \\MyNetworkServer\FullBackupShare\" & _
 oServer.Name & "\" & oDatabase.Name &
 "_" & Format(Now(), "yyyymmyy") & ".bak" &
vbCrLf  & vbCrLf
oBackup.Database = oDatabase.Name
 oBackup.Files = "\\MyNetworkServer\FullBackupShare\"
& oServer.Name & "\" & oDatabase.Name & "_" &
 Format(Now(), "yyyymmyy") & ".bak"
                    oBackup.SQLBackup oServer
                End If

        End If
    Next oDatabase

    oServer.DisConnect

Next oRserver
```

If OutputString has anything in it, this means something has been created:

```
If OutputString <> "" Then

Open "c:\NewDBs.txt" For Output As #1

Print #1, OutputString

End If

Exit Sub
Close #1

err_handler:
Resume Next

End Sub
```

This is a wonderfully simple and amazingly useful application. It enables you to be proactive in your duties over any number of servers. You complement this application by having SQL Server check for the existence of the log output file from the application, and if it finds the file, it sends it to you so you know what's going on.

Permissions for Backing Up the Database

BACKUP DATABASE and BACKUP LOG permissions default to members of the db_owner fixed database role, who can transfer permissions to other users, and members of the db_backupoperator fixed database role.

Permissions for Restoring the Database

If the database being restored doesn't exist, the user must have CREATE DATABASE permissions. If the database does exist, RESTORE permissions default to members of the sysadmin fixed server role and members of the db_owner fixed database role.

Summary

Doing backups and restores is something we believe strongly in. In this chapter, we showed you some useful applications in SQL-DMO. We didn't cover every option that you could possibly use for backups and restores, but we did cover those points we think are most relevant. We also managed to develop a learning tool as a side effect of the restore application. Being asked to restore a database we have no idea about is something we would like to avoid, as we said earlier, and thankfully we have by using the application in this chapter.

In the next chapter you're going to add users to the databases and the server. Once the users are in there, you'll look to give them some permissions.

CHAPTER 3

Managing Users of Your Database and Server

ONCE YOUR DATA IS inside SQL Server, it serves little purpose unless your users can view it. At the same time, you need to ensure that the data is accurate and true. To do this, you need to make sure that only those people who require access to your databases are given it and that the level of access they're given is necessary to complete their jobs—nothing more and nothing less. If someone needs to be able to read the data kept in your database and nothing more, then that's the level of access you should grant that person. If someone only needs to read data from certain tables, then you should restrict that person's access to only those particular tables. Should you require, you could even restrict people to viewing only certain columns on certain tables. In many companies, we've found that restricting users' access to databases involves a significant mindset shift and can be a painful exercise. Data security can often be seen as secondary to users being able to access it, so suddenly removing peoples' access can be quite a shock to them.

In this chapter, you'll create two applications in Visual Basic using SQL-DMO— namely, the Add User application and the Add Permissions application—to illustrate how to add users and give them permissions using the SQL-DMO library. As always, we show you how to do the same things using both Enterprise Manager and T-SQL.

This chapter covers the following topics:

- Adding users to the server

- Enabling users to use a database or databases

- Adding users to fixed server roles

- Creating roles within your databases

- Adding users to the roles you create within your databases

- Granting permissions at both the object level and the statement level

- Removing, revoking, and denying permissions

We begin by explaining some of the terminology that we use during the course of the chapter.

Database Terminology

It's important that you understand some database-related terms before you get too far into the chapter, so let's look at them now.

Login

When a user requires access to your databases, she first needs to be added to the Logins collection of your SQL Server. This doesn't mean she can access any of your data yet, just that she's granted access to the server. The only exception to this is if you've granted database access to the guest account, in which case the user can do what the guest account can do. Logins comes in two flavors: Standard and Windows Authentication. Windows Authentication means that you're granted access to the SQL Server by virtue of your Windows NT or Windows 2000 user account, or the role to which you belong. When you try to log into SQL Server, you don't need to give a password. A Standard login involves specifying a username and a password, both of which have been set up beforehand.

 NOTE   SQL Server Books Online clearly states in the "Logins – overview" section that a member of the sysadmin fixed server role needs to add logins to the server. This is incorrect. To be able to add logins to your SQL Server, you can be a member of either the sysadmin role or the securityadmin role.

User

If you want people to be able to access data in your databases, then you need to make the Login a user of the database. The user can also be a member of a database role. A login can take a completely different name within your database from that which it has as a Login. By convention, though, if you have an NT login of AM2\allanm, then your username would be allanm.

Fixed Server Role

Fixed server roles are as their name suggests: fixed. You can't add more of them, and you can't remove them either. They're there to perform server-wide functions. An example of their use may be that instead of granting sysadmin permissions to all of your DBA team, you could add the junior members to one of the other roles, and as their experience grows you add them to more. Table 3-1 shows the fixed server roles available in versions 7.0 and 2000 of SQL Server.

Table 3-1. Fixed Server Roles

SQL Server 7.0	SQL Server 2000
Sysadmin	Sysadmin
Serveradmin	Serveradmin
Setupadmin	Setupadmin
Processadmin	Processadmin
Dbcreator	Dbcreator
Diskadmin	Diskadmin
Securityadmin	Securityadmin
	Bulkadmin

Fixed server roles have a set group of permissions, and you can easily view what they are by doing any of the following.

T-SQL

```
EXEC sp_srvrolepermission <server role>
```

SQL-DMO

```
Private Sub EnumServerRolePermissioning(ServerName As String, sRole as string)
Dim dmo_server As SQLDMO.SQLServer
Dim dmo_login As SQLDMO.Login
Dim dmo_results As SQLDMO.QueryResults

Dim i As Integer

Set dmo_server = New SQLDMO.SQLServer

dmo_server.LoginSecure = True
dmo_server.Connect ServerName
```

In your SQL Server, if you navigate to the Security folder and then choose Server Roles, you'll see all the roles listed. If you right-click a role, choose Properties, and then select the Permissions tab, you'll see the screen shown in Figure 3-1.

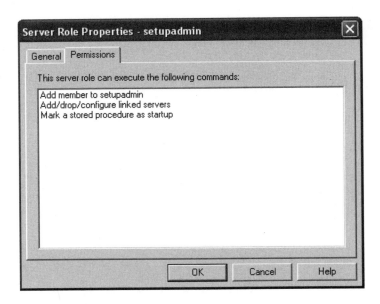

Figure 3-1. Server role permissions

In the following code, you assign the results of EnumServerRolePermission to an object of the type QueryResults. The QueryResults object holds data in the form of a table with rows and columns. All you need to do is enumerate through it and extract the values you require.

```
Set dmo_results =dmo_server.ServerRoles(sRole).EnumServerRolePermission
For i = 1 To dmo_results.Rows
 Debug.Print "Server Role: " & _
 sRole & "  has this permission: " & _
dmo_results.GetColumnString(i, 1)
        Next i

End Sub
```

NOTE There's nothing a member of the sysadmin role can't do. Even if you explicitly deny the login account the ability to do something, as long as the user is a member of this role, he'll be able to perform the task you denied.

In the Add User application in this chapter, we'll show you how to add logins to these roles.

Database Roles

Each database has a standard set of database roles. You can, however, create your own database roles. The Public database role, to which all users in a database are automatically added, can have its permissions changed. The following list contains the permissions you get by default:

db_owner

db_accessadmin

db_datareader

db_datawriter

db_ddladmin

db_securityadmin

db_backupoperator

db_denydatareader

db_denydatawriter

In the Add User application, we'll show you how to add new database roles to your databases and make your users members of them. Just as you can with server roles, you can see what permissions database roles have within your database.

T-SQL

```
EXEC sp_dbfixedrolepermission <rolename>
```

Using Enterprise Manager, you can only view the permissions of the Public role. If you try to view the permissions of the other roles, you'll find that the Permissions button is grayed out (see Figure 3-2).

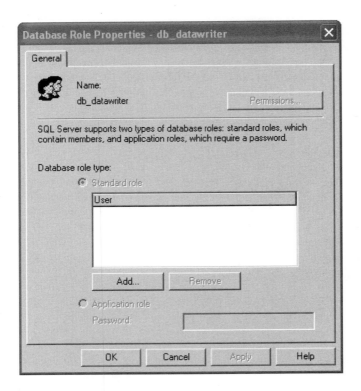

Figure 3-2. The Permissions button is grayed out.

Here's how to find the permissions for the Public role:

1. Navigate to your database.

2. Select the role.

3. Right-click the Public role and select Properties.

Figure 3-3 shows the permissions of the Public role.

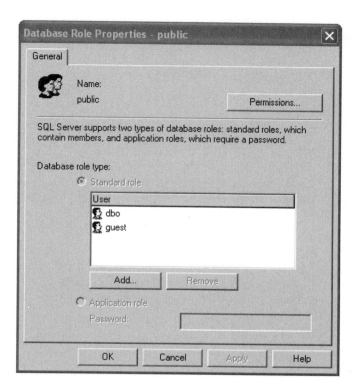

Figure 3-3. Permissions of the Public role

In the code that follows, you're going to go through the permissions that are granted to the fixed database role that you pass into the procedure.

SQL-DMO

```
Private Sub EnumDatabasesRolePermissions(ServerName As String, RoleName As String)
Dim dbrolePerms As SQLDMO.QueryResults
Dim i As Integer
Set server = New SQLDMO.SQLServer

server.LoginSecure = True
server.Connect ServerName

if RoleName <> "public" then
```

Again, here you assign the EnumFixedDatabaseRolePermission output to a QueryResults object.

```
Set dbrolePerms  = server.Databases("Pubs").DatabaseRoles _
(RoleName).EnumFixedDatabaseRolePermisson
  For i = 1 To dbrolePerms.Rows
Debug.Print "Role: " & RoleName  & " has " &_
 dbrolePerms.GetColumnString(i, 1) & " permission"
 Next I

End if

End Sub
```

NOTE   Although the Public role comes with every database (as do all the other roles mentioned in list earlier), it's still not considered a fixed database role as the others are.

There are two types of database roles, standard and application, and you'll learn the differences between them as you work through the applications in this chapter.

Statement Permissions

These are the permissions required to be able to execute statements such as CREATE TABLE, BACKUP DATABASE, and CREATE VIEW.

Object Permissions

Quite simply, you use object permissions when you grant, revoke, or deny SELECT, UPDATE, DELETE, or INSERT statements to be executed by a database user on tables and views in your database. You also use these permissions to execute a stored procedure.

GRANT, REVOKE, or DENY

It's worth explaining of the implications of these permissions. If a user's account has SELECT permissions on a table and you REVOKE those permissions, the user will still be able to view that table if he is a member of a group or role that has SELECT permissions on the table. If you DENY the permissions, then this takes precedence over all permissions granted elsewhere. The user will always be denied SELECT permissions on the table. If a user has been denied SELECT permissions on a table and you revoke the permissions, then the user no longer has SELECT permissions on the table but he can read it by virtue of any other roles or groups he belongs to.

Let's look at how you can grant the CREATE TABLE permission to a user, User1, in the Pubs database. You'll then give the same user SELECT privileges on the Authors table, deny the permissions, and then revoke the permissions.

T-SQL

```
USE PUBS

GRANT CREATE TABLE TO  User1

GRANT SELECT ON authors TO User1
DENY SELECT ON authors TO User1
REVOKE SELECT ON authors TO User1
```

For the CREATE TABLE permission in Enterprise Manager, you need to right-click the database and choose Properties. You then select the Permissions tab and click in the box (see Figure 3-4).

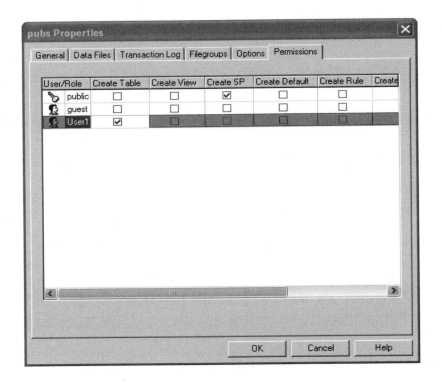

Figure 3-4. Granting the CREATE TABLE permission in the Pubs database

You can grant the permissions on the table in a couple of ways. You can right-click the table to select all tasks and manage permissions, double-click the table and click the Permissions button, or double-click the user and click the Permissions button. In Figure 3-5, we've chosen to view the permissions on the table, not the user.

To deny the permissions, simply click once again in the box (see Figure 3-6).

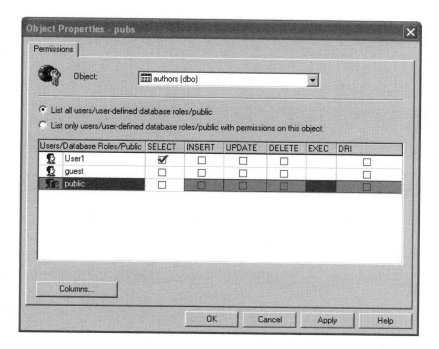

Figure 3-5. Granting SELECT permissions on the Authors table

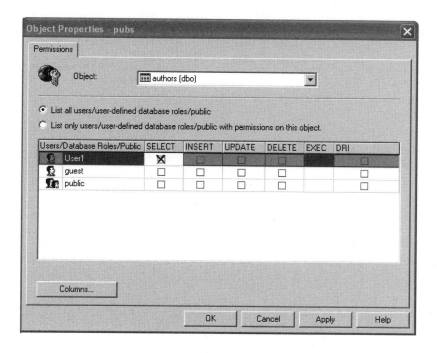

Figure 3-6. Denying SELECT permissions on the Authors table

If you remove the tick from the SELECT box in Figure 3-5 or the cross from the SELECT box in Figure 3-6, then you revoke SELECT permissions from the user. You can see the result of this in Figure 3-7.

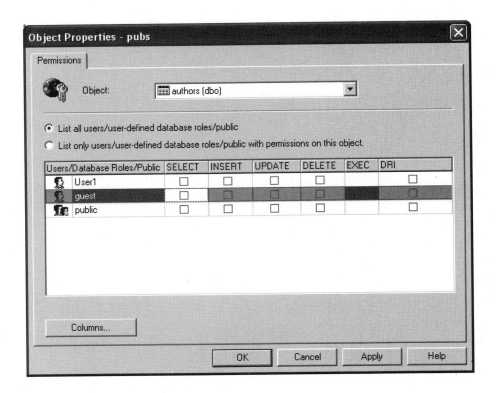

Figure 3-7. Revoking SELECT permissions on the Authors table

The first piece of code here will grant you the CREATE TABLE permission in the Pubs database.

SQL-DMO

```
Sub AssignStatementPermissionsToUser(ServerName As String,
DatabaseName As String, UserRoleName As String,
Permission As SQLDMO.SQLDMO_PRIVILEGE_TYPE)

Dim dmo_server As SQLDMO.SQLServer
Set dmo_server = New SQLDMO.SQLServer

dmo_server.LoginSecure = True
dmo_server.Connect ServerName
```

The Grant method of the Database object takes two parameters: the permission type and the person or role who needs it. The person or role who needs the permission must already be a user in your database.

```
dmo_server.Databases(DatabaseName).Grant Permission, UserRoleName

dmo_server.DisConnect
End Sub
```

Quite simply, you call this procedure with the following code:

```
AssignStatementPermissionsToUser "AM2", "Pubs", "User1", SQLDMOPriv_CreateTable
```

Here's how you grant SELECT permissions on a table:

```
Private Sub AddPermissionToTable(server As String,
dbName As String, TableName As String, Permission As SQLDMO.SQLDMO_PRIVILEGE_TYPE,
UserRoleName As String)
Dim dmo_server As SQLDMO.SQLServer
Dim dmoTable As SQLDMO.table

Set dmo_server = New SQLDMO.SQLServer
dmo_server.LoginSecure = True
dmo_server.Connect server

dmo_server.Databases(dbName).Tables(TableName).Grant Permission,
UserRoleName, , False
End Sub
```

The Grant method of the Table object is slightly different from the Grant method of the Database object. It takes four parameters:

- The permission

- The person or role who requires the permission

- Specification of particular columns you want to restrict the privileges to (if any)

- Indication of whether or not you want the user or role to be able to grant this permission to others

You call this procedure as follows:

```
AddPermissionToTable "AM2", "Pubs", "Authors", SQLDMOPriv_Select, "User1"
```

Denying SELECT Permissions on a Table

The following code shows how to deny SELECT permissions on a table. This is similar to the Grant method you saw in the previous section:

```
Sub DenypermissionFromUser(ServerName As String,
DatabaseName As String, tablename As String,
UserRoleName As String,
Permission As SQLDMO.SQLDMO_PRIVILEGE_TYPE)

Dim dmo_server As SQLDMO.SQLServer
Set dmo_server = New SQLDMO.SQLServer

dmo_server.LoginSecure = True
dmo_server.Connect ServerName

dmo_server.Databases(DatabaseName).Tables(tablename).Deny Permission, UserRoleName

End Sub
```

You call this procedure as follows:

```
DenypermissionFromUser "AM2", "Pubs", "Authors", "User1", SQLDMOPriv_Select
```

Revoking SELECT Permissions on a Table

This listing shows how to revoke SELECT permissions on a table:

```
Sub RevokepermissionFromUser(ServerName As String,
DatabaseName As String, tablename As String,
UserRoleName As String,
Permission As SQLDMO.SQLDMO_PRIVILEGE_TYPE)

Dim dmo_server As SQLDMO.SQLServer
Set dmo_server = New SQLDMO.SQLServer

dmo_server.LoginSecure = True
dmo_server.Connect ServerName

dmo_server.Databases(DatabaseName).Tables _
(tablename).Revoke Permission, UserRoleName

End Sub
```

You call this procedure as follows:

```
RevokepermissionFromUser "AM2", "Pubs", "Authors", "User1", SQLDMOPriv_Select
```

In Table 3-2, you can see the complete list of permissions you're able to use.

Table 3-2. List of Permissions

Constant	Value	Description
SQLDMOPriv_AllDatabasePrivs	130944	All database permissions
SQLDMOPriv_AllObjectPrivs	63	All applicable object permissions
SQLDMOPriv_CreateDatabase	256	Can create and own databases
SQLDMOPriv_CreateDefault	4096	Can create Default objects
SQLDMOPriv_CreateFunction	65366	Can create and own UserDefinedFunction objects
SQLDMOPriv_CreateProcedure	1024	Can create and own StoredProcedure objects
SQLDMOPriv_CreateRule	16384	Can create rules
SQLDMOPriv_CreateTable	128	Can create and own base tables
SQLDMOPriv_CreateView	512	Can create and own view tables
SQLDMOPriv_Delete	8	Can delete rows in a referenced table
SQLDMOPriv_DumpDatabase	2048	Can back up a database
SQLDMOPriv_DumpTable	32768	Can back up a referenced table
SQLDMOPriv_DumpTransaction	8192	Can back up a database transaction log
SQLDMOPriv_Execute	16	Can execute a referenced stored procedure
SQLDMOPriv_Insert	2	Can add rows to a referenced table

Table 3-2. List of Permissions (Continued)

Constant	Value	Description
SQLDMOPriv_References	32	Can grant declarative referential integrity (DRI) on a referenced table
SQLDMOPriv_Select	1	Can query a referenced table
SQLDMOPriv_Unknown	0	No privilege assigned, or unable to determine privilege on the referenced database or database object
SQLDMOPriv_Update	4	Can change row data in a referenced table

NOTE   The SQLDMOPriv_CreateFunction permission is a privilege only found in SQL Server 2000 because that's when Microsoft introduced user-defined functions (UDFs). UDFs are familiar to users of other database systems created by some guy named Larry Ellison.

The Applications

We've designed two simple applications that should help illustrate what we've covered so far in this chapter and a bit more. The first application, the Add User application, deals with the following:

- Adding a login

- Adding a user

- Adding a login to a server role

- Adding a user to a database role

- Creating a database role (application and standard)

- Removing a user

- Dropping a login

The second application, the Add Permissions application, deals with the following:

- Granting object permissions on tables in a database

- Revoking object permissions on tables in a database

The Add User Application

The Add User application allows you to do what its name suggests (i.e., add a user), and it also allows you to add a login. By now, you should know there's a difference between these two tasks. Let's dig straight in, then, and take a look at the application. Figure 3-8 shows the first screen of the Add User application.

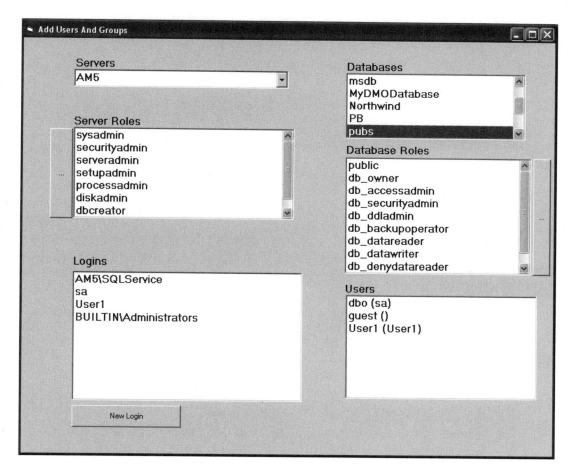

Figure 3-8. The first screen of the Add User application

The upcoming sections provide detailed explanations and code, and follow the structure of topics presented in the bulleted list in the last section.

Adding a Login

When you select your server, you can add a new login by clicking the New Login button. You're greeted by the screen shown in Figure 3-9.

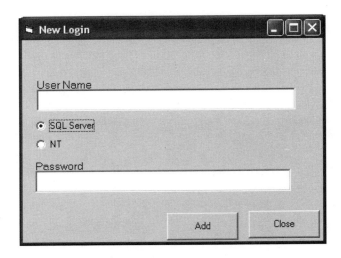

Figure 3-9. Adding a login

Enter a name in the User Name text box, and if you specify a SQL Server login, then supply a password in the Password text box. Here's the code that adds this login to your server in SQL-DMO.

SQL-DMO

```
Private Sub AddnewUser(UserName As String, NT-SQL As Integer,
Optional Password As String)
Dim exists As Integer
Dim oNewLogin As SQLDMO.Login
Set oNewLogin = New SQLDMO.Login
exists = 0
```

In the following code, you test whether or not the login you're passing already exists on the server. If it does, you quickly exit, assigning the value of 1 to your exists variable.

```
For Each oLogin In oServer.Logins
    If UCase(oLogin.Name) = UCase(UserName) Then
        exists = 1
        MsgBox "Login already exists", _
vbInformation, "Login already Exists"
        Exit Sub
    End If
Next oLogin
```

If the login doesn't exist, then you need to check if the login you want to add is a SQL Server login or an NT login. You pass a variable to the procedure, NT-SQL, to tell you which type of login you want to use.

```
If exists = 0 Then
    If NT-SQL = 1 Then
```

If NT-SQL = 1, then you set the name of the login to the name passed to the procedure, and you tell SQL Server that it's an NT login.

```
        oNewLogin.Name = UserName

oNewLogin.Type = SQLDMOLogin_NTUser
    Else
```

> **NOTE**   You could also specify a type of SQLDMOLogin_NTGroup if you're adding an NT group.

The following code indicates that you'll be adding a SQL Server login. Note the fact that you specify a password here.

```
        oNewLogin.Name = UserName
        oNewLogin.Type = SQLDMOLogin_Standard
        oNewLogin.SetPassword "", Password
    End If
End If
```

Finally, you add the login to the Logins collection of the server:

```
oServer.Logins.Add oNewLogin

End Sub
```

Here's how to do the exact same thing in T-SQL for both an NT login and a SQL Server login.

T-SQL: NT Login

```
 IF NOT  EXISTS (select * from master..sysxlogins where name = 'AM2\allanm')
BEGIN
    EXEC sp_addlogin 'AM2\allanm'
END
ELSE
BEGIN
    PRINT 'This login already Exists'
END
```

T-SQL: SQL Server Login

```
IF NOT EXISTS(select * from master..sysxlogins where name = 'allan')
BEGIN
    EXEC sp_addlogin 'allan','MyPassword'
END
ELSE
BEGIN
    PRINT 'This login already Exists'
END
```

To add a login using Enterprise Manager, navigate to the Security folder of your server and right-click the Logins icon. Select from the pop-up menu to add a new login and you'll see the screen in Figure 3-10.

Figure 3-10. Adding a login using Enterprise Manager

There isn't a big difference between the Add User application and Enterprise Manager, and the extra tabs you see in Figure 3-10 are dealt with in extra screens in the Add User application.

Removing a Login

In the Add User application, to delete a login, you select your server (this shows you the logins that exist on that server) and double-click the login you want to delete. The screen shown in Figure 3-11 appears.

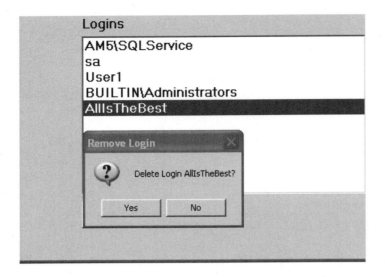

Figure 3-11. Removing a login

Here's the code you use to drop the login:

```
Private Function ShowIfWeCanDeleteLogin(LoginName As String) As Integer

Dim CanWe As Integer
Dim oDatabase As SQLDMO.Database
Dim oList As SQLDMO.SQLObjectList
Dim obj As Object
Dim oUsr As SQLDMO.User

CanWe = 1
```

Your ability to remove a login is hampered by the fact that a login may own objects within a database or the database itself, so the first thing you need to do is check if this is the case with the login you want to delete. The variable CanWe tells you whether or not you can delete a login. Initially, CanWe is set to 1 to indicate that you can delete the login, but if the username is found to own anything, then you set it to 0.

```
For Each oDatabase In oServer.Databases
    If UCase$(oDatabase.Owner) = UCase$(LoginName) Then
      CanWe = 0
    End If
```

Here's the meat of this procedure. You declare the variable oList to be of the type SQLObjectList, which holds the names of objects. You read into it what's returned from the ListOwnedObjects method of the User object. The method takes two parameters:

- *SQLDMO_OBJECT_TYPE:* What is the type of object you want to know about? In this case, you want to know about any type of object owned.

- *SQLDMO_OBJSORT_TYPE:* In what order do you want the results returned to you (e.g., date, name, owner, type)?

If the count of rows in the oList variable is greater than 0, the login owns something, so you can't remove it. The following code checks for objects owned by the login, and if it finds any, then it sets the value of the CanWe variable to 0, which indicates that you can't remove the login.

```
For Each oUsr In oDatabase.Users
    If UCase$(oUsr.Login) = UCase$(LoginName) Then
    Set oList = oServer.Databases(oDatabase.Name).Users _
(oUsr.Name).ListOwnedObjects(SQLDMOObj_AllDatabaseUserObjects, SQLDMOObjSort_Type)
            If oList.Count > 0 Then
                CanWe = 0
            End If
        End If
    Next oUsr
Next oDatabase
```

The function returns the value of the CanWe variable so that you can react to that in your call.

```
ShowIfWeCanDeleteLogin = CanWe

End Function
```

You can now call this procedure and remove the login using the following code:

```
Private Sub lstLogins_DblClick()

If MsgBox("Delete Login " & lstLogins.Text & "?", vbQuestion + vbYesNo, _
  "Remove Login") = vbNo Then
    Exit Sub
Else
    If ShowIfWeCanDeleteLogin(lstLogins.Text) = 1 Then
        oServer.Logins.Remove lstLogins.Text
        lstLogins.RemoveItem lstLogins.ListIndex
    Else
        MsgBox "Login Owns objects within 1 or more databases", _
vbInformation, "Removal Aborted"
    End If
End If

End Sub
```

The first thing you need to do in T-SQL is find out the security identifier (sid) of the login you want to remove.

```
Select sid from master..sysxlogins where name = 'MyUser'
```

You then need to find out if the user is a member of any databases on the server. You do that by executing this code in each database:

```
select name from <databasename>..sysusers
where sid = 0x07DB89A975DF72469D46AE31442A0DE5
and isaliased = 0
```

If the user is a member of that database, then you need to execute the following statement in the database as well:

```
select count(*) from sysobjects o where power(2, sysstat & 0xf) & 511 != 0
and not (OBJECTPROPERTY(id, N'IsDefaultCnst') = 1 and category & 0x0800 != 0)
and o.name not like N'#%' and uid = 6
```

If the count returned is greater than 0, the user owns something and you can't delete the login.

The long and the short of this process in Enterprise Manager is that if you want to check all databases on a server for objects owned by a particular login, then you're going to have to do a lot of clicking and staring at your screen, working through your database objects. There's no quick way of doing it—sorry!

Adding a User to a Fixed Server Role

In the application, you need to select a server and then select the login that you want to add to one of the fixed server roles. Once you've done so, click the button to the left of the list box showing the roles. The screen in Figure 3-12 will appear, and if the login is already a member of a role, then the box next to the role will be checked.

Figure 3-12. Adding a user to a fixed server role

In this section, you'll first learn how to determine if the login is already a member of a role. Then you'll learn how to remove the login from a role or add the login to a role.

Determining the Role

The point of the function is that you'll pass to it the login you want to check and the role you want to check it against. If the login is a member of that role, then the function will return true, and if the login isn't a member of that role, then the function will return false.

```
Private Function ShowSRoleLoginMemberOf(LoginName As String,
SRole As String) As Boolean
Dim i As Integer

ShowSRoleLoginMemberOf = False


Dim oQryresults As SQLDMO.QueryResults
```

The ServerRole object has an EnumServerRoleMember method. As its name implies, the EnumServerRoleMember method enumerates through the members of that role. Here you give it the name of the role you want to check. This method returns a QueryResults object. If you think of the QueryResults object as a virtual table, you can't go far wrong. You look through the rows returned and see if you can locate the login. If you find the login, then you return true; if you don't find the login, then you return false.

```
Set oQryresults = oServer.ServerRoles(SRole).EnumServerRoleMember

For i = 1 To oQryresults.Rows
        If oQryresults.GetColumnString(i, 1) = LoginName Then
            ShowSRoleLoginMemberOf = True
        End If

Next i

End Function
```

Here's the code to use when you call the function:

```
lstsroles.Clear
Dim i As Integer
```

All you do here is loop through the list box that's holding your server roles and pass the name of the role and the login selected on the application's first screen to the function just created. If the function returns true, then you check the box next to the role.

```
For i = 0 To lstsroles.ListCount - 1
    If ShowSRoleLoginMemberOf(frmAddGroups.lstLogins.Text, _
lstsroles.List(i)) = True Then
        lstsroles.Selected(i) = True
    End If
Next I
```

Two methods are available to you in T-SQL. In the first method, you create a table to hold the output of the stored procedure sp_helpsrvrolemember. If you don't specify a role to look in, for example:

```
EXEC sp_helpsrvrolemember 'sysadmin'
```

then the output will display the members of any server role that has members. You then query the table looking for your login:

```
CREATE TABLE SrvRoleMemberHolder
(
Role sysname,
member sysname,
membersid varbinary(85)
)

insert SrvRoleMemberHolder EXEC sp_helpsrvrolemember

select Role from SrvRoleMemberHolder where member = 'Our Login'
```

We think the second method is really quite cool. Because sp_helpsrvrolemember returns a resultset with columns, you can query it directly. First, allow your server to be queried as though it were a linked server:

```
EXEC sp_serveroption 'AM2','DATA ACCESS',true
```

You can then use OPENQUERY to build the results ready for you to read:

```
select * from openquery(AM2,'EXEC sp_helpsrvrolemember') where
MemberName = 'Our Login'
```

Once again, in Enterprise Manager, we can't say anything else but "Sorry." To look through the server roles and find the login, you'll need to open each role individually and look through the members' list.

Changing the Membership of Roles

In the application, you start as before by selecting a server, choosing a login, and clicking the button next to the list of server roles. If you want to add the login to a role or remove the login from a role, then you check or uncheck the box next to the role. The code to do so follows.

In this code, you have a function that takes the login name, role name, and a boolean value indicating the state of the check box you're passing:

```
Public Const IS_MEMBER = 1
Public Const NEEDS_ADDING = 2
Public Const NEEDS_DELETING = 3


Public Function ReturnValuesofSMembership(strLoginName As String,
strSRoleName As String, booChecked As Boolean) As Integer

Dim i As Integer
Dim booInList As Boolean

Dim oQList As SQLDMO.QueryResults
```

Here, as before, you're going to read in who is a member of the role that you've passed to the function as a parameter to a QueryResults object.

```
Set oQList = oServer.ServerRoles(strSRoleName).EnumServerRoleMember
```

You've declared the variable booInList as a boolean, and this will indicate whether or not your login is a member of the role already. (We assume it isn't.)

```
    booInList = False
```

In the following code, all you do is loop through the results, and if you find a match between your login name and the members of the role, then you set booInList to true:

```
    For i = 1 To oQList.Rows
        If UCase(Trim(oQList.GetColumnString(i, 1))) = _
UCase(Trim(strLoginName)) Then
            booInList = True
            Exit For
        End If
    Next I
```

If booInList is true and you've passed to the function booChecked as true, this means the user is a member of the role and you still want him or her to be:

```
If booInList = True And booChecked = True Then
     ReturnValuesofSMembership = IS_MEMBER
   End If
```

If booInList is true but booChecked isn't, it means the login was in the list but you want to remove it:

```
If booInList = True And booChecked = False Then
     ReturnValuesofSMembership = NEEDS_DELETING
   End If
```

If booInList is false and booChecked is true, it means the login wasn't previously a member of the role but you want to add it:

```
If booInList = False And booChecked = True Then
'not in the list and checkbox ticked = needs adding
         ReturnValuesofSMembership = NEEDS_ADDING
   End If
```

```
End Function
```

You would then call the procedure like this:

```
Dim j As Integer
Dim i As Integer

For j = 0 To lstsroles.ListCount - 1
```

You loop through the list of server roles, passing the name of the login from your main form and the name of the role, followed by an indication of whether or not the check box is checked. After that, you test your return value and take action. If the value is NEEDS_ADDING, then you do just that: You add the login to the role. If the function returns NEEDS_DELETING, then you remove the login.

```
Select Case ReturnValuesofSMembership _
(frmAddGroups.lstLogins.Text, lstsroles.List _
(j), lstsroles.Selected(j))

     Case NEEDS_ADDING
            oServer.ServerRoles(lstsroles.List(j)).AddMember _
frmAddGroups.lstLogins.Text

   Case NEEDS_DELETING
           oServer.ServerRoles(lstsroles.List(j)).DropMember  _
frmAddGroups.lstLogins.Text

End Select
Next j
```

If you want to add a login to a server role in T-SQL, the syntax is as follows:

```
sp_addsrvrolemember [@loginame =] 'login', [@rolename =] 'role'
```

If you want to remove a login from a role in T-SQL, you use the following:

```
sp_dropsrvrolemember [@loginame =] 'login', [@rolename =] 'role'
```

We're sure you realize by now that for most tasks, Enterprise Manager is the most "click-intensive" choice of the three available options, and when you try to add people to and remove from multiple server roles it once again proves to be so. On each server role you want to manipulate, you have to right-click and choose Properties or double-click. Once you select Add Member, the screen in Figure 3-13 appears.

Figure 3-13. Adding logins to and removing logins from server roles

Select a login to add and then click OK.

To remove a login from the role, simply highlight the login and click the Remove button.

Adding a User to a Database

Once you've added the logins, you need to start adding them to your databases. For this, you choose a server and then a database on that server. This will populate the Users list box at the bottom of the form with the existing users in that database. You then need a way to get a server login over to the new database. The way we've chosen to do this is when we drag the login over and drop it in the Users list box, we either add it to the database Users collection or if it already exists we pop up a box to give us this information.

Here's the code to use. You pass to this function the login name that you want to add and the database name you want to add the login to:

```
Private Function AddDatabaseUser(LoginName As String,
DatabaseName As String) As Integer
On Error GoTo err_handler
Dim oNewUser As SQLDMO.User
Set oNewUser = New SQLDMO.User

Dim exists As Integer

exists = 0
```

In the following code, you check all the users and see if their respective logins match the one you're trying to pass in. If one matches, then you set exists = 1 (true).

```
For Each oUser In oServer.Databases(DatabaseName).Users
    If UCase(oUser.Login) = UCase(LoginName) Then
        exists = 1
    End If
Next oUser
```

If you don't find the user, then you can add the user. You declare an object of the type **SQLDMO.User** to hold the new user details. Two properties are compulsory: login name and username. Here you set the login name to the name you pass to the procedure, and you set the username to one of two things:

- If the login you're trying to add is an NT login (characterized by the "\" in the login name), then you set the username to everything after the "\".

- If the login is a SQL Server user, then you set the username to the login name.

If the user is added, then you set the return value of the function to 1.

```
If exists = 0 Then
    oNewUser.Login = LoginName
    oNewUser.Name = IIf(InStr(1, LoginName, "\") > 0, _
Right(LoginName, Len(LoginName) - InStr(1, LoginName, "\")), _
LoginName)
    oServer.Databases(DatabaseName).Users.Add oNewUser
    MsgBox "New User " & oNewUser.Name & "(" & _
 (oNewUser.Login) & ") added", vbInformation,  & _
"New User Added"
    AddDatabaseUser = 1
    Exit Function
Else
    MsgBox "User already Exists", vbInformation, "User already Exists"
    AddDatabaseUser = 0
    Exit Function
End If

Exit Function

err_handler:
MsgBox "Error Adding User: " & Err.Description, vbCritical, "Error"
AddDatabaseUser = 0
Exit Function


End Function
```

Remember how we stated earlier that we would drag the login into the Users list box? Well here's the code. First, you do your routine to find out the username to add (if any). You form this by manipulating Data.GetData, which is the text of the login you're depositing in the Users list box. You then call your function, and if it returns a 1, then you add the login to the Users list box.

```
Private Sub lstUsers_OLEDragDrop(Data As DataObject,
Effect As Long, Button As Integer, Shift As Integer,
X As Single, Y As Single)
Dim UserToAdd As String
UserToAdd = IIf(InStr(1, Data.GetData(1), "\") > 0, _
Right(Data.GetData(1), Len(Data.GetData(1)) - _
InStr(1, Data.GetData(1), "\")), Data.GetData(1)) + & _
" (" + Data.GetData(1) + ")"



    If AddDatabaseUser(Data.GetData(1), lstDatabases.Text) = 1 Then
        lstUsers.AddItem UserToAdd
    End If


End Sub
```

When you want to add a login to the database in T-SQL, you need to check two things:

- Does the username already exist?

- Is the login already associated with a user?

Here's how you could check those two items:

```
if exists(select * from sysusers where name = 'Allanm')
begin


Print 'User Already Exists'
RETURN

end
else
if exists (select * from master..sysxlogins x join
sysusers s on x.sid = s.sid
where x.name = 'AM2\AllanMitchell')
begin

Print 'Login already associated with user in DB'
Return

end
```

```
else
begin
EXEC sp_adduser 'ALLAN\Allan Mitchell','Allanm'
End
```

In Enterprise Manager, you click the user's icon for the database you want to use. You then right-click in the right-hand pane and choose New Database User. Figure 3-14 shows the screen that appears.

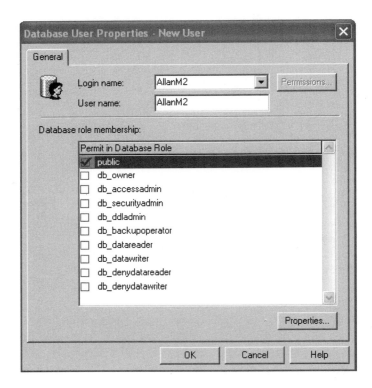

Figure 3-14. Adding a new database user

Drop down the list of server logins and add them. As you can see, you can also specify the login's name in the database.

Removing a User from a Database

The way you remove a user from a database in the application is to double-click the user you want to remove. The code behind this event will go through the database you selected and see if the user owns anything in there. If the user does own something, then you can't remove the user. This is very similar to the check you need to do to remove a login, except the check then needs to go through all the databases on the server.

Here's the code, including the calling code, you use to check if the user owns anything in the chosen database:

```
Private Function FindIfUserOwnsAnything(UserName As String,
DatabaseName As String) As Integer


On Error GoTo err_handler


Dim oList As SQLDMO.SQLObjectList
Dim obj As Object
Dim oUsr As SQLDMO.User

Set oUsr = New SQLDMO.User

FindIfUserOwnsAnything = 0
```

This function will return one of three values to the calling procedure:

- 0 means the user doesn't own anything and can be readily removed.

- 1 means the user does own something and can't be removed.

- 2 means an error has occurred.

You initially set the function's value to 0. You check the owner of the current database first, followed by all user objects to see if the user owns anything. As with the login removal routine, you read the results of the ListOwnedObjects method of the User object into a variable of the SQLDMO.SQLObjectList type. You then test to see if you have any rows in there, and if you do, then you know that the user owns something. You aren't concerned with what exactly the user owns, but you could easily change this and tell the person trying to remove the user where to look for the objects owned.

```
                    If UCase$(oServer.Databases _
(DatabaseName).Owner) = UCase$(UserName) Then
                    FindIfUserOwnsAnything = 1
                    Exit Function
                End If

        'Now the user objects

        For Each oUsr In oServer.Databases(DatabaseName).Users
            If UCase$(oUsr.Login) = UCase$(UserName) Then
                Set oList = oServer.Databases(DatabaseName).Users _
(oUsr.Name).ListOwnedObjects( _
SQLDMOObj_AllDatabaseUserObjects, SQLDMOObjSort_Type)
                    If oList.Count > 0 Then
                        FindIfUserOwnsAnything = 1
                        Exit Function
                    End If
            End If
        Next oUsr

Exit Function

err_handler:

FindIfUserOwnsAnything = 2
Exit Function


End Function
```

Now we'll go through the calling code. In the User list box in the application, you display the username as

```
UserName (LoginName)
```

so you need to trim it up to pass to your function. When you do, you end up with the variable NameToCheck.

You quite simply pass the name of the database and NameToCheck to the function and take action on the results.

```
Dim NameToCheck As String

NameToCheck = Mid(lstUsers.Text, 1, InStr(1, lstUsers.Text, "(") - 2)

If FindIfUserOwnsAnything _
(oServer.Databases _ (lstDatabases.Text).Users _
(NameToCheck).Login, lstDatabases.Text) = 0 Then

    lstUsers.RemoveItem lstUsers.ListIndex
    oServer.Databases(lstDatabases.Text).Users(NameToCheck).Remove
    MsgBox "User Removed", vbInformation, "User Removed"
ElseIf FindIfUserOwnsAnything(oServer.Databases _
(lstDatabases.Text).Users _
(NameToCheck).Login, lstDatabases.Text) = 1 Then
    MsgBox "This User Owns Objects", vbInformation, "Cannot Remove Login"
ElseIf FindIfUserOwnsAnything(oServer.Databases _
(lstDatabases.Text).Users _
(NameToCheck).Login, lstDatabases.Text) = 2 Then
    MsgBox "An Error Occurred"
End If
```

The syntax you use in T-SQL to remove a user from a database is as follows:

```
Use <databasename>
```

There are two ways to remove the user. The first is the one you need to use going forward:

```
sp_revokedbaccess [@name_in_db =] 'name'
```

The next method is used and provided for backward compatibility only:

```
sp_dropuser [@name_in_db =] 'user'
```

In Enterprise Manager, you have a couple of ways to remove a user from a database. If you right-click the user's icon, you see the options list shown in Figure 3-15. Select Delete to delete the user.

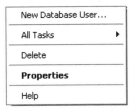

Figure 3-15. Removing a user, method 1

The second method is to navigate to the Security folder of your server and select the login that you know corresponds to the user you want to remove. Double-click the login and select the Database Access tab. All you do then is remove the checkmark next to the database that you intend to remove the user from.

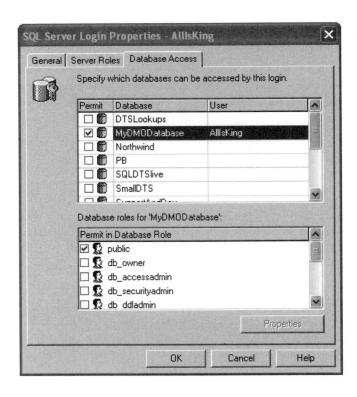

Figure 3-16. Removing a user, method 2

Adding/Removing a User to/from a Database Role

As mentioned at the beginning of the chapter, a database role is to users what a server role is to logins. Later in the chapter, you'll look at how to create new roles, both application and standard, but let's start by looking at how to add users to or remove users from database roles.

The first thing you need to do in the application is select a database and a user. You then click the button next to the list of database roles available, and the screen in Figure 3-17 appears.

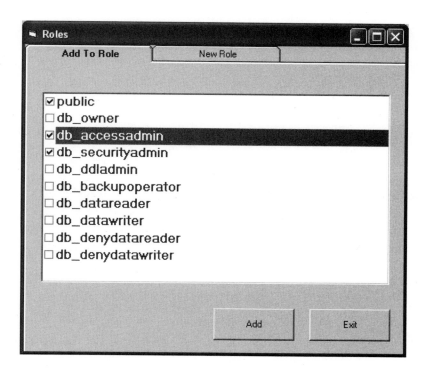

Figure 3-17. Adding a user to and removing a user from a database role

When the form opens, you need to place a checkmark next to the roles to which the user belongs. Here's the code to do that:

```
Private Function ShowRoleUserMemberOf(UserName As String,
DatabaseName As String, DBRole As String) As Boolean
Dim i As Integer
Dim j As Integer
ShowRoleUserMemberOf = False
```

You pass to the function the username you're interested in, the database name, and the role name you want to check. If the user is a member of that role, then the function will return true. You execute the EnumDatabaseRoleMember method of the role you want to look at and read the results into a QueryResults object, which as we mentioned earlier is similar to a table with columns and rows. You loop through the results and see if they contain the user.

```
Dim oQryresults As SQLDMO.QueryResults

Set oQryresults = oServer.Databases(DatabaseName).DatabaseRoles _
(DBRole).EnumDatabaseRoleMember

For i = 1 To oQryresults.Rows
        If oQryresults.GetColumnString(i, 1) = UserName Then
            ShowRoleUserMemberOf = True
        End If

Next i

End Function
```

The lstRoles list box has been prepopulated with a list of roles available in the database. You loop through each one and pass these details to your function, which will return either true or false. If the function returns true, then you need to place a checkmark next to that role.

```
For i = 0 To lstRoles.ListCount - 1
    If ShowRoleUserMemberOf(Left(frmAddGroups.lstUsers.Text, InStr(1,
frmAddGroups.lstUsers.Text, "(") - 2), _
frmAddGroups.lstDatabases.Text, lstRoles.List(i)) = True Then
        lstRoles.Selected(i) = True
    End If
Next I
```

To add a user to or remove a user from a role, you just check or uncheck the box next to the role. When you click the Add button, you'll commit the changes to the database.

The following code checks to see if you need to remove the user from a role or add the user to one or more roles. The function accepts the username, the database name, the role name, and whether or not the check box is checked as parameters from the application to determine what it needs to do.

```
Public Const IS_MEMBER = 1
Public Const NEEDS_ADDING = 2
Public Const NEEDS_DELETING = 3
Public Function ReturnValuesofMembership(strUserName As String,
strDatabaseName As String, strRoleName As String,
booChecked As Boolean) As Integer

Dim i As Integer
Dim booInList As Boolean



Dim oQList As SQLDMO.QueryResults

Set oQList = oServer.Databases(strDatabaseName).DatabaseRoles _
(strRoleName).EnumDatabaseRoleMember
```

Once you have read in the members of the role, you look for your user. You assume you won't find the user. If the user is in the list, then booInList is set to true.

```
    booInList = False

    For i = 1 To oQList.Rows
        If UCase(Trim(oQList.GetColumnString _
(i, 1))) = UCase(Trim(strUserName)) Then
            booInList = True
            Exit For
        End If
    Next I
```

Here's where you check to see what you need to do. If the user is in the list of members and the check box is checked, then the user still needs to be a user in the role.

```
    If booInList = True And booChecked = True Then
            ReturnValuesofMembership = IS_MEMBER
    End If
```

If the user is in the list but the check box is unchecked, then you need to signal for this user to be removed from the role.

```
    If booInList = True And booChecked = False Then
        ReturnValuesofMembership = NEEDS_DELETING
    End If
```

If the user isn't in the list but the check box is checked, then you want to add the user to the role.

```
If booInList = False And booChecked = True Then
'not in the list and checkbox ticked = needs adding
        ReturnValuesofMembership = NEEDS_ADDING
End If

End Function
```

Here's how you call the function. You loop through the list box of roles and pass the required parameters to the function:

```
Dim j As Integer
Dim i As Integer

For j = 0 To lstRoles.ListCount - 1

Select Case ReturnValuesofMembership _
(Left(frmAddGroups.lstUsers.Text, InStr _
(1, frmAddGroups.lstUsers.Text, "(") - 2), _
frmAddGroups.lstDatabases.Text, lstRoles.List _
(j), lstRoles.Selected(j))

    Case NEEDS_ADDING
          oServer.Databases _
(frmAddGroups.lstDatabases.Text).DatabaseRoles _
(lstRoles.List(j)).AddMember Left _
(frmAddGroups.lstUsers.Text, InStr(1, _
frmAddGroups.lstUsers.Text, "(") - 2)

    Case NEEDS_DELETING
          oServer.Databases _
(frmAddGroups.lstDatabases.Text).DatabaseRoles _
(lstRoles.List(j)).DropMember Left _
(frmAddGroups.lstUsers.Text, InStr _
(1, frmAddGroups.lstUsers.Text, "(") - 2)

End Select

Next j
```

Here's how you add a user to and remove a user from a database role using T-SQL. To add a user to a role, use this code:

```
sp_addrolemember [@rolename =] 'role', [@membername =] 'security_account'
```

To remove a user from a role, use this code:

```
sp_droprolemember [@rolename =] 'role', [@membername =] 'security_account'
```

Enterprise Manager is quite similar to the application, really. You navigate to the Security folder of your server and double-click the login of the user you want to add to a role. Go to the Database Access tab and select a database. In the bottom pane, you'll see the list of roles available, so put a checkmark in the corresponding box to add the user to the role, or remove the checkmark to remove the user from the role. When you saw how to remove a data user in Figure 3-16, you saw the exact same screen as you would see here, so we haven't duplicated it. The only difference there was you were removing the user, whereas here you're adding the user.

Creating a New Database Role

In the application, there's a New Role tab next to the tab where you added your users to the database roles (i.e., the Add to Role tab) that allows you to create a new database role. Figure 3-18 shows you how to add a new database role in the Add User application.

We mentioned earlier that there are two types of database roles, standard and application, and that we would explain them when you encountered them. Well, that time is now.

- *Standard role:* Has members. Doesn't have a password.

- *Application role:* Has no members. Has a password.

Users are added to standard database roles and the roles are granted permissions in your database. Application roles are granted access to your database, but you aren't allowed to add users to them. What happens is that a user will connect to SQL Server and activate the role. All permissions that the user has will be forgotten about and the only permissions the user will have are those of the role. This implementation is typically used when you want to let the application connect to SQL Server and have a common set of permissions. This means that while the user is using this one application, she can access the database. If she tries to access the database using another tool or creates an ODBC link, she'll be denied access. We'll show you a possible routine you could use in an application to call an application role.

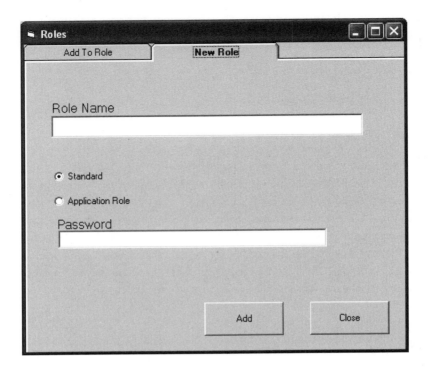

Figure 3-18. Adding a new database role using the Add User application

The procedure takes three parameters: the role name; the role type, of which there are two—standard (1) and application (0); and an optional password.

```
Private Sub AddDatabaseRole(rolename As String,
RoleType As Integer, DatabaseName As String,
Optional Password As String)


Dim exists As Integer

Dim onewdbrole As SQLDMO.DatabaseRole
Set onewdbrole = New SQLDMO.DatabaseRole
exists = 0
```

First, you need to check if the role you're about to add already exists.

```
For Each oDBRole In oServer.Databases(DatabaseName).DatabaseRoles
    If UCase(oDBRole.Name) = UCase(rolename) Then
        exists = 1
        MsgBox "Role already Exists", vbInformation, "Exists"
        Exit Sub
    End If
Next oDBRole
```

If the role doesn't exist, then you need to add it. Because the Add method of the DatabaseRoles collection expects a role to be passed, you need to set the properties of your role before you call the Add method. The only difference between the two implementations is that for the application role you specify a password.

```
If exists = 0 Then
    If RoleType = 1 Then
        onewdbrole.Name = rolename
        onewdbrole.AppRole = False
        oServer.Databases(DatabaseName).DatabaseRoles.Add onewdbrole
    ElseIf RoleType = 0 Then
        onewdbrole.Name = rolename
        onewdbrole.AppRole = True
        onewdbrole.Password = Password
        oServer.Databases(DatabaseName).DatabaseRoles.Add onewdbrole
    End If
End If
End Sub
```

Here's how you call the procedure. If you don't specify a password for an application database role, you pass a default of "Password."

```
Dim i As Integer
If txtRoleName.Text <> "" Then
    If optNormal.Value = True Then
        AddDatabaseRole txtRoleName.Text, 1, frmAddGroups.lstDatabases.Text
        ClearUp
    Else
        AddDatabaseRole txtRoleName.Text, 0,
frmAddGroups.lstDatabases.Text, IIf(txtPassword.Text <> "",
txtPassword.Text, "Password")

    End If

End If
```

This is how you would create standard and application database roles using T-SQL.

Standard Database Role in T-SQL

```
sp_addrole [ @rolename = ] 'role' [ , [ @ownername = ] 'owner' ]
```

Application Database Role in T-SQL

```
sp_addapprole [ @rolename = ] 'role'  , [ @password = ] 'password'
```

In Enterprise Manager, you select the database you want to add the role to and then choose the Roles collection. If you right-click in the right-hand pane and select New Database Role, you should see a screen similar to the one shown in Figure 3-19.

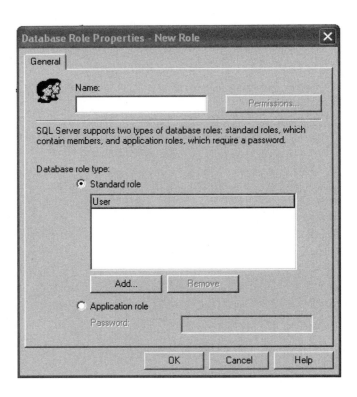

Figure 3-19. Adding a new database role in Enterprise Manager

If you select an application role, the Password box becomes available but the Add button to add users to the role becomes unavailable.

Earlier we said we would show you a possible way to activate the application role, so here it is. We mentioned that you connect to the server through the application, possibly using your NT account (or using a SQL login that the DBA has provided you with). The application will then trigger the application role and you will only then have the permissions of the role.

Activating an Application Role

The following code uses ActiveX data objects to connect to a server. Once the connection is established, it activates the application role.

```
Sub ActivateAppRole(servername As String,
AppRoleName As String,
ApprolePassword As String)

Dim cnString As String
Dim cn As ADODB.Connection

Set cn = New ADODB.Connection
cnString = "Provider = SQLOLEDB;Data Source = " & _
 servername & _
";initial catalog = MyDatabase;User ID = MyUser;Password = YouWish"

cn.Open cnString

cn.sp_setapprole AppRoleName, ApprolePassword

cn.Close
Set cn = Nothing
End Sub
```

The Permissions Application

This small application will enable you to add permissions to and revoke permissions from tables in the database of your choice. Figure 3-20 shows the first screen of the Permissions application.

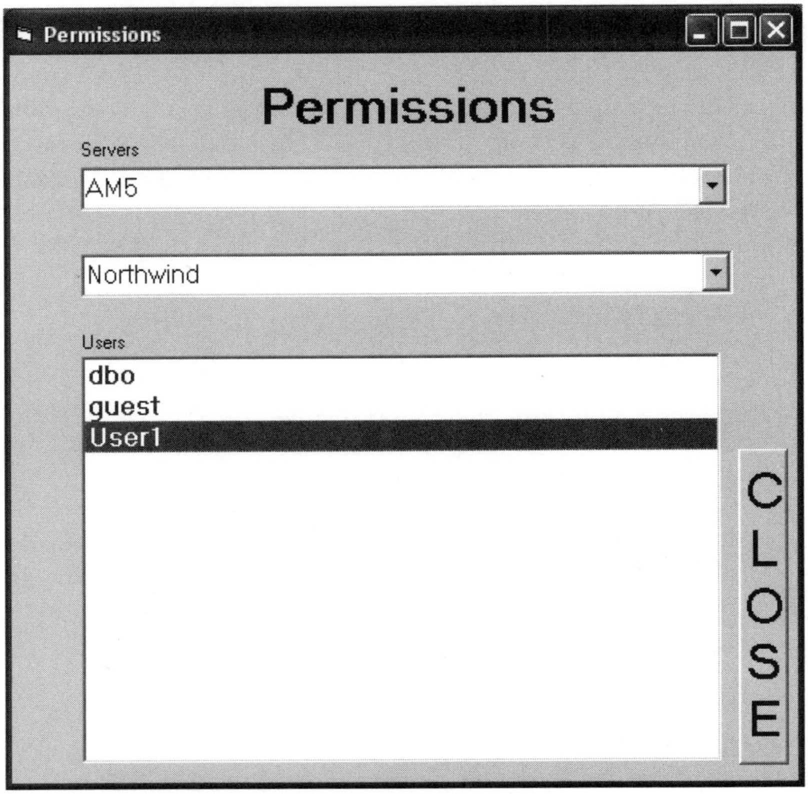

Figure 3-20. The first screen of the Permissions application

How does the application work, then? Well, you select a server and then a database from the lists. This will give you a list of users in that database. You then select a user and the screen in Figure 3-21 appears.

If you highlight a table, the check boxes to the right will show you what permissions the user has on that object. In Figure 3-21 you can see that the user has SELECT permissions on the Categories table.

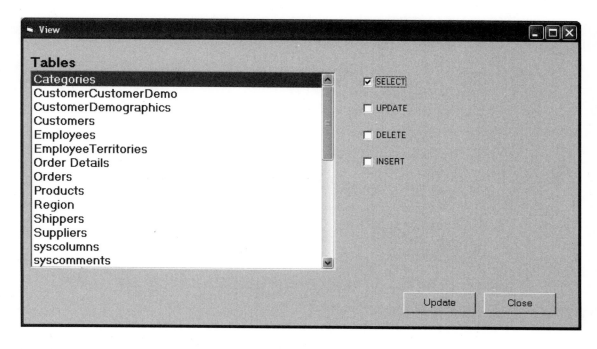

Figure 3-21. The adding permissions screen of the Add Permissions application

Showing Who Has Which Permissions on the Table

To show who has which permissions on the table, you pass the name of the database, the name of the user, and the table name to the procedure.

```
Private Sub ValidatePermissions(DatabaseName As String,
tableName As String, UserName As String)
Dim i As Integer
```

The variable oList that you can see is of the type SQLObjectList, and this can hold any type of object you may encounter or care to read into it. In this case, you just want to read in the permissions of your user on the table.

```
Set oList = oServer.Databases(DatabaseName).Tables _
(tableName).ListUserPermissions(UserName)
```

You then iterate through SQLObjectList looking for any permissions you may have. What you find depends on which check boxes you check.

```
For Each objPermission In oList

    Select Case objPermission.PrivilegeTypeName

    Case "Select"
    chkSelect.Value = vbChecked

    Case "Insert"
    chkInsert.Value = vbChecked

    Case "Update"
    chkUpdate.Value = vbChecked

    Case "Delete"
    chkDelete.Value = vbChecked

End Select

Next objPermission

End Sub
```

Changing the User's Permissions

What if you want to change the user's permissions? Remember in the Add User application how you found out which roles a user belonged to? Well, this is the same kind of thing. You check or uncheck the box next to the permission you want to change and then click the Update button.

```
Sub AlterPermissionOrNot(DatabaseName As String,
tableName As String, UserName As String)

Dim Sselect As Integer
Dim Iinsert As Integer
Dim Uupdate As Integer
Dim Ddelete As Integer
```

The following variables are used to hold whether or not you have the permissions on the table already:

```
Sselect = 0
Ddelete = 0
Iinsert = 0
Uupdate = 0
```

Again, you iterate through the Permissions collection in your SQLObjectList and set the corresponding variable to 1 if you have the permission and leave it at 0 if you don't have the permission.

```
For Each objPermission In oList

If objPermission.PrivilegeTypeName = "Select" Then
    Sselect = 1
End If

If objPermission.PrivilegeTypeName = "Update" Then
    Uupdate = 1
End If

If objPermission.PrivilegeTypeName = "Delete" Then
    Ddelete = 1
End If

If objPermission.PrivilegeTypeName = "Insert" Then
    Iinsert = 1
End If

Next objPermission
```

Checking for an Existing Permission

If you have the permission already and the variable is set to 1, but the check box corresponding to that permission is unchecked, it means that you want to revoke the permission. If you don't have the permission already and the variable is set to 0, but the check box corresponding to that permission is checked, it means you want to add the permission. The other variations require you to take no action (i.e., you have the permission and the check box is still checked, or you don't have the permission and the check box is still unchecked).

```
If Sselect = 1 And chkSelect.Value = vbUnchecked Then
    oServer.Databases(DatabaseName).Tables(tableName).Revoke _
SQLDMOPriv_Select, UserName
ElseIf Sselect = 0 And chkSelect.Value = vbChecked Then
    oServer.Databases(DatabaseName).Tables(tableName).Grant _
SQLDMOPriv_Select, UserName
End If


If Uupdate = 1 And chkUpdate.Value = vbUnchecked Then
    oServer.Databases(DatabaseName).Tables(tableName).Revoke _
SQLDMOPriv_Update, UserName
ElseIf Uupdate = 0 And chkUpdate.Value = vbChecked Then
    oServer.Databases(DatabaseName).Tables(tableName).Grant _
SQLDMOPriv_Update, UserName
End If


If Iinsert = 1 And chkInsert.Value = vbUnchecked Then
    oServer.Databases(DatabaseName).Tables(tableName).Revoke _
SQLDMOPriv_Insert, UserName
ElseIf Iinsert = 0 And chkInsert.Value = vbChecked Then
    oServer.Databases(DatabaseName).Tables(tableName).Grant _
SQLDMOPriv_Insert, UserName
End If


If Ddelete = 1 And chkDelete.Value = vbUnchecked Then
    oServer.Databases(DatabaseName).Tables(tableName).Revoke _
SQLDMOPriv_Delete, UserName
ElseIf Ddelete = 0 And chkDelete.Value = vbChecked Then
    oServer.Databases(DatabaseName).Tables(tableName).Grant _
SQLDMOPriv_Delete, UserName
End If

End Sub
```

To see a full range of the permissions you can grant on objects in your database, please refer back to Table 3-2.

Although we briefly covered how to give users permissions to your objects in T-SQL, we thought it would be useful to quickly reiterate them here. SQL Server Books Online gives the following syntax for GRANT:

```
GRANT
    {ALL [PRIVILEGES] | permission[,...n]}
    {
        [(column[,...n])] ON {table | view}
        | ON {table | view}[(column[,...n])]
        | ON {stored_procedure | extended_procedure}
    }
TO security_account[,...n]
[WITH GRANT OPTION]
[AS {group | role}]
```

Here's an example usage:

```
GRANT SELECT ON Authors TO MyUser
```

This example would grant you SELECT permissions on the whole of the Authors table. There may be occasions when you need to restrict the ability to select data from a table to certain columns, perhaps because you have salary information in there. Here's how you do that:

```
GRANT SELECT on Authors(au_id,au_fname) TO MyUser
```

We covered how to grant permissions in Enterprise Manager earlier in the chapter, and Figure 3-5 shows the results. There's only one thing we would like to add. The Figure 3-5 image was taken from version 7.0 of SQL Server. Version 7.0 allows you to operate at the table level, but remember, you may need to drill deeper. In version 7.0 we can find no way using Enterprise Manager to allocate permissions at the column level. In SQL Server 2000, however, things are a little different. Figure 3-22 shows in version 2000 the equivalent screen to Figure 3-5.

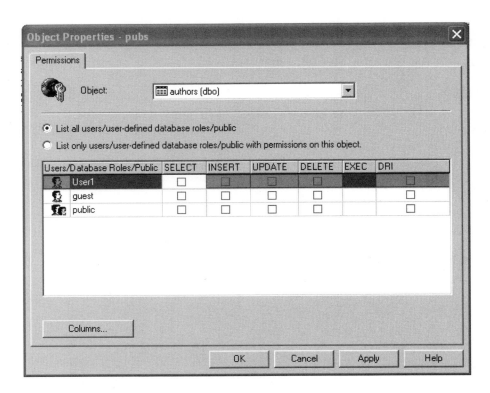

Figure 3-22. SQL Server 2000 permissions through Enterprise Manager

The main point here is the addition of the Columns button. If you click the Columns button, you can see on the screen in Figure 3-23 that you're able to add permissions at the column level.

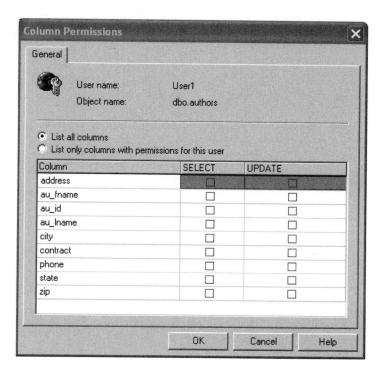

Figure 3-23. Enterprise Manager permissions on columns

Summary

This chapter gave you insight into just how easy it is to manage a user's permissions on objects through SQL-DMO. Probably the hardest part of all this is knowing what type of object will hold the list of things for you to check against (i.e., SQLObjectList or a QueryResults object). We built the Add User and Add Permissions applications very quickly, so you may want to add more features and make the applications more colorful.

In the next chapter, you'll look at OLE automation, which is leveraging the power of SQL-DMO in your T-SQL scripts. The next chapter promises to be a must for those who want added flexibility without the need for a graphical interface.

CHAPTER 4

Using SQL-DMO with OLE Automation

IF YOU'RE ONE OF THOSE people who does everything in T-SQL, never touching Enterprise Manager, then this chapter is for you. Using OLE automation and SQL-DMO is going to give your fingers and the keyboard a workout. In this chapter, we show you how to manipulate the SQL-DMO library using nothing more than good old T-SQL. We won't deny that in our experience there's a bit more code involved when you do things in T-SQL, but we think the extra code is well worth it, and once you get the hang of things you should have no problems with it. This chapter is heavy on examples and explanations, so you should find something here that you can either use directly or adapt for use in your own environment.

We're going to automate the manipulation of COM objects through a process called *OLE automation*. In our examples, we manipulate the SQL-DMO objects, but we could quite easily be using Microsoft Word, Excel, or even Data Transformation Services. It's our opinion that before you dive into OLE automation using T-SQL, you should experiment in Visual Basic or the programming language of your choice, as you'll then get a feel for the objects, properties, and methods available to you. We've found using SQL-DMO in a job to be extremely powerful.

As we mentioned earlier, some developers either don't use any RAD tools (such as Visual Basic or C++) or simply prefer to use T-SQL for everything. Also, if you code in T-SQL, it means you can nicely package the code up into stored procedures and keep them in your database. In the next release of SQL Server (post SQL Server 2000) it's expected that Microsoft will allow developers to save objects written in Visual Basic .NET (VB .NET) and C#, Microsoft's newest programming languages, onto the database server.

In this chapter, we're going to re-cover some ground to show you how to do things you've already looked at in T-SQL and OLE automation. We'll then move on to doing some really quite interesting things, including

- Adding a login and then adding that login to a database as a user

- Transferring a database from one server to another and specifying any options you want to use along the way

- Scripting out a database definition

- Pumping out all the data in a database's tables to text files (useful for small-scale disaster recovery)

- Running Database Console Commands (DBCCs) on all your tables (DBCC DBREINDEX, in this instance)

Using OLE

To use OLE in T-SQL, you need only know seven stored procedures. Table 4-1 lists these procedures. The syntax was taken straight from SQL Server Books Online.

 NOTE You can find out more about these stored procedures in SQL Server Books Online.

Table 4-1. OLE Stored Procedures

Procedure	Use	Syntax
sp_OACreate	Creates an instance of the OLE object	`sp_OACreate progid,	clsid,` ` objecttoken OUTPUT` ` [, context]`

sp_OAMethod	Calls a method of the OLE object	`sp_OAMethod objecttoken,`
		`    methodname`
		`    [ , returnvalue OUTPUT ]`
		`    [ , [ @parametername = ] parameter [ OUTPUT ]`
		`    [ ...n ] ]`

sp_OAGetProperty	Retrieves a property value from the OLE object	`sp_OAGetProperty objecttoken,`
		`    propertyname`
		`    [ , propertyvalue OUTPUT ]`
		`    [ , index...]`

sp_OASetProperty	Sets a property of the OLE object	`sp_OASetProperty objecttoken,`
		`    propertyname,`
		`    newvalue`
		`    [ , index... ]`

Table 4-1. OLE Stored Procedures (Continued)

Procedure	Use	Syntax
sp_OAStop	Stops execution of the OLE environment	`sp_OAStop`

sp_OAGetErrorInfo	Manipulates an error from the OLE object	`sp_OAGetErrorInfo [ objecttoken ]`
		`[ , source OUTPUT ]`
		`[ , description OUTPUT ]`
		`[ , helpfile OUTPUT ]`
		`[ , helpid OUTPUT ]`

sp_OADestroy	Destroys/cleans up your OLE objects	`sp_OADestroy objecttoken`

In the following sections, you're going to cover some of the same ground you covered in previous chapters, such as adding a login and a user to a server and a database, but you'll also cover some new ground, such as exporting the data and structure of your databases.

Adding a Login and a User

In Chapter 3, we covered adding users and logins to and removing users and logins from your SQL Servers in depth. However, as we mentioned in that chapter, we thought it would be useful to cover this again using OLE so you can start to recognize the format required using something you've already seen.

Adding a Login to SQL Server

Let's recap what needs to be done to add a login to your SQL Server. If you want to see a more comprehensive example, then turn to Chapter 3, where we take you though adding a user to a database and a whole lot more.

1. Log on to your SQL Server.

2. Create a Login object.

3. Give the Login object a name.

4. Decide what type of login it will be (Standard, NT User, or NT Group). If it's a Standard login, then give it a password (this isn't actually required, but it's preferable for security reasons).

5. Add the login to the Logins collection of SQL Server.

Adding a Login and a User in OLE

To add a login and a user in OLE, you have to first log into SQL Server using OLE.

```
declare @Databases int
declare @Server int
declare @rtn int
declare @transfer int
declare @specificDB int
DECLARE @output varchar(255)
DECLARE @hr int
DECLARE @source varchar(255)
DECLARE @description varchar(255)
DECLARE @Login int
DECLARE @Logins int
```

In the following code, you're creating the Server object and the Login object for later use. The OUTPUT parameters at the end are so you can reference this object later.

```
EXEC @rtn = sp_OACreate 'SQLDMO.SQLServer',@Server OUTPUT
EXEC @rtn = sp_OACreate 'SQLDMO.Login', @Login OUTPUT
```

Next, log into the server and use a trusted authentication, as in the following code:

```
EXEC @rtn = sp_OASetProperty @Server,'LoginSecure','True'
EXEC @rtn = sp_OAMethod @Server,'Connect',NULL,'AM2'
```

Now set the name of your login with this code:

```
EXEC @rtn = sp_OASetProperty @Login,'Name','AllanSQL'
```

Create your error-checking procedure here:

```
IF @rtn <> 0
BEGIN
    EXEC sp_OAGetErrorInfo @Login, @source OUT, @description OUT
    SELECT @output = '  Source: ' + @source
    PRINT @output
    SELECT @output = '  Description: ' + @description
    PRINT END
@output
```

NOTE   If you don't explicitly capture errors when you use OLE through
T-SQL, then you have none returned. It's different from using most
other tools in this way. As with a lot of errors, the code may be a little
undecipherable. We discovered a Microsoft Knowledge Base article
((which you can find on MSDN)) that provides more detail: "INFO:
Underlying OLE and OLEDB Provider Errors Are Exposed Through
ADO" (Q168354).

Here you set the type of login you want to add:

```
EXEC @rtn = sp_OASetProperty @Login,'Type',2
IF @rtn <> 0
BEGIN
    EXEC sp_OAGetErrorInfo @Login, @source OUT, @description OUT
    SELECT @output = '  Source: ' + @source
    PRINT @output
    SELECT @output = '  Description: ' + @description
    PRINT @output
END
```

NOTE   You use the numeric values of the login types as opposed to their
constants, as you would when using Visual Basic. If you attempt to use
the constant, you'll receive an error of "Type Mismatch."

Give your new login a password:

```
EXEC @rtn = sp_OAMethod @Login,
'SetPassword',NULL,@OldPassword = '',
@NewPassword = 'Allan'
IF @rtn <> 0
BEGIN
    EXEC sp_OAGetErrorInfo @Login, @source OUT,
 @description OUT
    SELECT @output = '  Source: ' + @source
    PRINT @output
    SELECT
    @output = '  Description: ' + @description
     PRINT @output
END
```

Next, grab a handle on the Logins collection of your SQL Server:

```
EXEC @rtn = sp_OAGetProperty @Server,'Logins', @Logins OUTPUT
IF @rtn <> 0
BEGIN
    EXEC sp_OAGetErrorInfo @Server, @source OUT,
@description OUT
    SELECT @output = '  Source: ' + @source
    PRINT @output
    SELECT
    @output = '  Description: ' + @description
    PRINT @output
END
```

Now add your new login to the Logins collection:

```
EXEC @rtn = sp_OAMethod @Logins,'Add',NULL,@login
IF @rtn <> 0
BEGIN
    EXEC sp_OAGetErrorInfo @Logins, @source OUT,
 @description OUT
    SELECT @output = '  Source: ' + @source
    PRINT @output
    SELECT @output = '  Description: ' + @description
    PRINT @output
END
```

Finally, clean up:

```
EXEC sp_OADestroy @logins
EXEC sp_OADestroy @login
EXEC sp_OADestroy @server
```

As you can see, you use a lot more code to add a login using this method than you do using standard T-SQL, and quite clearly, if you were thinking of adding a user, you would probably do it using one of the other methods. This example was meant to give you a gentle introduction to the way you write these procedures and how they should look when they're used. Figure 4-1 shows the Logins tree in Enterprise Manager.

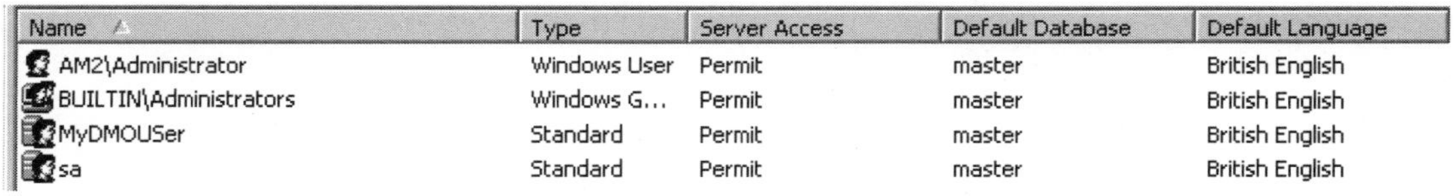

Name	Type	Server Access	Default Database	Default Language
AM2\Administrator	Windows User	Permit	master	British English
BUILTIN\Administrators	Windows G...	Permit	master	British English
MyDMOUSer	Standard	Permit	master	British English
sa	Standard	Permit	master	British English

Figure 4-1. The SQL Server Logins tree

Transferring a Database

We've all had the need to move a database either onto the same server under a different name or onto another server altogether. You have a few ways to do this:

- Backup and restore

- Data Transformation Services (DTS)

- Scripting and the bulk copy program (BCP)

We're going to show you an alternative to these methods. This alternative involves using DMO and the Transfer object to move a database from one server to another. With this method, you can elect to take as much or as little of the database as you want. If bells are going off now inside your head, then yes, it's the same as the DTS transfer of objects.

The very first thing you need to do is create your database on the destination server if it doesn't exist already. You can use Enterprise Manager, T-SQL, the Visual Basic examples using the DMO library we mentioned in Chapter 1, or T-SQL and DMO.

You can easily put the following code into a stored procedure, and when you want to transfer a database, you simply pass the necessary values to it. It really is that easy.

```
declare @hr int
declare @source varchar(100)
declare @description varchar(100)
declare @SQLServer int
declare @DatabaseNew int
declare @DBFile int
declare @LogFile int
declare @DBFileCollection INT
declare @DBLogCollection INT
declare @filegroup int
declare @tlog int
declare @DBCollection INT
declare @output varchar(200)
```

Transferring a Database with DMO and the Transfer Object

To transfer a database with DMO and the Transfer object, begin by creating and logging onto your SQL Server using trusted authentication. Here's the code to do so:

```
EXEC @hr = sp_OACreate 'SQLDMO.SQLServer', @SQLServer OUT
IF @hr <> 0
BEGIN
    EXEC sp_OAGetErrorInfo @SQLServer, @source OUT, @description OUT
    SELECT @output = ' Source: ' + @source
    PRINT @output
    SELECT @output = ' Description: ' + @description
    PRINT @output
END


EXEC @hr = sp_OASetProperty @SQLServer ,'LoginSecure','True'
IF @hr <> 0
BEGIN
    EXEC sp_OAGetErrorInfo @SQLserver, @source OUT, @description OUT
    SELECT @output = ' Source: ' + @source
    PRINT @output
    SELECT @output = ' Description: ' + @description
    PRINT @output
END
```

```
EXEC @hr = sp_OAMethod @SQLServer,'Connect',null,@ServerName = 'ALLAN\REPLINSTANCE'
IF @hr <> 0
BEGIN
    EXEC sp_OAGetErrorInfo @SQLserver, @source OUT, @description OUT
    SELECT @output = '  Source: ' + @source
    PRINT @output
    SELECT @output = '  Description: ' + @description
    PRINT @output
END
```

You now need to create a database and set the name. Here's how:

```
EXEC @hr = sp_OACreate 'SQLDMO.Database' , @DatabaseNew OUT
IF @hr <> 0
BEGIN
    EXEC sp_OAGetErrorInfo @DatabaseNew, @source OUT, @description OUT
    SELECT @output = '  Source: ' + @source
    PRINT @output
    SELECT @output = '  Description: ' + @description
    PRINT @output
END
EXEC sp_OASetProperty @DatabaseNew, 'Name', 'TEST_SCRIPT'
```

Next, you need to initialize the data file and set the properties:

```
EXEC  @hr = sp_OACreate 'SQLDMO.DBFile' ,@DBFile OUT
IF @hr <> 0
BEGIN
    EXEC sp_OAGetErrorInfo @DBFile, @source OUT,
 @description OUT
    SELECT @output = '  Source: ' + @source
    PRINT @output
    SELECT @output = '  Description: ' + @description
    PRINT @output
END

EXEC @hr = sp_OASetProperty @DBFile , 'Name', 'TEST_SCRIPT_DAT'
EXEC @hr = sp_OASetProperty @DBFile ,
 'PhysicalName',
'C:\Program Files\Microsoft SQLServer\MSSQL\data\TEST_SCRIPT.mdf'
EXEC @hr = sp_OASetProperty @DBFile , 'Size', 30
```

At this point, you must initialize the log file and set the properties:

```
EXEC  @hr = sp_OACreate 'SQLDMO.LogFile' , @LogFile OUT
IF @hr <> 0
BEGIN
    EXEC sp_OAGetErrorInfo @LogFile, @source OUT,
@description OUT
    SELECT @output = '  Source: ' + @source
    PRINT @output
    SELECT @output = '  Description: ' + @description
    PRINT @output
END

EXEC @hr = sp_OASetProperty @LogFile , 'Name', 'TEST_SCRIPT_Log'
EXEC @hr = sp_OASetProperty @LogFile ,
'PhysicalName', 'C:\Program Files\Microsoft SQL Server\MSSQL\data\TEST_SCRIPT.ldf'
EXEC @hr = sp_OASetProperty @LogFile , 'Size', 7
```

Now you need to add the log file and the data file to their respective collections. The database data file will be added to the Primary file group.

```
EXEC @hr = sp_OAGetproperty @DatabaseNew ,
'FileGroups("Primary").DBFiles',@FileGroup OUT
EXEC @hr = sp_OAMethod @Filegroup , 'Add',NULL, @DBFile

EXEC @hr = sp_OAGetProperty @DatabaseNew , 'TransactionLog.LogFiles',@tlog OUT
EXEC @hr = sp_OAMethod @tlog , 'Add',NULL,@LogFile
```

Here you add the database to the Databases collection of SQL Server:

```
EXEC @hr = sp_OAGetProperty @SQLServer,'Databases',@DBCollection OUTPUT
IF @hr <> 0
BEGIN
    EXEC sp_OAGetErrorInfo @SQLServer, @source OUT,
 @description OUT
    SELECT @output = '  Source: ' + @source
    PRINT @output
    SELECT @output = '  Description: ' + @description
    PRINT @output
END
```

```
EXEC @hr = sp_OAMethod @DBCollection ,'Add',NULL,@DatabaseNew
IF @hr <> 0
BEGIN
    EXEC sp_OAGetErrorInfo @SQLServer, @source OUT,
 @description OUT
    SELECT @output = '  Source: ' + @source
    PRINT @output
    SELECT @output = '  Description: ' + @description
    PRINT @output
END
```

Transferring Your Source Database

Now you come to transferring your database from its source to the destination. The following code sample will do this for you:

```
declare @Databases int
declare @Server int
declare @transfer int
declare @specificDB int
DECLARE @output varchar(255)
DECLARE @hr int
DECLARE @source varchar(255)
DECLARE @description varchar(255)
```

To transfer your source database, follow these steps. First, get a handle onto the server where the source database is located:

```
EXEC @hr = sp_OACreate 'SQLDMO.SQLServer', @Server OUTPUT
IF @hr <> 0
BEGIN
    EXEC sp_OAGetErrorInfo @Server, @source OUT,
 @description OUT
    SELECT @output = '  Source: ' + @source
    PRINT @output
    SELECT @output = '  Description: ' + @description
    PRINT @output
END
```

You now need to create a Transfer object that will do the bulk of the work later on:

```
EXEC @hr = sp_OACreate 'SQLDMO.Transfer', @transfer OUTPUT
IF @hr <> 0
BEGIN
    EXEC sp_OAGetErrorInfo @transfer, @source OUT,
 @description OUT
    SELECT @output = ' Source: ' + @source
    PRINT @output
    SELECT @output = ' Description: ' + @description
    PRINT @output
END
```

Next, you log onto the source server:

```
EXEC @hr = sp_OASetProperty @Server ,'LoginSecure','True'
IF @hr <> 0
BEGIN
    EXEC sp_OAGetErrorInfo @server, @source OUT,
 @description OUT
    SELECT @output = ' Source: ' + @source
    PRINT @output
    SELECT @output = ' Description: ' + @description
    PRINT @output
END
EXEC @hr = sp_OAMethod @Server,'Connect',null,@ServerName = 'ALLAN'
IF @hr <> 0
BEGIN
    EXEC sp_OAGetErrorInfo @server, @source OUT, @description OUT
    SELECT @output = ' Source: ' + @source
    PRINT @output
    SELECT @output = ' Description: ' + @description
    PRINT @output
END
```

You need to find the database you want to transfer in the Databases collection of the source server. You first get a handle onto the Databases collection, and once you have that, then you can locate the specific database within it.

```
EXEC @hr = sp_OAGetProperty @Server,'Databases',@Databases OUTPUT
IF @hr <> 0
BEGIN
    EXEC sp_OAGetErrorInfo @server, @source OUT, @description OUT
    SELECT @output = '  Source: ' + @source
    PRINT @output
    SELECT @output = '  Description: ' + @description
    PRINT @output
END


EXEC @hr = sp_OAMethod @databases, 'Item', @specificDB OUTPUT, 'Pubs'
IF @hr <> 0
BEGIN
    EXEC sp_OAGetErrorInfo @databases, @source OUT, @description OUT
    SELECT @output = '  Source: ' + @source
    PRINT @output
    SELECT @output = '  Description: ' + @description
    PRINT @output
END
```

You now need to define the items that you want to transfer. There are many more items besides the ones we've defined here.

 NOTE   You can find a fuller list of items you can transfer in SQL Server Books Online.

```
EXEC @hr= sp_OASetProperty @transfer, 'CopySchema',1
EXEC @hr= sp_OASetProperty @transfer, 'CopyAllObjects',1
EXEC @hr= sp_OASetProperty @transfer, 'CopyData',1
EXEC @hr= sp_OASetProperty @transfer, 'DropDestObjectsFirst',1
EXEC @hr= sp_OASetProperty @transfer, 'DestServer','ALLAN\REPLINSTANCE'
EXEC @hr= sp_OASetProperty @transfer, 'DestDatabase','TEST_SCRIPT'
EXEC @hr= sp_OASetProperty @transfer, 'DestUseTrustedConnection',1
EXEC @hr= sp_OASetProperty @transfer, 'IncludeLogins',1
EXEC @hr= sp_OASetProperty @transfer, 'IncludeUsers',1
EXEC @hr= sp_OASetProperty @transfer, 'DropDestObjectsFirst',1
```

Finally, you transfer the database:

```
EXEC @hr = sp_OAMethod @specificdb,'Transfer',NULL,@transfer
```

Then you clean up after yourself:

```
EXEC sp_OADestroy @specificDB
EXEC sp_OADestroy @Databases
EXEC sp_OADestroy @transfer
EXEC sp_OADestroy @Server
```

Remember that we mentioned at the beginning of the "Transferring a Database" section that this method is the same as the DTS transfer objects task? Figure 4-2 shows the graphical equivalent.

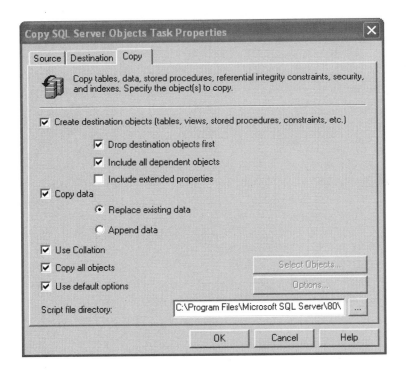

Figure 4-2. The DTS transfer objects task

Creating a Database Script

It can be very useful to have at your disposal a script for quickly re-creating your database either for disaster recovery purposes or so you can re-create the database on a different server. Although we show you how to do this in greater detail when we cover DBScripter in Chapter 9, the next piece of code is a very easy way of getting your database definition up and running quickly. The code is very similar in that you just used to transfer a database to a different server.

```
declare @Databases int
declare @Server int
declare @rtn int
declare @transfer int
declare @specificDB int
DECLARE @output varchar(255)
DECLARE @hr int
DECLARE @src varchar(255)
DECLARE @descr varchar(255)
declare @method varchar(200)
declare @DatabaseName varchar(20)
```

Let's go through the steps you need to complete in order to create a database script. First, you create the objects you're going to use later on:

```
EXEC @rtn = sp_OACreate 'SQLDMO.SQLServer', @Server OUTPUT
If @rtn <> 0
BEGIN
EXEC sp_OAGetErrorInfo @Server,@Src OUTPUT, @Descr OUTPUT
Print '1.  Source of Failure = ' + @src
Print 'Description of Failure = ' + @Descr
END




EXEC @rtn = sp_OACreate 'SQLDMO.Transfer', @transfer OUTPUT
If @rtn <> 0
BEGIN
EXEC sp_OAGetErrorInfo @transfer,@Src OUTPUT, @Descr OUTPUT
Print '2.  Source of Failure = ' + @src
Print 'Description of Failure = ' + @Descr
END
```

When you connect to a server, it's going to require you to log in. In the following code, you set the way you want to log in as Windows Authentication:

```
EXEC @rtn = sp_OASetProperty @Server , 'LoginSecure','True'
If @rtn <> 0
BEGIN
EXEC sp_OAGetErrorInfo @Server,@Src OUTPUT, @Descr OUTPUT
Print '3.  Source of Failure = ' + @src
Print 'Description of Failure = ' + @Descr
END
```

You've set the properties necessary to connect to the server, so in the following code sample you actually establish the connection:

```
EXEC @rtn = sp_OAMethod @Server,'Connect',null,'ALLAN'
If @rtn <> 0
BEGIN
EXEC sp_OAGetErrorInfo @Server,@Src OUTPUT, @Descr OUTPUT
Print '4.  Source of Failure = ' + @src
Print 'Description of Failure = ' + @Descr
END

set @DatabaseName = 'Pubs'
```

Here you set a pointer to the specific database you're interested in scripting:

```
set @Method = 'Databases(' + @DatabaseName + ')'
```

```
EXEC @rtn = sp_OAGetProperty @Server,@method , @Specificdb OUT
If @rtn <> 0
BEGIN
EXEC sp_OAGetErrorInfo @Server,@Src OUTPUT, @Descr OUTPUT
Print '5.  Source of Failure = ' + @src
Print 'Description of Failure = ' + @Descr
END
```

You want to script out everything, so indicate that to the Transfer object:

```
EXEC @rtn= sp_OASetProperty @transfer, 'CopyAllObjects',1
```

Finally, you get to scripting out the database. Option 2 tells SQL Server to use a single file to script out to. You could quite easily change this so that each object type is scripted to a separate file.

```
EXEC @rtn = sp_OAMethod @specificdb,
'ScriptTransfer',NULL,
@transfer, 2 ,
'c:\MyDMOTransfer.txt'
If @rtn <> 0
BEGIN
EXEC sp_OAGetErrorInfo @Server,@Src OUTPUT, @Descr OUTPUT
Print '6.  Source of Failure = ' + @src
Print 'Description of Failure = ' + @Descr
END


EXEC sp_OADestroy @specificDB
EXEC sp_OADestroy @Databases
EXEC sp_OADestroy @transfer
EXEC sp_OADestroy @Server
```

Exporting All of Your Data to Text Files

It can, in some cases, be extremely useful to have text files that contain the data from your database's tables in comma-delimited format. You could use these files in a small-scale disaster recovery situation. Text files zip up very tightly, and therefore you can store quite a few revisions of your data using very little hard drive space. Another possible use is when you want to easily restore only one table from a backup. If you want to restore only one table from last night's backup in SQL Server 7.0 and 2000, then you need to restore the whole backup to another server and then DTS the data over to your live server. Here's the code that you could use to perform this action:

```
DECLARE @Server INT
DECLARE @Bulk_Copy_Object INT
DECLARE @DataBaseCollection INT
DECLARE @item INT
DECLARE @Src varchar(100)
DECLARE @Descr varchar(100)
DECLARE @Rtn INT
declare @TablesCollection INT
declare @DatabaseTablesCounter INT
declare @GeneralCounter INT
```

```
declare @GeneralMethod varchar(100)
declare @TableRef INT
declare @TableName varchar(50)
declare @FileDestinationName varchar(200)
declare @outputRowCounter int
declare @COMMA_DELIMITED int



set @COMMA_DELIMITED = 1
```

Here are the steps you need to complete to export data to text files. First, create the objects for use later:

```
EXEC @rtn = sp_OACreate "SQLDMO.SQLServer",@Server OUTPUT
If @rtn <> 0
BEGIN
EXEC sp_OAGetErrorInfo @Server,@Src OUTPUT, @Descr OUTPUT
Print '1.  Source of Failure = ' + @src
Print 'Description of Failure = ' + @Descr
END
```

This listing shows the BulkCopy object:

```
EXEC @rtn = sp_OACreate "SQLDMO.BulkCopy",@Bulk_Copy_Object OUTPUT
If @rtn <> 0
BEGIN
EXEC sp_OAGetErrorInfo @Server,@Src OUTPUT, @Descr OUTPUT
Print '1.  Source of Failure = ' + @src
Print 'Description of Failure = ' + @Descr
END
```

Next, you choose how you're going to log on. In the following code, you're going to log onto the server using Windows Authentication:

```
EXEC @rtn = sp_OASetProperty @Server, 'LoginSecure','True'
If @rtn <> 0
BEGIN
EXEC sp_OAGetErrorInfo @Server,@Src OUTPUT, @Descr OUTPUT
Print '2.  Source of Failure = ' + @src
Print 'Description of Failure = ' + @Descr
END
```

In the following code snippet, you actually establish the connection:

```
Exec @rtn = sp_OAMethod @Server,"Connect" , NULL , "(local)"
If @rtn <> 0
BEGIN
EXEC sp_OAGetErrorInfo @Server,@Src OUTPUT, @Descr OUTPUT
Print '3.  Source of Failure = ' + @src
Print 'Description of Failure = ' + @Descr
END
```

What type of file do you want to pump to? Here we've chosen to pump out to a comma-delimited text file, but you could easily change that value to TAB, which is also the default, by specifying 2 as the value.

```
EXEC @rtn = sp_OASetProperty @Bulk_Copy_Object, 'DataFileType',@COMMA_DELIMITED
If @rtn <> 0
BEGIN
EXEC sp_OAGetErrorInfo @Bulk_Copy_Object,@Src OUTPUT, @Descr OUTPUT
Print '4.  Source of Failure = ' + @src
Print 'Description of Failure = ' + @Descr
END
```

Get a handle to the Databases collection:

```
Exec @rtn = sp_OAGetProperty @Server, 'Databases',@DatabaseCollection OUTPUT
If @rtn <> 0
BEGIN
EXEC sp_OAGetErrorInfo @Server,@Src OUTPUT, @Descr OUTPUT
Print '5.  Source of Failure = ' + @src
Print 'Description of Failure = ' + @Descr
END
```

Once inside the collection, you look for a reference to your database (in this case, Northwind), but you can easily have this as a parameter:

```
Exec @rtn = sp_OAMethod @DataBaseCollection, 'item',@item out, 'pubs'
If @rtn <> 0
BEGIN
EXEC sp_OAGetErrorInfo @DataBaseCollection,@Src OUTPUT, @Descr OUTPUT
Print '6.  Source of Failure = ' + @src
Print 'Description of Failure = ' + @Descr
END
```

Once you're inside the database itself, you look for a handle on the Tables collection:

```
Exec @rtn = sp_OAGetProperty @item, 'tables',@TablesCollection OUTPUT
If @rtn <> 0
BEGIN
EXEC sp_OAGetErrorInfo @item,@Src OUTPUT, @Descr OUTPUT
Print '7.  Source of Failure = ' + @src
Print 'Description of Failure = ' + @Descr
END
```

You're going to be looping through the tables in Northwind using a while loop, so you need to know how many tables you have in Northwind:

```
Exec
@rtn = sp_OAGetProperty @TablesCollection, 'Count',@DatabaseTablesCounter OUTPUT
If @rtn <> 0
BEGIN
EXEC sp_OAGetErrorInfo @TablesCollection,@Src OUTPUT, @Descr OUTPUT
Print '8.  Source of Failure = ' + @src
Print 'Description of Failure = ' + @Descr
END
```

Print out a little message to the screen to indicate the count:

```
print CAST(@DatabaseTablesCounter as varchar(4)) + ' tables are in the database'
```

You're now going to loop through the tables. In the following code, you declare a variable, @GeneralCounter, to be incremented each time you pick up a new table. You want to carry on looping while this value is less than the value of @DatabaseTablesCounter, which holds the count of tables in total.

```
set @generalCounter  =1


While @GeneralCounter <= @DatabasetablesCounter
    BEGIN
```

You need to know the table name so you can name your destination file, and also so you can grab a reference to it from the Tables collection.

```
set @GeneralMethod = 'Tables(' + cast(@GeneralCounter as varchar(4)) + ').Name'
Exec @rtn = sp_OAGetProperty @item,
@GeneralMethod,@TableName OUTPUT
  If @rtn <> 0
    BEGIN
    EXEC sp_OAGetErrorInfo @item,@Src OUTPUT, @Descr OUTPUT
    Print '9.  Source of Failure = ' + @src
    Print 'Description of Failure = ' + @Descr
    Print 'Description of Failure = ' + @Descr
    END
```

Here's where you find a reference to the table:

```
Exec @rtn = sp_OAMethod @item, 'Tables',@tableref out, @TableName
If @rtn <> 0
BEGIN
EXEC sp_OAGetErrorInfo @item,@Src OUTPUT, @Descr OUTPUT
Print '10.  Source of Failure = ' + @src
Print 'Description of Failure = ' + @Descr
END
```

Next, you set the name of your destination file:

```
SET @FileDestinationName = 'f:\BCPData\[' + @TableName + '].txt'
EXEC @rtn = sp_OASetProperty @Bulk_Copy_Object,
'DataFilePath',@FileDestinationName
If @rtn <> 0
BEGIN
EXEC sp_OAGetErrorInfo @Bulk_Copy_Object,@Src OUTPUT, @Descr OUTPUT
Print '11.  Source of Failure = ' + @src
Print 'Description of Failure = ' + @Descr
END
```

Finally, you export your data using the ExportData method of the Table object:

```
Exec @rtn = sp_OAMethod @Tableref,
'ExportData',@OutputRowCounter OUT,
 @Bulk_Copy_Object
print @rtn
If @rtn <> 0
BEGIN
EXEC sp_OAGetErrorInfo @TableRef,@Src OUTPUT, @Descr OUTPUT
Print '12.  Source of Failure = ' + @src
Print 'Description of Failure = ' + @Descr
END


Print CAST(@OutputRowCounter as varchar(10)) +
' rows were exported for table ' +
@TableName
```

Remember that you need to increase the table counter by 1 each time:

```
SET @GeneralCounter = @GeneralCounter + 1

End
```

Running Database Console Commands

Database Console Commands (DBCCs) can perform a multitude of tasks on your database and its objects. These tasks range from validation commands to maintenance routines. DBCCs check to make sure that the health of your database objects is as it should be and how you would want it. You can perform a raft of different checks on your database, but we've chosen to illustrate DBCC DBREINDEX(). This procedure will re-index one or more indexes on your database tables.

When you initially create your indices, the data is laid very nicely across your database pages. As time goes on and you move data in and out of your database or you update existing data, the index pages can become fragmented and this, as you know from hard disk drive fragmentation, causes a performance hit. The code is very similar to the code you used to export your tables' data, so we'll only show the differences here. The full code is available in the Downloads section of the Apress Web site (http://www.apress.com).

The first thing you need to do is check if the table you're looking at is a system table. You can't issue DBCC DBREINDEX() against a system table.

```
Exec @rtn = sp_OAGetProperty @tableref, 'SystemObject',@IsSystemObject OUTPUT
   If @rtn <> 0
BEGIN
EXEC sp_OAGetErrorInfo @tableref,@Src OUTPUT, @Descr OUTPUT
Print '9.  Source of Failure = ' + @src
Print 'Description of Failure = ' + @Descr
END
```

If you're not looking at a system table, then you want to proceed as follows:

```
If @IsSystemObject = 'False'

BEGIN
```

All this next piece of code does is set up the statement you'll execute:

```
SET @ProcToRun = 'DBCC DBREINDEX([' + @tablename + '])'
Exec @rtn = sp_OAMethod @item,
'ExecuteWithResultsAndMessages',
@results OUTPUT , @ProcToRun ,
NULL,@msgs OUT
If @rtn <> 0
BEGIN
EXEC sp_OAGetErrorInfo @Server,@Src OUTPUT, @Descr OUTPUT
Print '7.  Source of Failure = ' + @src
Print 'Description of Failure = ' + @Descr
END


END

Print 'Returning results of DBCC DBREINDEX from ' + @tablename
Print @msgs
```

NOTE The code you've just seen had us stumped for days. The reason was that ExecuteWithResultsAndMessages returns an object of type QueryResults. We created the object up front as we do when we create a SQL Server, but all we kept getting was "Invalid Class String." This indicates that a library hasn't been registered or that we're making up a fictional object class. We went through creating the very same procedure in Visual Basic and VBScript, and both were happy with QueryResults. We e-mailed SQL Server MVP Ron Talmage to see if he knew what was going on. He actually dug up a very interesting point as a side effect of trying to help us: OLE automation isn't supported when you're using fibers in SQL Server. We then talked to a friend of ours, SQL Server MVP Hilary Cotter, who did a bit of digging and came up with more or less the code you see here. The idea is to just let the object types work themselves out without trying to influence them, rather like self-determination. Thanks, Hilary and Ron.

Summary

Depending on what it is you're doing, OLE automation can involve quite a bit of typing. We think it's worth it, though, for the power of what you can do. We also like to use OLE automation because we can keep our objects on the database server in SQL Server, and we're then less likely to put the code somewhere and completely forget about it. OLE automation doesn't need to stop here. You can perform many other tasks with it, such as manipulating the file system or Excel spreadsheets. We love OLE automation, and hopefully we've given you some ideas of how to apply it in your environments.

CHAPTER 5

Jobs, Alerts, and Operators

WHILE WRITING THIS CHAPTER, we quickly realized why people say you shouldn't attempt to create jobs using T-SQL until you have a solid grasp of what it is you want to do in Enterprise Manager. The options are vast and at times difficult to understand. We hope, though, that if you try to create jobs with T-SQL, you'll save yourself some hard work by using the tables and code in this chapter as templates.

Creating jobs in SQL-DMO is no easier. Many times, we've scratched our heads wondering why a job was created with incorrect options, when it was because the same piece of code may mean different things based on the code before it.

In this chapter, we've created some applications to illustrate how to create your jobs using SQL-DMO, and we've provided tables detailing the options we didn't use. We'll break you in gently, but you might get a little dazed in the middle. By the time you get to the end of the chapter, though, everything should be as clear as spring water.

We'll start by defining the concepts we're going to discuss in the chapter, and then we'll cover the following topics:

- Adding an operator to SQL Server

- Viewing your jobs

- Adding a job

- Creating an alert

Defining General Concepts

Before we start running off into the chapter, we'll define some terms and concepts that we're going to use in this chapter.

What Is a Job?

A *job* is nothing more than one or two steps grouped together and then scheduled using SQL Server Agent to execute at a time you specify. You can schedule the job to execute on a recurring schedule, when the CPU becomes idle, or when SQL Server Agent starts up. If you want to schedule anything in SQL Server, the whole process is managed by SQL Server Agent. You can group jobs into categories, which will help you organize your jobs logically (although this is optional). If you have a multistep job, you can have flow control within the steps—for example, upon completion of one step, depending on whether it succeeded or failed, you can jump to whatever step you require. This will become clearer in the applications we present in this chapter. You can perform different types of steps within a job, and these steps are listed here:

- *TransactSQL (default):* This step will allow you to enter T-SQL commands in the step.

- *Snapshot Replication:* This step allows you to manipulate any Snapshot Replication publications you may have on your server.

- *Merge Replication:* This step allows you to manipulate any Merge Replication publications you may have on your server.

- *Transactional Replication:* This step allows you to manipulate any Transactional Replication publications you may have on your server.

- *Replication Distribution:* This step allows you to manipulate any Replication Distribution publications you may have on your server.

- *Operating System (CmdExec):* This allows you to enter operating system commands just as you would if you were entering them in a DOS window.

- *ActiveX Script:* This step lets you add some ActiveX scripts to the step of your job.

What Is an Operator?

An *operator* is a person (or people) you want notified of events in SQL Server. Examples of the events you might notify the operator of are a job failing and an alert being fired. You can notify an operator in three ways:

- *E-mail:* Providing you have a mail client on the server that supports Messaging Application Programming Interface (MAPI), you can send your operator an e-mail.

- *Pager:* Many technicians carry pagers, which you can use to notify them of a job. You send your operator a page in the same way you send him or her an e-mail.

- *Net send:* This option is only available on NT-based operating systems. It pops up a message box on the operator's designated workstation.

What Is an Alert?

An *alert* is an event that causes a reaction to be fired in SQL Server and lets you take action. You can have SQL Server fire an alert when the transaction log is full or a database has suffered a critical failure. In addition to the standard methods of notifying someone of an alert, you can have a job respond to the alert. This is very useful when the alert is in response to a full transaction log, for example.

Adding an Operator to SQL Server

In this section, you'll learn how to add an operator to SQL Server. You'll want to have at least one operator on your system before you move on to create any alerts or jobs.

Adding an Operator Using Enterprise Manager and T-SQL

Let's first examine how to add an operator using Enterprise Manager and T-SQL before you add one using SQL-DMO.

In Enterprise Manager, you'll need to navigate down the tree of your SQL Server until you come to the Management folder. Once you've opened that folder, you'll see the icon for SQL Server Agent. Expand the SQL Server Agent icon. The center icon of the three is for operators. If you right-click the operator icon, you'll see the option to add a new operator. After you choose to add a new operator, you're greeted by the screen shown in Figure 5-1.

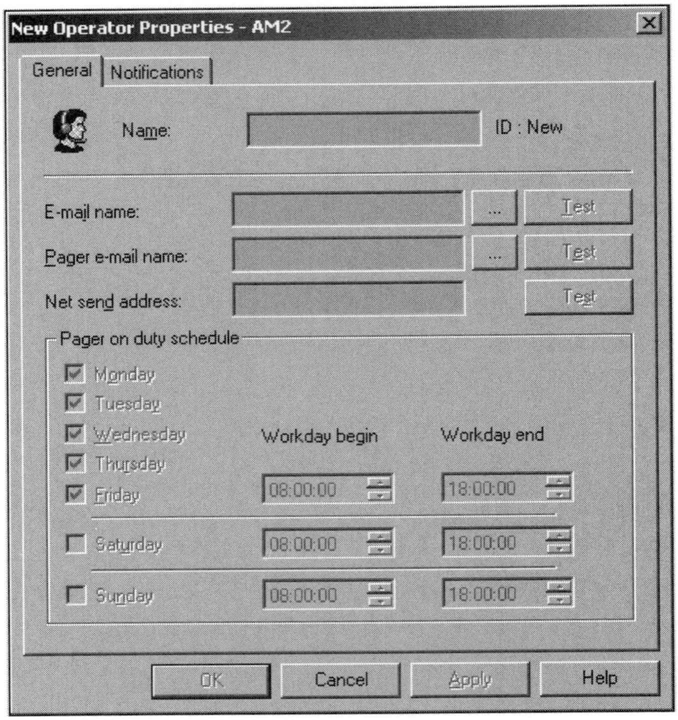

Figure 5-1. Adding an operator

On this first screen you can take a very good guess as to what each box means. The one thing we find interesting about this setup, though, is that if you enter the operator's pager number, the series of check boxes to indicate the days the operator is available becomes visible. You're allowed to specify a start and end time of day individually for Saturdays and Sundays but not for weekdays. During the week, SQL Server assumes that the operator will be available in the same time frame each day.

The Notifications tab (see Figure 5-2) details the list of jobs and alerts that you want this operator to be notified of and the method of notification.

As you can see, there's a radio button at the top of the form to allow you to switch between the available alerts and jobs.

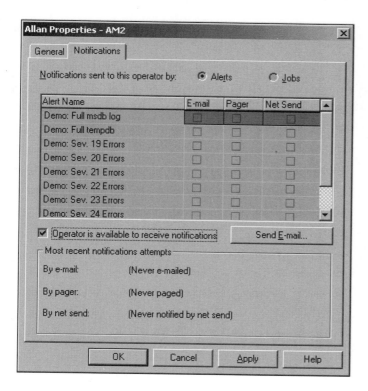

Figure 5-2. Notifying the operator in Enterprise Manager

Now we'll show you how to add an operator with T-SQL. The syntax for adding an operator using T-SQL is really quite simple. The following code was taken straight from SQL Server Books Online.

T-SQL

```
sp_add_operator [@name =] 'name'
    [, [@enabled =] enabled]
    [, [@email_address =] 'email_address']
    [, [@pager_address =] 'pager_address']
    [, [@weekday_pager_start_time =] weekday_pager_start_time]
    [, [@weekday_pager_end_time =] weekday_pager_end_time]
    [, [@saturday_pager_start_time =] saturday_pager_start_time]
    [, [@saturday_pager_end_time =] saturday_pager_end_time]
    [, [@sunday_pager_start_time =] sunday_pager_start_time]
    [, [@sunday_pager_end_time =] sunday_pager_end_time]
    [, [@pager_days =] pager_days]
    [, [@netsend_address =] 'netsend_address']
    [, [@category_name =] 'category']
```

We want to tell you about a few things about this code that some people might view as deliberately misleading. We, on the other hand, consider these issues to be something to figure out during long, cold winter nights:

- SQL Server Books Online says that if the e-mail address is a physical address and not an alias (i.e., allan@allisonmitchell.com), you must enclose it in square brackets, like this: [allan@allisonmitchell.com]. This is incorrect.

- The format for start times and end times is HHMMSS.

- Pager days are the result of adding together the values in Table 5-1.

SQL Server stores the days that an operator is available for paging by adding the numeric values you see in Table 5-1 together for the days the operator should be available.

Table 5-1. Pager Days

Numeric Value	Description
1	Sunday
2	Monday
4	Tuesday
8	Wednesday
16	Thursday
32	Friday
64	Saturday

So, if you wanted your operator to be available on Monday, Wednesday, and Saturday, you would enter a value of 74 (2+8+64).

Adding an Operator Using SQL-DMO

We've built an application that allows you to add an operator to SQL Server and also to define when and how the operator should be available. The application demonstrates how to use SQL-DMO to accomplish this.

Figure 5-3 shows how to define an operator using our application.

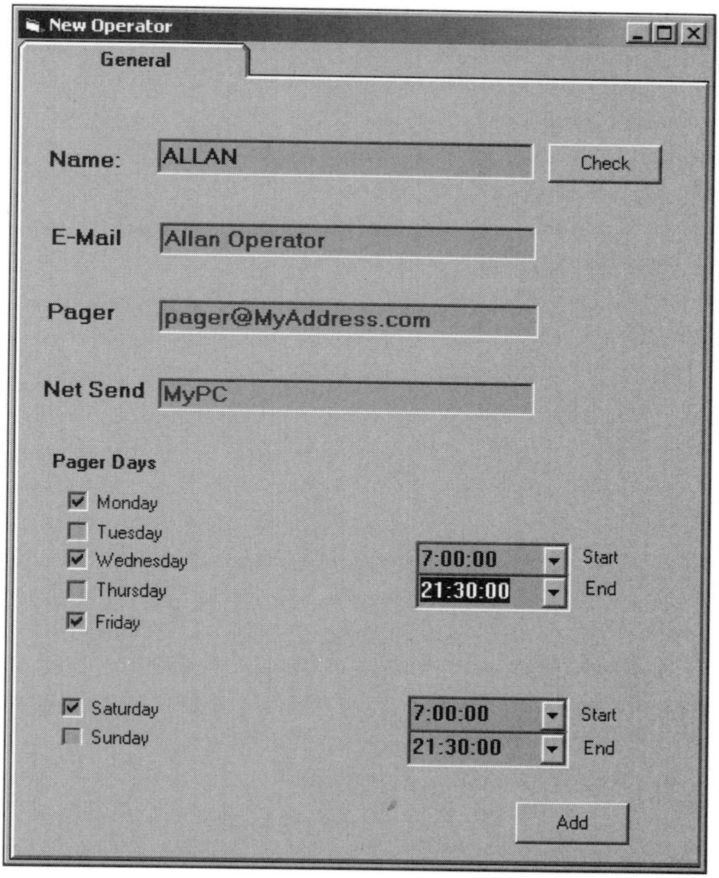

Figure 5-3. Adding an operator using our application in SQL-DMO

This application answers four essential questions:

1. Does the operator already exist?

2. Have you got any pager days during the week?

3. Have you got any pager days on a weekend?

4. If you have days for paging, what are they?

You handle all of this when you click the Add button. In the following sections, we show the code for and explain the meaning of each of the four application parts.

Determining If the Operator Already Exists

To determine if the operator already exists, you loop through the Operators collection of the JobServer object and look for the name of the operator that you're passing as a parameter to the function. If you find it, you set the function to return true, and if you don't find it, you set the function to return false. Here's the code:

```
Private Function CheckOperators(strOperatorName As String) As Boolean

CheckOperators = False

For Each oOperator In oServer.JobServer.Operators
    If oOperator.Name = strOperatorName Then
        CheckOperators = True
        MsgBox "An Operator With That " & _
"Name Already Exists", vbInformation, _
"Already Exists"
    End If
Next oOperator


End Function
```

Determining If You Have Pager Days During the Week

You look at the Checked property of each of the check boxes that are for days of the week, and if any one of them is checked, then you return true. Here's the code:

```
Private Function HaveWeGotPagerDaysInWeek() As Boolean

HaveWeGotPagerDaysInWeek = False

If chkMonday.Value = vbChecked
Or chkTuesday.Value = vbChecked
Or chkWednesday.Value = vbChecked
Or chkThursday.Value = vbChecked
 Or chkFriday.Value = vbChecked Then
    HaveWeGotPagerDaysInWeek = True
End If

End Function
```

Determining If You Have Pager Days on a Weekend

To determine if you have pager days on a weekend, follow the same procedure for checking for days of the week, except obviously the days of the week themselves are different. Here's the code:

```
Private Function HaveWeGotPagerDaysInWeekend() As Boolean

HaveWeGotPagerDaysInWeekend = False

If chkSaturday.Value = vbChecked Or chkSunday.Value Then
    HaveWeGotPagerDaysInWeekend = True
End If

End Function
```

Determining Your Days for Paging

To determine what days you have for paging, loop through all the check boxes on the page and look at their Checked property. If the check box is checked, then you add its Tag properties together and return that as the value of the function. Here's the code:

```
Private Function CheckPagerDays() As Integer


Dim ctl As Control

CheckPagerDays = 0

For Each ctl In frmNewOperator.Controls
    If TypeOf ctl Is CheckBox Then
        If ctl.Value = vbChecked Then
            CheckPagerDays = CheckPagerDays + ctl.Tag
        MsgBox CheckPagerDays
        End If
    End If
Next ctl



End Function
```

We chose to look at the integer values of the days of the week and add them together, but we could quite easily have used the constants that are available. Table 5-2 shows those constants.

Table 5-2. SQL-DMO Weekday Constants

Constant	Value	Description
SQLDMOWeek_EveryDay	127	All days
SQLDMOWeek_Sunday	1	Sunday
SQLDMOWeek_Monday	2	Monday
SQLDMOWeek_Tuesday	4	Tuesday
SQLDMOWeek_Wednesday	8	Wednesday
SQLDMOWeek_Thursday	16	Thursday
SQLDMOWeek_Friday	32	Friday
SQLDMOWeek_Saturday	64	Saturday
SQLDMOWeek_WeekDays	62	Monday, Tuesday, Wednesday, Thursday, and Friday
SQLDMOWeek_WeekEnds	65	Saturday and Sunday
SQLDMOWeek_Unknown	0	None specified

The Complete Code

The code listings that follow will bring together everything we've discussed thus far.

In the following code, you define the operator. You give the operator a name, an e-mail address, and a pager number. If the operator has a pager, you also define when the operator is available to be contacted by the pager.

```
Private Sub cmdAdd_Click()

On Error GoTo err_handler
```

If the name of the operator already exists or the user hasn't supplied a name, then you need to exit the routine.

```
If txtName.Text = "" Or CheckOperators(txtName.Text) = True Then
    Exit Sub
Else

Set oOperator = New SQLDMO.Operator

With oOperator
    .Name = txtName

    If txtmail.Text <> "" Then

        .EmailAddress = txtmail.Text

    End If

    If txtPager.Text <> "" Then
        .PagerAddress = txtPager.Text
        .PagerDays = CheckPagerDays

            If HaveWeGotPagerDaysInWeek = True Then
                .WeekdayPagerStartTime = cboWeekdayStart.Text
                .WeekdayPagerEndTime = cboWeekDayEnd.Text
            End If

            If HaveWeGotPagerDaysInWeekend = True Then
                .SaturdayPagerStartTime = cboWeekendStart.Text
                .SaturdayPagerEndTime = cboWeekendEnd.Text
                .SundayPagerStartTime = cboWeekendStart.Text
                .SundayPagerEndTime = cboWeekendEnd.Text
            End If
    End If

End With

End If
```

Adding Your Operator

After you've defined all the properties of your operator, you add him or her to the Operators collection of the JobServer object.

```
oServer.JobServer.Operators.Add oOperator

Exit Sub

err_handler:

MsgBox Err.Description
Exit Sub

End Sub
```

Viewing Your Jobs

From time to time you're going to need to look at a job and find out things about it. Some examples of the kinds of things you might need to know are as follows:

- Why did the job fail?

- On which step did the job fail?

- When is the job scheduled to run?

- What exactly does the job do?

Let's look now at how you can view the details of your jobs with Enterprise Manager and T-SQL.

Viewing Jobs with Enterprise Manager

In Enterprise Manager, as when you added an operator, you need to navigate to the Management folder. Select the SQL Server Agent icon, and then select the last of the three icons, the Jobs icon. On our server, we have a job called Backup Databases that we're going to use here to illustrate how to view the various properties of jobs.

Even before you open up a job, you can see some useful information on the first screen. Figure 5-4 shows Enterprise Manager when we've clicked jobs in the left-hand pane. As you can see, any jobs already defined on the server are displayed in the pane to the right.

Name	Category	Enabled	Runnable	Sched...	Status	Last Run Status (Start Date)	Next Run Date
A	Database Maintenance	No	No (Add s...	Yes	Not Running	Unknown	(Date and Time are not available)
Backup Databases	Database Maintenance	Yes	Yes	Yes	Not Running	Succeeded (31/01/2002 19:55:06)	(09/02/2002 19:00:00)

Figure 5-4. Job information from Enterprise Manager

If any of our jobs had failed, the icon would have changed to a red circle with a white cross in it. You can double-click the job to see some more of the properties of the job. Figure 5-5 shows the Steps tab of the job creation screen. Here you can view, create, edit, and delete steps in your job.

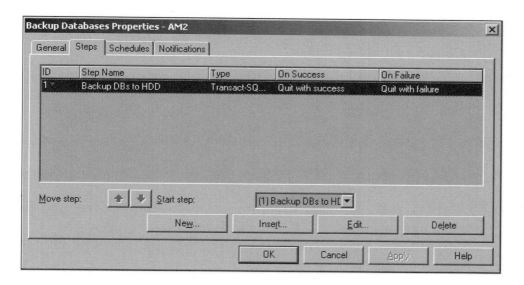

Figure 5-5. The Steps tab

If you double-click the job step you're interested in, you get to see the command of the step. We'll show you how to enter details in here later when we show you how to create a new job in Enterprise Manager. Figure 5-6 shows you the Schedules tab of the job creation screen.

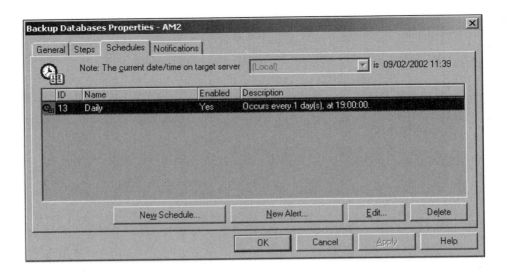

Figure 5-6. The Schedules tab

Click the Notifications tab to view the Notifications screen shown in Figure 5-7. Here you decide who to alert, how to alert him or her, and the reason for the alert.

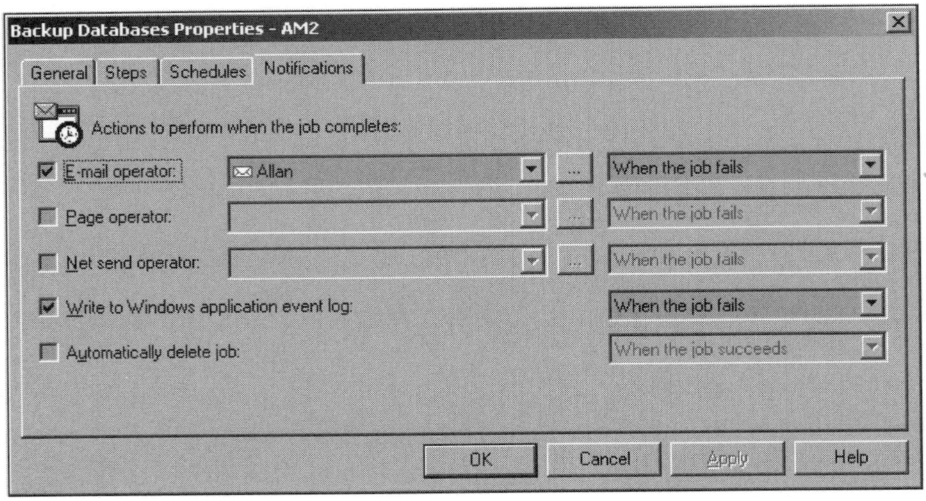

Figure 5-7. The Notifications tab

If you want to see the job history, then you need to right-click the job and select View Job History. This brings up a screen like the one in Figure 5-8. Note that on this screen we've checked the "Show step details" box in the top right corner so we can see an expanded view of the steps.

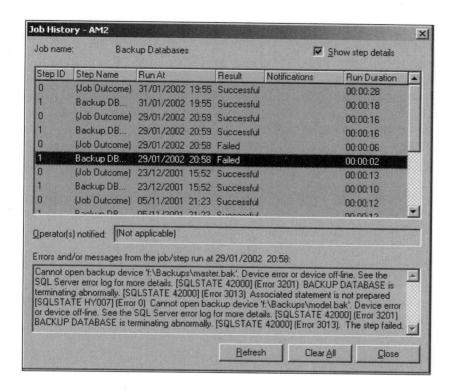

Figure 5-8. Viewing the job history in Enterprise Manager

Viewing Jobs with T-SQL

Viewing jobs with T-SQL involves a lot less clicking than viewing jobs with Enterprise Manager, but it's a little less intuitive in that it gives you all the information you need to work with but not in a manner you can easily use. Here's what we mean: Besides the information for the job history, you can execute one statement and get everything you need. The following code listing was taken from SQL Server Books Online:

```
sp_help_job [ [ @job_id = ] job_id ]
    [ , [ @job_name = ] 'job_name' ]
    [ , [ @job_aspect = ] 'job_aspect' ]
    [ , [ @job_type = ] 'job_type' ]
    [ , [ @owner_login_name = ] 'login_name' ]
    [ , [ @subsystem = ] 'subsystem' ]
    [ , [ @category_name = ] 'category' ]
    [ , [ @enabled = ] enabled ]
    [ , [ @execution_status = ] status ]
    [ , [ @date_comparator = ] 'date_comparison' ]
    [ , [ @date_created = ] date_created ]
    [ , [ @date_last_modified = ] date_modified ]
    [ , [ @description = ] 'description_pattern' ]
```

NOTE   You can specify job_id or job_name, but you can't specify both.

Job_aspect determines how many resultsets you have returned from the procedure. The default is NULL, which means you have all of the four possible resultsets returned. The possible options are listed in Table 5-3.

Table 5-3. Job Aspect Types

Value	Description
ALL	Job aspect information
JOB	Job information
SCHEDULES	Schedule information
STEPS	Job step information
TARGETS	Target information

NOTE   The stored procedure sp_help_job consists of other stored procedures, including sp_help_jobstep and sp_help_jobschedule, which give you details of the job's steps and the job's schedule(s), respectively.

The output from sp_help_jobschedule takes a little bit of deciphering. We've decided to explain the meanings when we deal with adding a job schedule in T-SQL later in the chapter. Now all that's left to do is look at the job's history. You do that using the following stored procedure, which comes directly from SQL Server Books Online:

```
sp_help_jobhistory [ [ @job_id = ] job_id ]
    [ , [ @job_name = ] 'job_name' ]
    [ , [ @step_id = ] step_id ]
    [ , [ @sql_message_id = ] sql_message_id ]
    [ , [ @sql_severity = ] sql_severity ]
    [ , [ @start_run_date = ] start_run_date ]
    [ , [ @end_run_date = ] end_run_date ]
    [ , [ @start_run_time = ] start_run_time ]
    [ , [ @end_run_time = ] end_run_time ]
    [ , [ @minimum_run_duration = ] minimum_run_duration ]
    [ , [ @run_status = ] run_status ]
    [ , [ @minimum_retries = ] minimum_retries ]
    [ , [ @oldest_first = ] oldest_first ]
    [ , [ @server = ] 'server' ]
    [ , [ @mode = ] 'mode' ]
```

If you don't specify a job, you get all jobs. You can customize the output by restricting your search criteria. For example, say you wanted to see all instances of when the Backup Databases job had executed and the outcome was failure. Table 5-4 shows you the possible values you could use and their meanings.

Table 5-4. Job History Outcomes

Value	Description
0	Failed
1	Succeeded
2	Retry
3	Cancelled
4	In progress
5	Unknown

Your request would look like this:

```
EXEC msdb..sp_help_jobhistory
    @job_name = 'Backup Databases',
@run_status = 0
```

Next, you'll learn how to view jobs with SQL-DMO.

Viewing Jobs with SQL-DMO

Now you'll look at jobs in SQL-DMO with our application. Figure 5-9 shows the jobs on our server in the application.

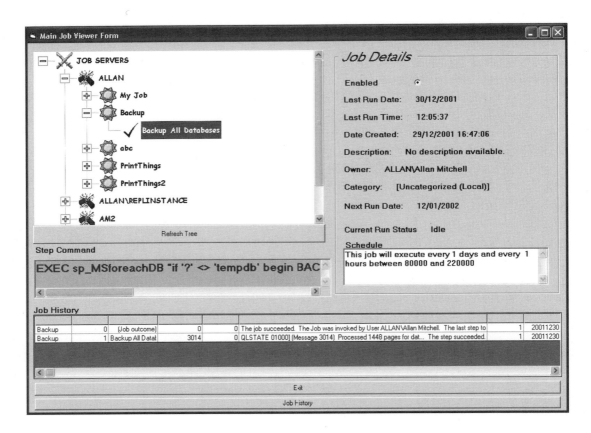

Figure 5-9. Viewing jobs in our application

The application indicates which jobs are on which servers, the job steps, the job details, the step details, and finally, the job outcomes. The application works as follows:

1. You expand a server to show all the jobs on the server.

2. You click the name of a job to populate the Job Details section.

3. You click the Job History button when a job is highlighted to view its history.

4. You expand a job to show the job steps.

5. You click a job step to show the step's command.

We take you through these steps in the following sections.

Showing All Jobs

Here's how we created the application to show all the jobs using SQL-DMO:

```
Private Sub LoadJobList(strServerclicked As String,
 strServerKey As String,
 intCountOfChildren As Integer,
 strFirstChildName As String,
intFirstChildIndex As Integer)


On Error GoTo err_handler
```

Checking What Server You're Logged Onto

You need to check if the server you're logged onto is the server you last used. If it isn't, you log onto it, and if it is, you carry on. Here's the code:

```
If strLastServerLoggedOnTo = "GOBBLEDYGOOK" Then
    oServer.LoginSecure = True
    oServer.Connect strServerclicked
    strLastServerLoggedOnTo = strServerclicked
ElseIf strServerclicked <> strLastServerLoggedOnTo Then
    oServer.DisConnect
    oServer.LoginSecure = True
    oServer.Connect strServerclicked
    strLastServerLoggedOnTo = strServerclicked
End If
```

Checking If Your Node Is Prepopulated

Next, you check if the node has children and you make sure that the first node's text isn't DUMMY. If it is, then it's prepopulated, so you'll need to get out. Here's how:

```
If intCountOfChildren > 0 And strFirstChildName <> "DUMMY" Then
    Exit Sub
End If
```

Populating Your Node

If the first node is DUMMY, then you attempt a population. You do this by removing the first node (the DUMMY node). You want to show a different icon in the tree next to the job depending on the last outcome of the job. You loop through each job on the JobServer object and check its last outcome. Table 5-5 lists possible job outcomes.

Table 5-5. Possible Job Outcomes

Constant	Value	Description
SQLDMOJobOutcome_Cancelled	3	Execution cancelled by user action
SQLDMOJobOutcome_Failed	0	Execution failed
SQLDMOJobOutcome_InProgress	4	Job or job step is executing
SQLDMOJobOutcome_Succeeded	1	Execution succeeded
SQLDMOJobOutcome_Unknown	5	Unable to determine execution state

In the following rather large code listing, you populate the tree with your jobs from the server. You also determine here whether the job failed. This has relevance because you display different icons based on job outcomes.

```
If strFirstChildName = "DUMMY" Then
    tv1.Nodes.Remove intFirstChildIndex
        For Each oJob In oServer.JobServer.Jobs
    If oJob.LastRunOutcome = _
SQLDMOJobOutcome_Succeeded Or oJob.LastRunOutcome = _
SQLDMOJobOutcome_Unknown Then
                tv1.Nodes.Add "SERVER_" & _
 strServerclicked, tvwChild, "JOB_" & _
strServerclicked &_
 "_" & oJob.Name, oJob.Name, _
 il1.ListImages(3).Key
            ElseIf oJob.LastRunOutcome = SQLDMOJobOutcome_Failed Then
                tv1.Nodes.Add "SERVER_" & _
 strServerclicked, tvwChild, "JOB_" & _
strServerclicked & "_" & oJob.Name, oJob.Name, il1.ListImages(4).Key
            End If


            tv1.Nodes.Add "JOB_" & _
strServerclicked & "_" & oJob.Name, _
tvwChild, "DUMMY_" & strServerclicked & _
 "_" & oJob.Name, "DUMMY"
        Next oJob
End If


Exit Sub


err_handler:
tv1.Nodes.Remove intFirstChildIndex
tv1.Nodes.Add "SERVER_" & strServerclicked, _
tvwChild, "ERROR_" & strServerclicked, _
"ERROR LOGGING INTO SERVER"


Exit Sub
End Sub
```

Showing the Job's Details

OK, so you have your jobs in the tree. Now you need to be able to click a job and see the details of that job. Here's how you do it:

```
Private Sub ShowJobDetails(strServer As String, JobName As String)

Dim strCurrentRunStatus As String

If strServer <> strLastServerLoggedOnTo Then
    oServer.DisConnect
    oServer.LoginSecure = True
    oServer.Connect strServer
    strLastServerLoggedOnTo = strServer
End If
```

Here you're checking if the job is enabled:

```
If oServer.JobServer.Jobs(JobName).Enabled = True Then
    optEnabled.Value = True
Else
    optEnabled.Value = False
End If
```

In the following code you pick up the details of the job, and in some cases, you format it into a style you can understand:

```
lblDateCreated = "Date Created:     " &
oServer.JobServer.Jobs(JobName).DateCreated
lblDescription = "Description:      "
& oServer.JobServer.Jobs(JobName).Description
lblLastRunDate = "Last Run Date:       &Mid(oServer.JobServer.Jobs _
(JobName).LastRunDate, 7, 2)
& "/" & Mid(oServer.JobServer.Jobs(JobName).LastRunDate, 5, 2)
& "/" & Left(oServer.JobServer.Jobs(JobName).LastRunDate, 4)
lblLastRunTime = "Last Run Time:     " & Mid(oServer.JobServer.Jobs _
(JobName).LastRunTime, 1, 2)
& ":" & Mid(oServer.JobServer.Jobs(JobName).LastRunTime, 3, 2)
& ":" & Mid(oServer.JobServer.Jobs(JobName).LastRunTime, 5, 2)
lblOwner = "Owner:        " & oServer.JobServer.Jobs(JobName).Owner
lblCategory = "Category:      " &_
 oServer.JobServer.Jobs(JobName).Category
lblNextRunDate = "Next Run Date:      " & Mid(oServer.JobServer.Jobs _
(JobName).NextRunDate, 7, 2)
```

```
& "/" & Mid(oServer.JobServer.Jobs(JobName).NextRunDate, 5, 2)
& "/" &
Left(oServer.JobServer.Jobs(JobName).NextRunDate, 4)
```

Here you're checking what the job is currently doing:

```
Select Case oServer.JobServer.Jobs(JobName).CurrentRunStatus

Case 0
strCurrentRunStatus = "Unknown - Probably never run"
Case 1
strCurrentRunStatus = "Executing"
Case 2
strCurrentRunStatus = "Waiting for worker thread"
Case 3
strCurrentRunStatus = "Between retries"
Case 4
strCurrentRunStatus = "Idle"
Case 5
strCurrentRunStatus = "Suspended"
Case 6
strCurrentRunStatus = "Waiting for Step to Finish"
Case 7
strCurrentRunStatus = "Performing Completion Actions"
End Select

lblCurrentRunStatus = "Current Run Status        " & strCurrentRunStatus
```

In the following line of code, we refer to showing the job's schedule. The procedure itself appears in the next section, "Determining the Job's Schedule."

```
txtSchedule.Text = ShowJobSchedule(strServer, JobName)


End Sub
```

Determining the Job's Schedule

The following procedure is where you work out what the schedule of the job is by interpreting the values that SQL Server gives you:

```
Public Function ShowJobSchedule( _
strServerclicked As String, Job As String)
As String

Dim strFrequencyInterval As String
Dim strFreqTypeConstant As String
Dim strFreqInterval As String
Dim strSubType As String
Dim strCompleteScheduleString As String
Dim freqRelativeInterval As String
```

Before you get all excited about a schedule, let's find out if the job has one:

```
If oServer.JobServer.Jobs(Job).HasSchedule = False Then
    ShowJobSchedule = "No Schedule Available"
    Exit Function
End If
```

Determining When Your Job Executes

Here you decide on whether the job executes only once in a time period, at hourly intervals, or every *n* many minutes:

```
Select Case
oServer.JobServer.Jobs(Job).JobSchedules(1).Schedule.FrequencySubDay
Case 0
strSubType = "Unknown"
Case 1
strSubType = "Once"
Case 4
strSubType = "Minutes"
Case 8
strSubType = "Hourly"
End Select
```

Here you're going to find out whether a job executes one time only, daily, weekly, monthly, when SQL Server Agent starts, or when the CPU becomes idle. The code will also indicate at what periods within those intervals the job fires. The tables to interpret the values appear after this code, so you may need to revisit this listing later to completely understand how a job schedule works. Different values can and often do mean different things depending on the setting preceding them. The reason we

present the information in this way is because it will link cleanly with following
sections, which cover adding a job, adding job steps, and defining a schedule.

```
Select Case oServer.JobServer.Jobs(Job).JobSchedules(1).Schedule.FrequencyType
Case 0
strFreqTypeConstant = "Unknown"
Case 1
strFreqTypeConstant = "One Time"
strCompleteScheduleString = & _
"This job will execute Once only on: " &
oServer.JobServer.Jobs(Job).JobSchedules _ (1).Schedule.ActiveStartDate & "
at: " & oServer.JobServer.Jobs(Job).JobSchedules &_
(1).Schedule.ActiveStartTimeOfDay
Case 4
strFreqTypeConstant = "Daily"

If strSubType = "Once" Then
    strCompleteScheduleString = _
"This job will execute every " & _
oServer.JobServer.Jobs(Job).JobSchedules &_
(1).Schedule.FrequencyInterval & " days at " &
oServer.JobServer.Jobs(Job).JobSchedules &_
(1).Schedule.ActiveStartTimeOfDay
ElseIf strSubType = "Minutes" Then
        strCompleteScheduleString = _
"This job will execute every " & oServer.JobServer.Jobs(Job).JobSchedules &_
(1).Schedule.FrequencyInterval & " days and every  " &
oServer.JobServer.Jobs(Job).JobSchedules &_
(1).Schedule.FrequencySubDayInterval & " minutes between " &
oServer.JobServer.Jobs(Job).JobSchedules &_
(1).Schedule.ActiveStartTimeOfDay & " and " &
oServer.JobServer.Jobs(Job).JobSchedules &_
(1).Schedule.ActiveEndTimeOfDay
ElseIf strSubType = "Hourly" Then
 strCompleteScheduleString = "This job will execute every " &
oServer.JobServer.Jobs(Job).JobSchedules &_
(1).Schedule.FrequencyInterval & " days and every  " &
oServer.JobServer.Jobs(Job).JobSchedules &_
(1).Schedule.FrequencySubDayInterval & _
" hours between " & _
oServer.JobServer.Jobs(Job).JobSchedules &_
(1).Schedule.ActiveStartTimeOfDay & " and " &
oServer.JobServer.Jobs(Job).JobSchedules &_
(1).Schedule.ActiveEndTimeOfDay
End If
```

```
Case 8
strFreqTypeConstant = "Weekly"

If (oServer.JobServer.Jobs(Job).JobSchedules &_
(1).Schedule.FrequencyInterval And 1) Then
strFrequencyInterval = _
strFrequencyInterval + "Sunday,"
End If


If (oServer.JobServer.Jobs(Job).JobSchedules &_
(1).Schedule.FrequencyInterval And 2) Then
strFrequencyInterval = _
strFrequencyInterval + "Monday,"
End If


If (oServer.JobServer.Jobs(Job).JobSchedules &_
(1).Schedule.FrequencyInterval And 4) Then
strFrequencyInterval = _
strFrequencyInterval + "Tuesday,"
End If


If (oServer.JobServer.Jobs(Job).JobSchedules &_
(1).Schedule.FrequencyInterval And 8) Then
strFrequencyInterval = _
strFrequencyInterval + "Wednesday,"
End If


If (oServer.JobServer.Jobs(Job).JobSchedules &_
(1).Schedule.FrequencyInterval And 16) Then
strFrequencyInterval = _
strFrequencyInterval + "Thursday,"
End If


If (oServer.JobServer.Jobs(Job).JobSchedules &_
(1).Schedule.FrequencyInterval And 32) Then
strFrequencyInterval = _
strFrequencyInterval + "Friday,"
End If


If (oServer.JobServer.Jobs(Job).JobSchedules &_
(1).Schedule.FrequencyInterval And 64) Then
strFrequencyInterval = _
strFrequencyInterval + "Saturday,"
End If
```

```
        If strSubType = "Once" Then
            strCompleteScheduleString = _
        "This job will execute on " & _
        Left(strFrequencyInterval, _
        Len(strFrequencyInterval) - 1) & " once only at " & _
        oServer.JobServer.Jobs(Job).JobSchedules &_
        (1).Schedule.ActiveStartTimeOfDay
        ElseIf strSubType = "Minutes" Then
                strCompleteScheduleString = &_
        "This job will execute on " & _
        Left(strFrequencyInterval,
        Len(strFrequencyInterval) - 1) & _
        " and every  " & _
        oServer.JobServer.Jobs(Job).JobSchedules &_
        (1).Schedule.FrequencySubDayInterval & _
        " minutes between " & _
        oServer.JobServer.Jobs(Job).JobSchedules &_
        (1).Schedule.ActiveStartTimeOfDay & " and " &
        oServer.JobServer.Jobs(Job).JobSchedules &_
        (1).Schedule.ActiveEndTimeOfDay
        ElseIf strSubType = "Hourly" Then
                strCompleteScheduleString = _
        "This job will execute on " & _
        Left(strFrequencyInterval, _
        Len(strFrequencyInterval) - 1) & " and every  " &
        oServer.JobServer.Jobs(Job).JobSchedules&_
        (1).Schedule.FrequencySubDayInterval & _
        " hours between " & _
        oServer.JobServer.Jobs(Job).JobSchedules &_
        (1).Schedule.ActiveStartTimeOfDay & " and " & &
        oServer.JobServer.Jobs(Job).JobSchedules &_
        (1).Schedule.ActiveEndTimeOfDay
        End If


Case 16
strFreqTypeConstant = "Monthly"

If strSubType = "Once" Then
    strCompleteScheduleString = "This job will execute on day " &
oServer.JobServer.Jobs(Job).JobSchedules &_
(1).Schedule.FrequencyInterval & _
" of the month every " & oServer.JobServer.Jobs(Job).JobSchedules &_
(1).Schedule.FrequencyRecurrenceFactor & _
" months once only at " & oServer.JobServer.Jobs(Job).JobSchedules &_
```

```
(1).Schedule.ActiveStartTimeOfDay
ElseIf strSubType = "Minutes" Then
        strCompleteScheduleString = "This job will execute on day " &
oServer.JobServer.Jobs(Job).JobSchedules &_ (1).Schedule.FrequencyInterval &
" of the month every " & oServer.JobServer.Jobs(Job).JobSchedules &_
(1).Schedule.FrequencyRecurrenceFactor & " months every  " &
oServer.JobServer.Jobs(Job).JobSchedules &_
(1).Schedule.FrequencySubDayInterval & " minutes between " &
oServer.JobServer.Jobs(Job).JobSchedules &_ (1).Schedule.ActiveStartTimeOfDay
& " and " & oServer.JobServer.Jobs(Job).JobSchedules &_
(1).Schedule.ActiveEndTimeOfDay
ElseIf strSubType = "Hourly" Then
        strCompleteScheduleString = "This job will execute on day " &
oServer.JobServer.Jobs(Job).JobSchedules &_ (1).Schedule.FrequencyInterval &
 " of the month every " & oServer.JobServer.Jobs(Job).JobSchedules &_
(1).Schedule.FrequencyRecurrenceFactor & " months every  " &
oServer.JobServer.Jobs(Job).JobSchedules &_
(1).Schedule.FrequencySubDayInterval & " hours between " &
oServer.JobServer.Jobs(Job).JobSchedules &_ (1).Schedule.ActiveStartTimeOfDay
& " and " & oServer.JobServer.Jobs(Job).JobSchedules &_
(1).Schedule.ActiveEndTimeOfDay
End If
Case 32
strFreqTypeConstant = "Monthly Relative"

If oServer.JobServer.Jobs(Job).JobSchedules &_
(1).Schedule.FrequencyInterval = 1 Then
    strFrequencyInterval = "Sunday"
ElseIf oServer.JobServer.Jobs(Job).JobSchedules &_
(1).Schedule.FrequencyInterval = 2 Then
    strFrequencyInterval = "Monday"
ElseIf oServer.JobServer.Jobs(Job).JobSchedules &_
(1).Schedule.FrequencyInterval = 3 Then
    strFrequencyInterval = "Tuesday"
ElseIf oServer.JobServer.Jobs(Job).JobSchedules &_
(1).Schedule.FrequencyInterval = 4 Then
    strFrequencyInterval = "Wednesday"
ElseIf oServer.JobServer.Jobs(Job).JobSchedules &_
(1).Schedule.FrequencyInterval = 5 Then
    strFrequencyInterval = "Thursday"
ElseIf oServer.JobServer.Jobs(Job).JobSchedules &_
(1).Schedule.FrequencyInterval = 6 Then
    strFrequencyInterval = "Friday"
ElseIf oServer.JobServer.Jobs(Job).JobSchedules &_
```

```
        (1).Schedule.FrequencyInterval = 7 Then
            strFrequencyInterval = "Saturday"
    ElseIf oServer.JobServer.Jobs(Job).JobSchedules &_
    (1).Schedule.FrequencyInterval = 8 Then
            strFrequencyInterval = "Day"
    ElseIf oServer.JobServer.Jobs(Job).JobSchedules &_
    (1).Schedule.FrequencyInterval = 9 Then
            strFrequencyInterval = "Weekday"
    ElseIf oServer.JobServer.Jobs(Job).JobSchedules &_
    (1).Schedule.FrequencyInterval = 10 Then
            strFrequencyInterval = "Weekendday"
    End If


    If oServer.JobServer.Jobs(Job).JobSchedules &_
    (1).Schedule.FrequencyRelativeInterval = 1 Then
            freqRelativeInterval = "First"
    ElseIf oServer.JobServer.Jobs(Job).JobSchedules &_
    (1).Schedule.FrequencyRelativeInterval = 2 Then
            freqRelativeInterval = "Second"
    ElseIf oServer.JobServer.Jobs(Job).JobSchedules &_
    (1).Schedule.FrequencyRelativeInterval = 4 Then
            freqRelativeInterval = "Third"
    ElseIf oServer.JobServer.Jobs(Job).JobSchedules &_
    (1).Schedule.FrequencyRelativeInterval = 8 Then
            freqRelativeInterval = "Fourth"
    ElseIf oServer.JobServer.Jobs(Job).JobSchedules &_
    (1).Schedule.FrequencyRelativeInterval = 16 Then
            freqRelativeInterval = "Last"
    End If



    If strSubType = "Once" Then
        If strFrequencyInterval = "Day" Then
            strCompleteScheduleString = _
    "This job executes on the " & _
    freqRelativeInterval & " day of every " &
    oServer.JobServer.Jobs(Job).JobSchedules &_
    (1).Schedule.FrequencyRecurrenceFactor & " months once only at " &
    oServer.JobServer.Jobs(Job).JobSchedules &_ (1).Schedule.ActiveStartTimeOfDay
        Else
            strCompleteScheduleString = "This job executes on the " &
    freqRelativeInterval & " " & _
    strFrequencyInterval & " of every " &
```

```
oServer.JobServer.Jobs(Job).JobSchedules &_
(1).Schedule.FrequencyRecurrenceFactor & _
" months once only at " & oServer.JobServer.Jobs(Job).JobSchedules &_
(1).Schedule.ActiveStartTimeOfDay
    End If

ElseIf strSubType = "Minutes" Then
    If strFrequencyInterval = "Day" Then
        strCompleteScheduleString = "This job executes on the " &
freqRelativeInterval & " day of every " &
oServer.JobServer.Jobs(Job).JobSchedules &_
(1).Schedule.FrequencyRecurrenceFactor & " months every  " &
oServer.JobServer.Jobs(Job).JobSchedules &_
(1).Schedule.FrequencySubDayInterval & " minutes between " &
oServer.JobServer.Jobs(Job).JobSchedules &_ (1).Schedule.ActiveStartTimeOfDay
& " and " & oServer.JobServer.Jobs(Job).JobSchedules &_
(1).Schedule.ActiveEndTimeOfDay
    Else
        strCompleteScheduleString = _
"This job executes on the " & freqRelativeInterval &
" " & _
strFrequencyInterval & " of every " & _
 oServer.JobServer.Jobs(Job).JobSchedules &_
(1).Schedule.FrequencyRecurrenceFactor & " months every  " &
oServer.JobServer.Jobs(Job).JobSchedules &_
(1).Schedule.FrequencySubDayInterval & " minutes between " &
oServer.JobServer.Jobs(Job).JobSchedules &_ (1).Schedule.ActiveStartTimeOfDay
& " and " & oServer.JobServer.Jobs(Job).JobSchedules &_
(1).Schedule.ActiveEndTimeOfDay
    End If

ElseIf strSubType = "Hourly" Then
    If strFrequencyInterval = "Day" Then
        strCompleteScheduleString = _
"This job executes on the " & freqRelativeInterval & _
" day of every " & oServer.JobServer.Jobs(Job).JobSchedules &_
(1).Schedule.FrequencyRecurrenceFactor & " months every  " &
oServer.JobServer.Jobs(Job).JobSchedules &_
(1).Schedule.FrequencySubDayInterval & " hours between " &
oServer.JobServer.Jobs(Job).JobSchedules &_ (1).Schedule.ActiveStartTimeOfDay
& " and " & oServer.JobServer.Jobs(Job).JobSchedules &_
(1).Schedule.ActiveEndTimeOfDay
```

```
       Else
           strCompleteScheduleString = "This job executes on the " &
    freqRelativeInterval & " " & _
    strFrequencyInterval & " of every " &
    oServer.JobServer.Jobs(Job).JobSchedules &_
    (1).Schedule.FrequencyRecurrenceFactor & " months every  " &
    oServer.JobServer.Jobs(Job).JobSchedules &_
    (1).Schedule.FrequencySubDayInterval & " hours between " &
    oServer.JobServer.Jobs(Job).JobSchedules &_ (1).Schedule.ActiveStartTimeOfDay
    & " and " & oServer.JobServer.Jobs(Job).JobSchedules &_
    (1).Schedule.ActiveEndTimeOfDay
       End If
    End If


    Case 64
    strFreqTypeConstant = "Autostart"
        strCompleteScheduleString = _
    "This job will execute when the SQL Server Agent Starts Up"
    Case 128
    strFreqTypeConstant = "On Idle"
        strCompleteScheduleString = "This job will execute when the CPU becomes idle"
    End Select


    ShowJobSchedule = strCompleteScheduleString

    End Function
```

Showing the Steps of a Job

You've got your job, and you've got the job's details. Now you need to see what steps compose that job. Here's the code:

```
Private Sub LoadJobStepList(JobName As String,
 strServer As String,
strJobKey As String, intCountOfChildren As Integer,
strFirstChildName As String,
intFirstChildIndex As Integer)

On Error GoTo err_handler
```

```
If strServer <> strLastServerLoggedOnTo Then
    oServer.DisConnect
    oServer.LoginSecure = True
    oServer.Connect strServer
    strLastServerLoggedOnTo = strServer
End If
```

This situation is very similar to when you were populating the jobs of the server. When you added the list of jobs you also added a DUMMY node underneath it to show the cross in the tree.

```
If intCountOfChildren > 0 And strFirstChildName <> "DUMMY" Then
    Exit Sub
End If
```

```
If strFirstChildName = "DUMMY" Then
    tv1.Nodes.Remove intFirstChildIndex
        For Each oJobStep In oServer.JobServer.Jobs(JobName).JobSteps
    If oJobStep.LastRunOutcome = SQLDMOJobOutcome_Succeeded Or _
oJobStep.LastRunOutcome = SQLDMOJobOutcome_Unknown Then
        tv1.Nodes.Add strJobKey, tvwChild, _
"JOBSTEP_" & JobName & "_" & oJobStep.Name, _
oJobStep.Name, il1.ListImages(5).Key
            ElseIf oJobStep.LastRunOutcome = SQLDMOJobOutcome_Failed Then
        tv1.Nodes.Add strJobKey, _
 tvwChild, "JOBSTEP_" & JobName & "_" & _
oJobStep.Name, oJobStep.Name, _
 il1.ListImages(6).Key
    End If
    Next oJobStep
End If
```

```
Exit Sub

err_handler:

Exit Sub
End Sub
```

Showing the Step's Command

When you click the job step itself you want to see what the text of the command is, and this is where you do it. It's quite an easy thing to do and it involves simply finding out the command property of your job, the name of which you pass to the procedure.

```
Public Sub ShowJobCommand(strServer As String, _
strJob As String, strJobStep As String)

On Error GoTo err_handler

Dim strStepCommand As String
txtStepCommand = ""


If strServer <> strLastServerLoggedOnTo Then
    oServer.DisConnect
    oServer.LoginSecure = True
    oServer.Connect strServer
    strLastServerLoggedOnTo = strServer
End If

strStepCommand = oServer.JobServer.Jobs(strJob).JobSteps(strJobStep).Command

txtStepCommand.Text = strStepCommand


Exit Sub

err_handler:
MsgBox "error"
Exit Sub

End Sub
```

Showing the Job's History

Last but not least, you show the previous outcomes of the job. To do so, you're going to read into a QueryResults object the outcome of the EnumJobHistory method of the JobServer object. This takes a parameter of a JobHistoryFilter object, and it's this object that will filter what you see. Once you set the properties of the JobFilter, you filter the results to show only certain things. Table 5-6, taken from SQL Server Books Online, shows the possible options available to you.

Table 5-6. EnumJobHistory Results

Column	Datatype	Description
instance_id	integer	System-generated identifier for execution attempt.
job_id	uniqueidentifier	System-generated job identifier.
job_name	nvarchar(129)	Job name.
message	nvarchar(1025)	When applicable, text of a SQL Server message raised by the step.
operator_emailed	nvarchar(129)	When applicable, operator receiving e-mail notification of job completion.
operator_netsent	nvarchar(129)	When applicable, operator receiving network pop-up message notification of job completion.
operator_paged	nvarchar(129)	When applicable, operator receiving page notification of job completion.
retries_attempted	integer	Number of times SQL Server Agent attempted execution of the step. This is 0 when the step executed successfully on the first attempt or no retry attempts are specified for the job step.
run_date	integer	Date on which execution occurred, formatted as described in Remarks.
run_duration	integer	Execution duration expressed as a number of seconds.
run_status	integer	Execution outcome interpreted using SQLDMO_JOBOUTCOME_TYPE.
run_time	integer	Time at which execution occurred, formatted as described in Remarks.
server	nvarchar(31)	Target server name.

Table 5-6. EnumJobHistory Results (Continued)

Column	Datatype	Description
sql_message_id	integer	When applicable, the SQL Server message number of the message raised by the step.
sql_severity	integer	When applicable, the severity of a SQL Server message raised by the step.
step_id	integer	User-specified step identifier. The result set lists each job step and its outcome.
step_name	nvarchar(129)	Job step name.

Some entries in Table 5-6 reference "Remarks." This is the definition of Remarks from SQL Server Books Online: The result set column run_date represents the execution date as a scaled long integer. The integer is built as a sum of the year scaled by 10000, the month scaled by 100, and the day. For example, the date April 19, 1997 is represented by the long integer value 19970419. The result set column run_time represents execution time as a scaled long integer. The integer is built as a sum of the hour scaled by 10000, the minute scaled by 100, and the seconds. The value uses a 24-hour clock. For example, the time 1:03:09 P.M. is represented by the long integer value 130309.

The following code listing deals with displaying the outcome of a particular job on a particular server:

```
Private Sub ShowJobHistory(ServerName As String, _
JobName As String, booFailedOrAll As Boolean)

Dim oJobHistory As SQLDMO.QueryResults
Dim i As Integer
Dim j As Integer


fg_JobHistory.Rows = 1

oServer.JobServer.JobHistoryFilter.JobName = JobName

If booFailedOrAll = True Then
    oServer.JobServer.JobHistoryFilter.OutcomeTypes = SQLDMOJobOutcome_Failed
End If
```

```
Set oJobHistory = oServer.JobServer.EnumJobHistory _
(oServer.JobServer.JobHistoryFilter)


    For i = 1 To oJobHistory.Rows
        fg_JobHistory.AddItem _
oJobHistory.GetColumnString(i, 3) & vbTab & oJobHistory.GetColumnString(i, 4)
& vbTab & oJobHistory.GetColumnString(i, 5) & vbTab &
oJobHistory.GetColumnString(i, 6) & vbTab & oJobHistory.GetColumnString(i, 7)
& vbTab & oJobHistory.GetColumnString(i, 8) & vbTab &
oJobHistory.GetColumnString(i, 9) & vbTab & oJobHistory.GetColumnString(i, 10)
    Next i

End Sub
```

Adding a Job

You've seen how to add a new operator and how to view jobs and their details. It's now time to learn how you can add your own jobs to SQL Server. This section is littered with tables because we have quite a bit of interpreting to do and tables are one of the best ways to explain things, along with some examples. We'll first discuss adding a job in Enterprise Manager and T-SQL.

Adding a Job in Enterprise Manager

This process is similar to examining the details of the job. You right-click the Jobs icon and select New Job. The screen you saw when you were viewing job properties appears, except none of the boxes is filled in. Figure 5-10 shows the General tab, which is the first tab you see when you create a job.

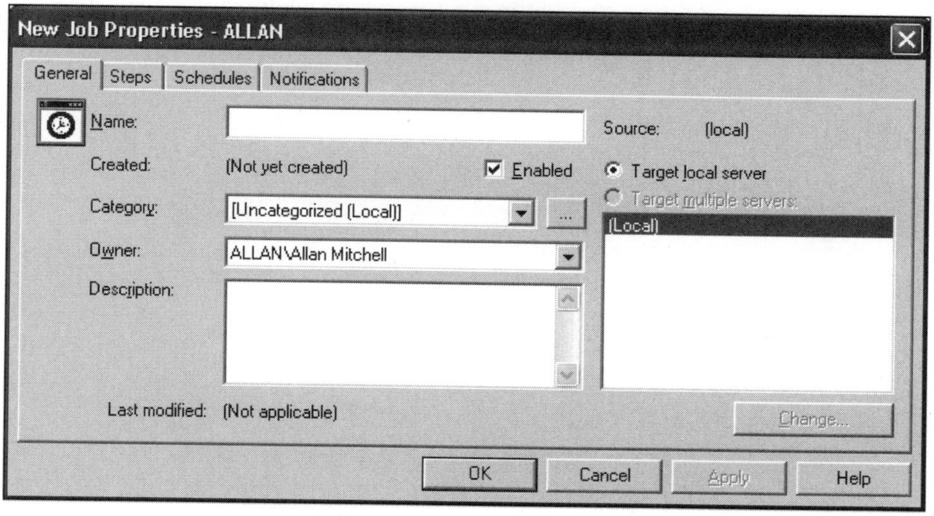

Figure 5-10. Defining the new job

On this screen, you give the job a name, indicate if the job is enabled, and optionally give the job a description. Adding a description is polite, as it may help others who come along after you who need a quick idea of what the job actually does. A job has to consist of at least one step, so you can move on to the Steps tab to add one (see Figure 5-11).

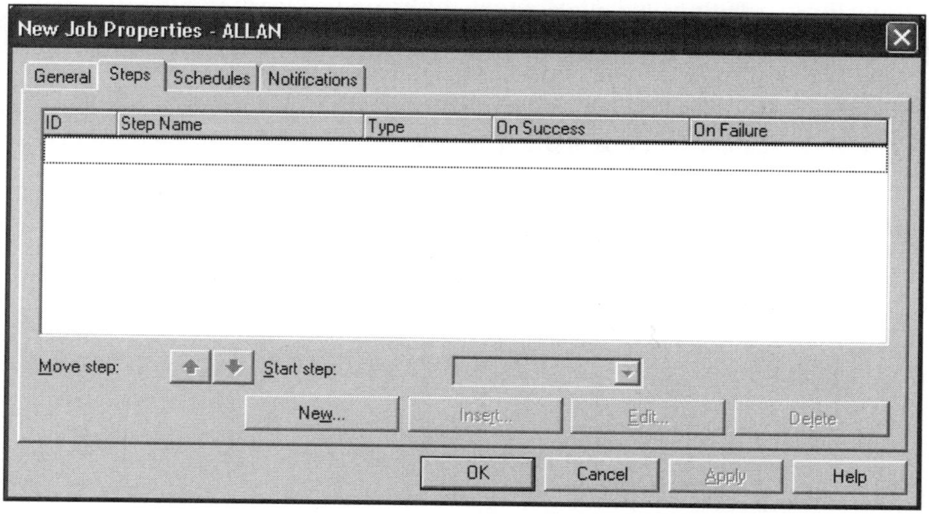

Figure 5-11. Adding a job step

In addition to adding a step to the job, this screen allows you to move existing steps about and set the start step. Click the New button to define your job step. Figure 5-12 shows the different types of steps that you can use in a job.

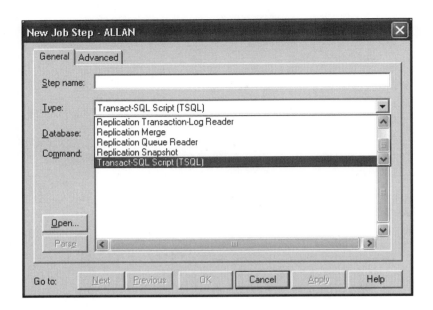

Figure 5-12. Defining the job step

Figure 5-12 shows the first page of defining your step. On it, you can give the step a name and choose what type of step it should be. Look back in the section "What Is a Job?" for a list of the options, the database the command executes in, and the command itself. When you've created the step, you can do some things with workflow, such as deciding where to go in the job depending on the outcome of the step. Figure 5-13 shows you the screen where you can define flow control.

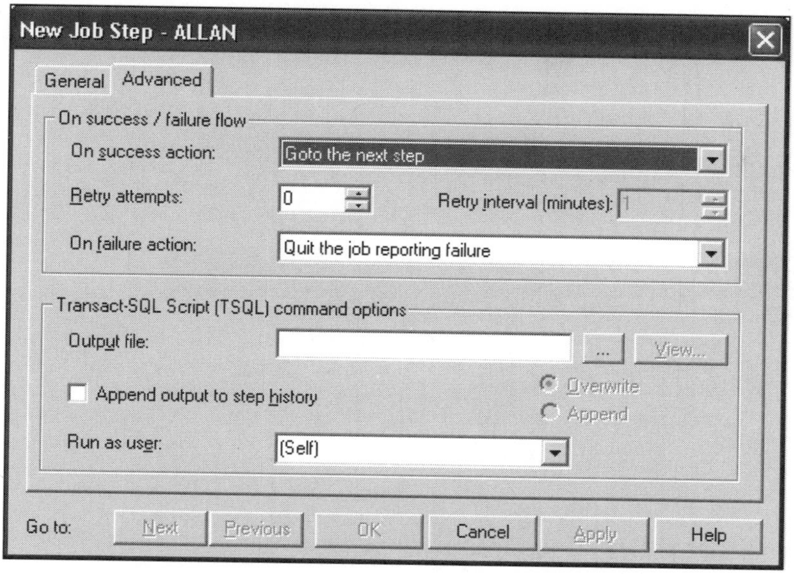

Figure 5-13. Determining job step flow control

On the Advanced tab, you can indicate what happens when the step succeeds or fails. You can also enter a file name that's written to with execution details of the step. We find this to be very useful in debugging problem job steps.

On the Schedules tab, you can define when the job should execute. Figure 5-14 shows the initial screen for adding a new schedule.

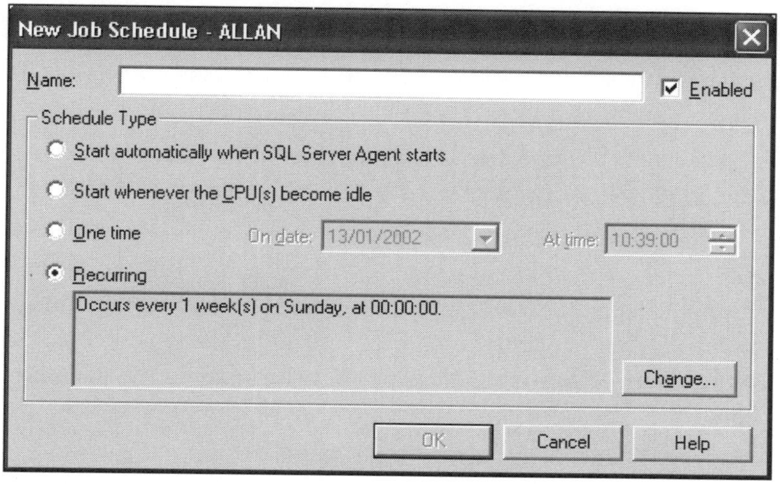

Figure 5-14. Adding a new schedule

If you click the Schedules tab and then click the New Schedule button to add a new schedule, the screen in Figure 5-14 appears. You give the schedule a name and then choose one of the options for when the job executes. The first three options are self-explanatory, but the fourth option warrants a closer look. If you choose it and then click the Change button, the screen in Figure 5-15 appears.

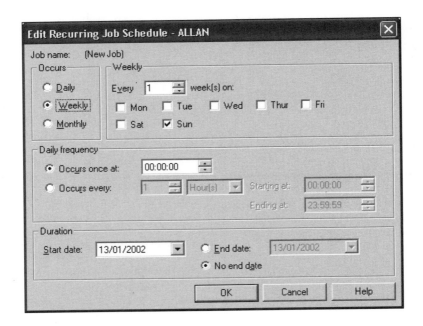

Figure 5-15. Defining a recurring scheduled job

Figure 5-15 shows you how you can define a recurring scheduled job. You can define a quite intricate schedule of execution if you want. However, you can't define a schedule like the following:

> *Execute every day of the week between 08:00 hours and 17:00 hours every 3 hours except on Wednesday, when we want it to execute every 2 hours.*

To define a schedule like this, you would need to define two job schedules: one that executes every day except Wednesday and one that executes on Wednesday.

Moving on from the Schedules tab, you come to the Notifications tab. This is where you get to define who, if anyone, you want to tell about the job outcome. In the screen shown in Figure 5-16, you define who you're going to notify, on what outcome, and how.

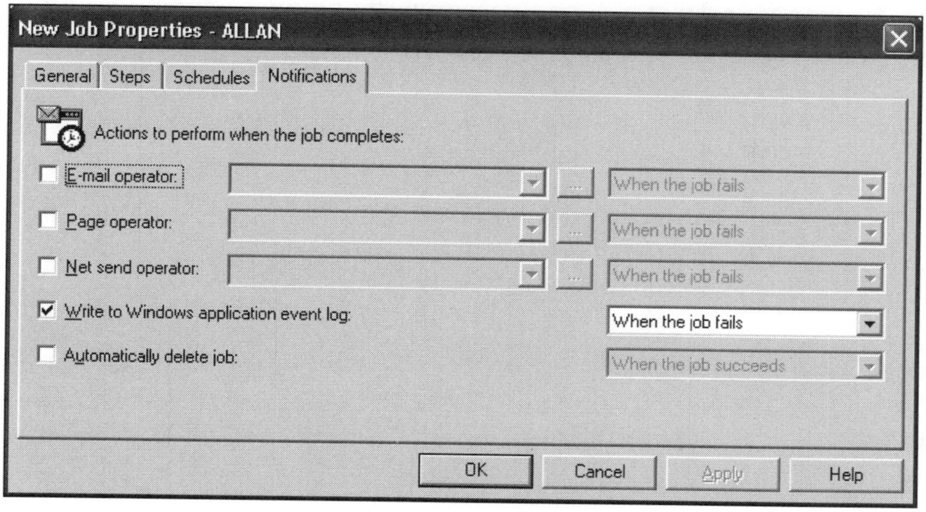

Figure 5-16. Who you gonna call (in Enterprise Manager)?

Adding a Job in T-SQL

Defining a job, job steps, and the schedule using T-SQL involves three stored procedures. In this section we go through each one in turn and provide you with those all-important interpretation tables we mentioned earlier. Here's the code to add a job in T-SQL:

```
sp_add_job [ @job_name = ] 'job_name'
    [ , [ @enabled = ] enabled ]
    [ , [ @description = ] 'description' ]
    [ , [ @start_step_id = ] step_id ]
    [ , [ @category_name = ] 'category' ]
    [ , [ @category_id = ] category_id ]
    [ , [ @owner_login_name = ] 'login' ]
    [ , [ @notify_level_eventlog = ] eventlog_level ]
    [ , [ @notify_level_email = ] email_level ]
    [ , [ @notify_level_netsend = ] netsend_level ]
    [ , [ @notify_level_page = ] page_level ]
    [ , [ @notify_email_operator_name = ] 'email_name' ]
    [ , [ @notify_netsend_operator_name = ] 'netsend_name' ]
    [ , [ @notify_page_operator_name = ] 'page_name' ]
    [ , [ @delete_level = ] delete_level ]
    [ , [ @job_id = ] job_id OUTPUT ]
```

We have a few things to point out regarding the preceding listing:

- Job_name is compulsory, which seems reasonable to us.

- Enabled is either 1 or 0 (1 = Yes, 0 = No).

- Start_step_id defaults to 1, but you can change this.

The page, e-mail, and net send levels are listed in Table 5-7.

Table 5-7. Levels

Value	Description
0	Never
1	Success
2	Failure
3	Always

Let's look at adding a job for which you have the following requirements:

- If the job fails, you e-mail the operator.

- If the job succeeds, you net send the operator.

- If the job completes, you page the operator.

- You never want to make an entry in the event log.

- The job will be owned by "sa."

Here's the code:

```
EXEC msdb..sp_add_job
     @job_name = 'My T-SQL Job'
   , @enabled = 1
   , @description = 'Job Created in T-SQL'
   , @owner_login_name = 'sa'
   , @notify_level_eventlog = 0
   , @notify_level_email = 2
   , @notify_level_netsend = 1
   , @notify_level_page = 3
   , @notify_email_operator_name = 'ALLAN'
   , @notify_netsend_operator_name = 'ALLAN'
   , @notify_page_operator_name = 'ALLAN'
```

The following code segment from SQL Server Books Online shows how to add a step to a job using T-SQL:

```
sp_add_jobstep [ @job_id = ] job_id | [ @job_name = ] 'job_name'
   [ , [ @step_id = ] step_id ]
   { , [ @step_name = ] 'step_name' }
   [ , [ @subsystem = ] 'subsystem' ]
   [ , [ @command = ] 'command' ]
   [ , [ @additional_parameters = ] 'parameters' ]
   [ , [ @cmdexec_success_code = ] code ]
   [ , [ @on_success_action = ] success_action ]
   [ , [ @on_success_step_id = ] success_step_id ]
   [ , [ @on_fail_action = ] fail_action ]
   [ , [ @on_fail_step_id = ] fail_step_id ]
   [ , [ @server = ] 'server' ]
   [ , [ @database_name = ] 'database' ]
   [ , [ @database_user_name = ] 'user' ]
   [ , [ @retry_attempts = ] retry_attempts ]
   [ , [ @retry_interval = ] retry_interval ]
   [ , [ @os_run_priority = ] run_priority ]
   [ , [ @output_file_name = ] 'file_name' ]
   [ , [ @flags = ] flags ]
```

You can specify either a job's ID or its name—not both. Step_id is the step's sequence, and subsystem is taken from one of the options in Table 5-8.

Table 5-8. Subsystems

Value	Description
'ACTIVESCRIPTING'	Active script
'CMDEXEC'	Operating-system command or executable program
'DISTRIBUTION'	Replication Distribution Agent job
'SNAPSHOT'	Replication Snapshot Agent job
'LOGREADER'	Replication Log Reader Agent job
'MERGE'	Replication Merge Agent job
'T-SQL' (default)	Transact-SQL statement

The command is the text of what you want the step to do. For us, one of the best things here is that some runtime tokens are exposed, which are very useful. Table 5-9 presents the token values. Later we'll provide you with a possible use for them.

Table 5-9. Tokens

Value	Description
[A-DBN]	Database name. If the job is run by an alert, this token automatically replaces the version 6.5 [DBN] token during the conversion process.
[A-SVR]	Server name. If the job is run by an alert, this token automatically replaces the version 6.5 [SVR] token during the conversion process.
[A-ERR]	Error number. If the job is run by an alert, this token automatically replaces the version 6.5 [ERR] token during the conversion process.
[A-SEV]	Error severity. If the job is run by an alert, this token automatically replaces the version 6.5 [SEV] token during the conversion process.
[A-MSG]	Message text. If the job is run by an alert, this token automatically replaces the version 6.5 [MSG] token during the conversion process.

Table 5-9. Tokens (Continued)

Value	Description
[DATE]	Current date (in YYYYMMDD format).
[JOBID]	Job ID.
[MACH]	Computer name.
[MSSA]	Master SQLServerAgent service name.
[SQLDIR]	The directory in which SQL Server is installed. By default, this value is C:\Program Files\Microsoft SQL Server\MSSQL.
[STEPCT]	A count of the number of times this step has executed (excluding retires). This can be used by the step command to force termination of a multistep loop.
[STEPID]	Step ID.
[TIME]	Current time (in HHMMSS format).
[STRTTM]	The time (in HHMMSS format) that the job began executing.
[STRTDT]	The date (in YYYYMMDD format) that the job began executing.

When an alert fires, you may want to log details from the alert, such as where, when, what, and how many times. Using these tokens you can log alert details quite easily.

When it completes, a job step can take a variety of courses. It may be that if the step fails, you'll want to back out everything you've just done. Table 5-10 shows the job workflow options.

Table 5-10. Success and Failure Actions

Value	Description (Action)
1 (default)	Quit with success
2	Quit with failure
3	Go to next step
4	Go to step on_success_step_id

The flags parameter determines whether you append to your job step output file or you start a new job step output file every time the step executes. Table 5-11 contains the possible output file options.

Table 5-11. Possible Output File Options

Value	Description
0 (default)	No options set
2	Append to output file
4	Overwrite output file

The following is an example of adding a job step with some of the possible options for adding a job step completed:

- You want to quit the job if the step fails reporting failure.

- You want to quit the job if the step succeeds reporting success.

- You want to write out to a text file, and each time the step executes the step history is appended to the file.

```
EXEC msdb..sp_add_jobstep
        @job_name =  'My T-SQL Job'
    ,  @step_id =  1
    ,  @step_name =  'The first step'
    ,  @subsystem =  'T-SQL'
    ,  @command =  'SELECT * FROM authors'
    ,  @on_success_action =  1
    ,  @on_fail_action =  2
    ,  @output_file_name =  'c:\JobOutput.txt'
    ,  @flags =  2
```

The following code adds a schedule to a job. The listing was taken from SQL Server Books Online.

```
sp_add_jobschedule [ @job_id = ] job_id, | [ @job_name = ] 'job_name',
    [ @name = ] 'name'
    [ , [ @enabled = ] enabled ]
    [ , [ @freq_type = ] freq_type ]
    [ , [ @freq_interval = ] freq_interval ]
    [ , [ @freq_subday_type = ] freq_subday_type ]
    [ , [ @freq_subday_interval = ] freq_subday_interval ]
    [ , [ @freq_relative_interval = ] freq_relative_interval ]
    [ , [ @freq_recurrence_factor = ] freq_recurrence_factor ]
    [ , [ @active_start_date = ] active_start_date ]
    [ , [ @active_end_date = ] active_end_date ]
    [ , [ @active_start_time = ] active_start_time ]
    [ , [ @active_end_time = ] active_end_time ]
```

This is where things become a little more confusing. First, we'll show you a list of possible values and then we'll provide a few examples and explanations to show you how to use them. Table 5-12 shows the frequency types for your jobs. These are the same options that you saw on the opening screen for adding a new schedule, and if you chose a schedule, yo saw them on the choose schedule screen as well.

Table 5-12. Frequency Types

Value	Description
1	Once
4	Daily
8	Weekly
16	Monthly
32	Monthly, relative to freq_interval
64	Run when SQLServerAgent service starts
128	Run when the computer is idle

Table 5-13 shows you the possible values for freq_interval depending on what you have set for the frequency type.

Table 5-13. Frequency Interval Values

Value of freq_type	Effect on freq_interval
1 (once)	freq_interval is unused.
4 (daily)	Every freq_interval days.
8 (weekly)	freq_interval is one or more of the following (combined with an OR logical operator): 1 = Sunday 2 = Monday 4 = Tuesday 8 = Wednesday 16 = Thursday 32 = Friday 64 = Saturday
16 (monthly)	On the freq_interval day of the month.
32 (monthly relative)	freq_interval is one of the following: 1 = Sunday 2 = Monday 3 = Tuesday 4 = Wednesday 5 = Thursday 6 = Friday 7 = Saturday 8 = Day 9 = Weekday 10 = Weekend day
64 (when SQLServerAgent service starts)	freq_interval is unused.
128	freq_interval is unused.

Table 5-14 shows you the values for the FrequencySubDay type. This relates to whether you want a schedule to execute at a given time or on a recurring schedule of *n* minutes or hours between each execution.

Table 5-14. FrequencySubDay Type Values

Value	Description (Unit)
1	At the specified time
4	Minutes
8	Hours

You set the frequency relative interval on the day relative to the start of the month you want the job to execute. Table 5-15 lists the frequency relative interval values.

Table 5-15. Frequency Relative Interval Values

Value	Description (Unit)
1	First
2	Second
4	Third
8	Fourth
16	Last

Now for those examples:

1. A job that executes every time SQL Server Agent starts.

2. A job that executes every second day, every 2 hours between 8:00 A.M. and 8:00 P.M.

3. A job that executes every third week on Wednesday and Saturday once only at 2:00 P.M.

4. A job that executes on the first Sunday of every second month every 20 minutes between 7:00 A.M. and 10:00 A.M.

Here's the code for the first example:

```
EXEC msdb..sp_add_jobschedule
    @job_name =  'My T-SQL Job'
    ,  @name = 'SQL Agent Startup schedule'
    ,  @enabled =  1
    ,  @freq_type =  64
```

Here's the code for the second example:

```
sp_add_jobschedule
    @job_name =  'My T-SQL Job'
    ,  @name =  'second day two hours eight to eight'
    ,  @enabled =  1
    ,  @freq_type =  4
    ,  @freq_interval =  2
    ,  @freq_subday_type =  8
    ,  @freq_subday_interval =  2
    ,  @active_start_time =  080000
    ,  @active_end_time =  200000
```

Here's the code for the third example:

```
EXEC msdb.. sp_add_jobschedule  @job_name =  'My T-SQL Job',
    @name =  'every third week on wed and sat once at 2PM'
    ,  @enabled =  1
    ,  @freq_type =  8
    ,  @freq_interval =  72
    ,  @freq_subday_type =  1
    ,  @freq_recurrence_factor =  3
    ,  @active_start_time =  140000
```

And here's the code for the fourth example:

```
sp_add_jobschedule  @job_name =  'My T-SQL Job',
    @name =  'first sunday of every two months every 20 mins between 7AM and 10AM'
    ,  @enabled =  1
    ,  @freq_type =  32
    ,  @freq_interval =  1
    ,  @freq_subday_type =  4
    ,  @freq_subday_interval =  20
    ,  @freq_relative_interval =  1
    ,  @freq_recurrence_factor =  2
    ,  @active_start_time =  070000
    ,  @active_end_time =  100000
```

Adding a Job in SQL-DMO

To illustrate how to add a job using SQL-DMO, we have again created an application. Let's look at how to perform each part of the job in turn. The way the application works is that on each screen you need to complete the action as opposed to setting things up so that at the end you can click one button and it adds everything then.

Creating the Job Itself

Using the JobBuilder application, you can build your own jobs. Figure 5-17 shows that our application is equivalent to the one you see in SQL Server.

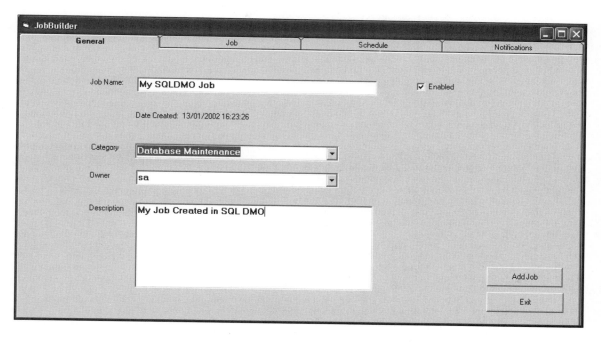

Figure 5-17. Defining a job in SQL-DMO

When you click the Add Job button on this screen, you create a job, take its details from the controls on this form, and add it to the Jobs collection of the JobServer.

```
If txtJobName.Text <> "" And JobExists(txtJobName.Text) = False Then
    Set ojob = New SQLDMO.Job
    ojob.Name = txtJobName.Text
    ojob.Category = cboCategory.Text
    ojob.Owner = cboOwner.Text
    ojob.Description = txtDescription.Text

    If chkEnabled.Value = vbChecked Then
        ojob.Enabled = True
    Else
        ojob.Enabled = False
    End If


    oServer.JobServer.Jobs.Add ojob
    strJobName = ojob.Name
End If
```

Figure 5-18 shows how you can define a T-SQL job step for your job using the application.

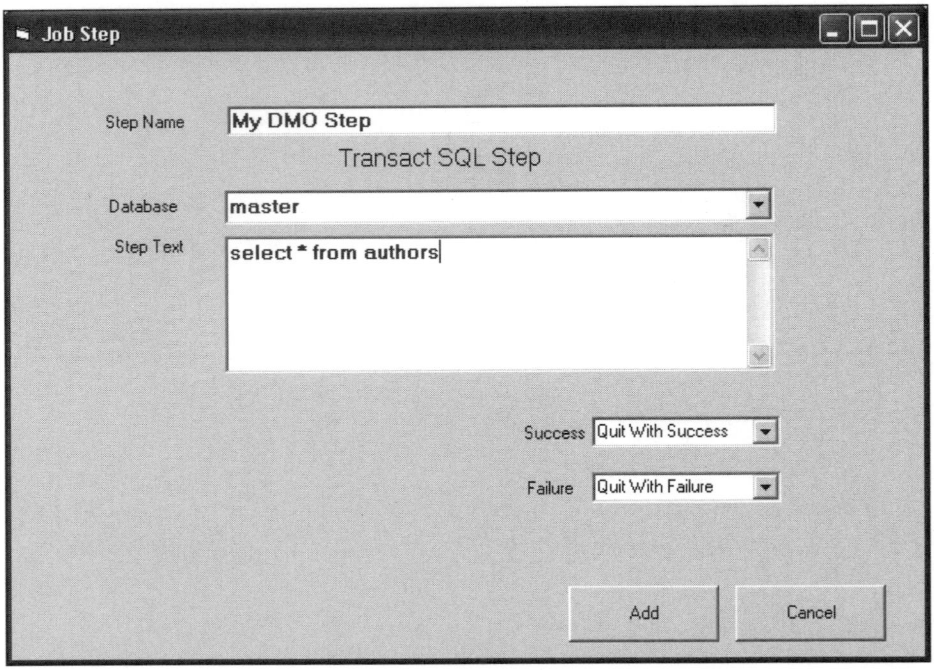

Figure 5-18. Adding a step

Most of the specifications of the step should look familiar now that you've created jobs in T-SQL.

```
Private Sub GetJobStepCredentials()
Dim OjobSuccessAction As SQLDMO.SQLDMO_JOBSTEPACTION_TYPE
Dim OjobFailureAction As SQLDMO.SQLDMO_JOBSTEPACTION_TYPE
```

Although we used the integer values for the SQLDMO_JOBSTEPACTION_TYPE, we could just as easily have used the constants in Table 5-16.

Table 5-16. Constants for Step Completion

Constant	Value	Description
SQLDMOJobStepAction_GotoStep	4	Continue execution at the next identified step.
SQLDMOJobStepAction_GotoNextStep	3	Continue execution at the next sequential step.
SQLDMOJobStepAction_QuitWithFailure	2	Terminate job execution, reporting failure.
SQLDMOJobStepAction_QuitWithSuccess	1	Terminate job execution, reporting success.
SQLDMOJobStepAction_Unknown	0	Job step logic is unassigned for the referenced job step.

The following code listing defines what you'll want to do when the step finishes executing and for each particular possible outcome.

```
Select Case cboOnSuccessAction.Text

Case "Quit With Success"
OjobSuccessAction = 1
Case "Quit With Failure"
OjobSuccessAction = 2
Case "Goto Next Step"
OjobSuccessAction = 3
End Select
```

```
Select Case cboOnfailureAction.Text

Case "Quit With Success"
OjobFailureAction = 1
Case "Quit With Failure"
OjobFailureAction = 2
Case "Goto Next Step"
OjobFailureAction = 3
End Select




Set OJobStep = New SQLDMO.JobStep


OJobStep.stepid = stepid + 1
OJobStep.Name = txtStepName.Text
OJobStep.DatabaseName = cboDatabase.Text
OJobStep.SubSystem = "T-SQL"
OJobStep.Command = txtStepText.Text
OJobStep.OnSuccessAction = OjobSuccessAction
OJobStep.OnFailAction = OjobFailureAction


oServer.JobServer.Jobs(strJobName).JobSteps.Add OJobStep
AddToStepList stepid, OJobStep.Name, _
OJobStep.SubSystem, cboOnSuccessAction.Text, cboOnfailureAction.Text

stepid = stepid + 1

Unload Me



End Sub
```

Adding a Schedule in SQL-DMO

On the Schedule tab you define when you want the job to run, just as you do in
Enterprise Manager. Figure 5-19 shows the Schedule tab.

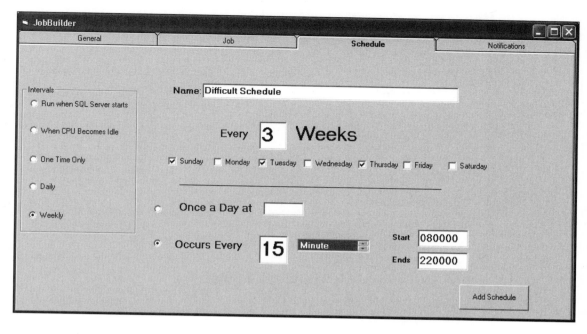

Figure 5-19. Defining a schedule

Just as we did for the options for scheduling a job in T-SQL, we present here a number of tables showing the equivalent values in SQL-DMO.

Table 5-17 contains the constants and values you can use to tell a job schedule when it should be used. FrequencyType is at the top of the job schedule hierarchy.

Table 5-17. FrequencyType

SQL-DMO Constant	Value	Description
SQLDMOFreq_Autostart	64	The scheduled activity is started when the SQLServerAgent service starts.
SQLDMOFreq_Daily	4	The schedule is evaluated daily.
SQLDMOFreq_Monthly	16	The schedule is evaluated monthly.
SQLDMOFreq_MonthlyRelative	32	The schedule is evaluated relative to a part of a month, such as the second week.
SQLDMOFreq_OneTime	1	The scheduled activity will occur once at a scheduled time or event.

Table 5-17. FrequencyType (Continued)

SQL-DMO Constant	Value	Description
SQLDMOFreq_OnIdle	128	The SQLServerAgent service will schedule the activity for any time during which the processor is idle.
SQLDMOFreq_Unknown	0	No schedule frequency, or frequency not applicable.
SQLDMOFreq_Valid	255	Mask to test schedule frequency validity.
SQLDMOFreq_Weekly	8	The schedule is evaluated weekly.

Table 5-18 shows the SQL-DMO constants you can use to determine when a job should execute for daily, weekly, or monthly jobs.

Table 5-18. Frequency Intervals

FrequencyType Value	FrequencyInterval Value
SQLDMOFreq_Daily	Positive, long integer that represents a number of day units. For example, when FrequencyInterval is 3, the scheduled activity occurs every third day.
SQLDMOFreq_Weekly	Bit-packed long integer. Values are interpreted using SQLDMO_WEEKDAY_TYPE naming the days of the week. Combine values using an OR logical operator to set more than a single day. For example, combine SQLDMOWeek_Tuesday and SQLDMOWeek_Friday to schedule an activity for Tuesday and Friday.
SQLDMOFreq_Monthly	Positive, long integer that represents the ordinal day of the month on which the schedule is active. For example, 4 specifies the fourth day of the month.
SQLDMOFreq_MonthlyRelative	Positive, long integer that represents a day of the week or a generic indication of a day. Values are interpreted using SQLDMO_MONTHDAY_TYPE.

The FrequencyRecurrenceFactor property is evaluated for Schedule objects with the FrequencyType values SQLDMOFreq_Monthly, SQLDMOFreq_MonthlyRelative, or SQLDMOFreq_Weekly. Table 5-19, which we've taken from SQL Server Books Online, shows those constants.

Table 5-19. FrequencyRecurrenceFactor

FrequencyType Value	Action
SQLDMOFreq_Monthly	Set FrequencyInterval to indicate the day of the month on which the activity occurs.
SQLDMOFreq_MonthlyRelative	Set FrequencyInterval to indicate the single day of the week on which the activity occurs. Set FrequencyRelativeInterval to indicate the day of the week relative to the start of the month.
SQLDMOFreq_Weekly	Set FrequencyInterval to indicate the day(s) of the week on which the activity occurs.

The constants listed in Table 5-20 simply list when the job schedule should fire relative to the first day of the month.

Table 5-20. FrequencyRelativeInterval

Constant	Value	Description
SQLDMOFreqRel_First	1	The event is scheduled to occur on the first subunit.
SQLDMOFreqRel_Fourth	8	The event is scheduled to occur on the fourth subunit.
SQLDMOFreqRel_Last	16	The event is scheduled to occur on the last subunit.
SQLDMOFreqRel_Second	2	The event is scheduled to occur on the second subunit.
SQLDMOFreqRel_Third	4	The event is scheduled to occur on the third subunit.

If the job should fire daily, then the FrequencySubDay constants in Table 5-21 indicate at which interval during the day it should fire.

Table 5-21. FrequencySubDay Property

Constant	Value	Description
SQLDMOFreqSub_Hour	8	Schedule reflects an activity scheduled using an hour as the unit.
SQLDMOFreqSub_Minute	4	Schedule reflects an activity scheduled using a minute as the unit.
SQLDMOFreqSub_Once	1	Schedule reflects an activity that occurs once on a scheduled unit.
SQLDMOFreqSub_Unknown	0	Subunits are invalid for the scheduled activity.
SQLDMOFreqSub_Valid	13	Mask to test schedule subfrequency validity.

Which option button you choose on this form depends on which one of these functions/procedures you call.

Execute When the SQL Server Agent Starts

The following code deals with how you schedule a job to be executed when SQL Server Agent starts:

```
Private Sub SQLServerStartSchedule(strschedulename As String)

oJobSchedule.Schedule.FrequencyType = SQLDMOFreq_Autostart
oJobSchedule.Name = strschedulename


With oServer.JobServer.Jobs(strJobName)
    .BeginAlter
    .JobSchedules.Add oJobSchedule
    .DoAlter
End With
End Sub
```

The schedule is set to fire when the CPU becomes idle:

```
Private Sub CPUIdleSchedule(strschedulename As String)
oJobSchedule.Schedule.FrequencyType = SQLDMOFreq_OnIdle
oJobSchedule.Name = strschedulename


With oServer.JobServer.Jobs(strJobName)
    .BeginAlter
    .JobSchedules.Add oJobSchedule
    .DoAlter

End With
End Sub
```

The schedule executes one time only:

```
Private Sub OneTimeOnlySchedule( _
strschedulename As String,
strWhen As String, strAtTime As String)
oJobSchedule.Schedule.FrequencyType = SQLDMOFreq_OneTime
oJobSchedule.Schedule.ActiveStartDate = strWhen
oJobSchedule.Schedule.ActiveStartTimeOfDay = strAtTime
oJobSchedule.Name = strschedulename

With oServer.JobServer.Jobs(strJobName)
    .BeginAlter
    .JobSchedules.Add oJobSchedule
    .DoAlter
End With
End Sub
```

The schedule will execute on a daily schedule:

```
Private Sub DailySchedule( _
strschedulename As String,
intDailyInterval As Integer,
 booOnce As Boolean,
Optional strOnceOnlyTime As String,
Optional intRecurrenceInterval As Integer,
Optional intMinHour As Integer,
Optional strStartTime As String,
Optional strEndTime As String)

oJobSchedule.Schedule.FrequencyType = SQLDMOFreq_Daily
oJobSchedule.Schedule.FrequencyInterval = intDailyInterval
oJobSchedule.Name = strschedulename
```

The following code lets you know if the job is due to fire at one time only during a period or if it's on a recurring schedule:

```
If booOnce = True Then
    oJobSchedule.Schedule.ActiveStartTimeOfDay = strOnceOnlyTime
Else

    oJobSchedule.Schedule.FrequencySubDayInterval = intRecurrenceInterval

    If intMinHour = 1 Then 'Minute
        oJobSchedule.Schedule.FrequencySubDay = SQLDMOFreqSub_Minute
    Else
        oJobSchedule.Schedule.FrequencySubDay = SQLDMOFreqSub_Hour
    End If

    oJobSchedule.Schedule.ActiveStartTimeOfDay = strStartTime
    oJobSchedule.Schedule.ActiveEndTimeOfDay = strEndTime

End If

oServer.JobServer.Jobs(strJobName).BeginAlter
    oServer.JobServer.Jobs(strJobName).JobSchedules.Add oJobSchedule
    oServer.JobServer.Jobs(strJobName).DoAlter
End Sub
```

The following code executes on a weekly schedule. When you call this procedure, one of the things you need to do is pass the days of the week on which this job will execute. You can do so quite simply as follows:

```
Private Function DaysOfWeekToRun() As Integer

DaysOfWeekToRun = 0

If chkSunday.Value = vbChecked Then
    DaysOfWeekToRun = DaysOfWeekToRun + 1
End If

If chkMonday.Value = vbChecked Then
    DaysOfWeekToRun = DaysOfWeekToRun + 2
End If

If chkTuesday.Value = vbChecked Then
    DaysOfWeekToRun = DaysOfWeekToRun + 4
End If
```

```
If chkWednesday.Value = vbChecked Then
    DaysOfWeekToRun = DaysOfWeekToRun + 8
End If


If chkThursday.Value = vbChecked Then
    DaysOfWeekToRun = DaysOfWeekToRun + 16
End If


If chkFriday.Value = vbChecked Then
    DaysOfWeekToRun = DaysOfWeekToRun + 32
End If


If chkSaturday.Value = vbChecked Then
    DaysOfWeekToRun = DaysOfWeekToRun + 64
End If
End Function




Private Sub WeeklySchedule(strschedulename As String, intWeeklyInterval As Integer,
booOnce As Boolean, Optional strOnceOnlyTime As String,
Optional intRecurrenceInterval As Integer,
Optional intMinHour As Integer,
Optional strStartTime As String,
Optional strEndTime As String,
Optional intOnDays As Integer)


oJobSchedule.Schedule.FrequencyType = SQLDMOFreq_Weekly
oJobSchedule.Schedule.FrequencyInterval = intOnDays
oJobSchedule.Name = strschedulename
oJobSchedule.Schedule.FrequencyRecurrenceFactor = intWeeklyInterval

If booOnce = True Then
    oJobSchedule.Schedule.ActiveStartTimeOfDay = strOnceOnlyTime
Else



    If intMinHour = 1 Then
        oJobSchedule.Schedule.FrequencySubDay = SQLDMOFreqSub_Minute
    Else
        oJobSchedule.Schedule.FrequencySubDay = SQLDMOFreqSub_Hour
    End If
```

```
                    oJobSchedule.Schedule.ActiveStartTimeOfDay = strStartTime
                    oJobSchedule.Schedule.ActiveEndTimeOfDay = strEndTime
                    oJobSchedule.Schedule.FrequencySubDayInterval = intRecurrenceInterval

            End If

            oServer.JobServer.Jobs(strJobName).BeginAlter
                    oServer.JobServer.Jobs(strJobName).JobSchedules.Add oJobSchedule
                    oServer.JobServer.Jobs(strJobName).DoAlter


            End Sub
```

In Figure 5-20 we define, using the application, whom to notify and when.

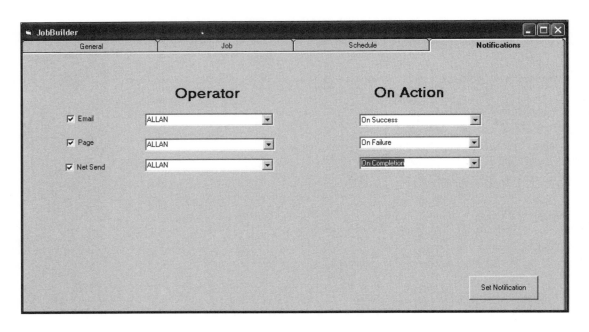

Figure 5-20. Notifying the operator of the outcome in SQL-DMO

The following code listing shows how to set the notifications in the application:

```
Private Sub AnyNotifications()

Dim oOutcomeLevel As SQLDMO.SQLDMO_COMPLETION_TYPE
```

The following section of code shows how to set up a mail notification for the job outcome:

```
If chkEmail.Value = vbChecked
And cboMailLevel.Text <> ""
And cboEmailOperator.Text <> "" Then

Select Case cboMailLevel.Text

    Case "On Success"
    oOutcomeLevel = 1
    Case "On Failure"
    oOutcomeLevel = 2
    Case "On Completion"
    oOutcomeLevel = 3
End Select

    oServer.JobServer.Jobs(strJobName).BeginAlter
        oServer.JobServer.Jobs(strJobName).EmailLevel = oOutcomeLevel
        oServer.JobServer.Jobs(strJobName).OperatorToEmail = "ALLAN"
    oServer.JobServer.Jobs(strJobName).DoAlter

End If
```

The following section of code shows how to set up a pager notification for the job outcome:

```
If chkPage.Value = vbChecked And
cboPagelevel.Text <> ""
And cboPageOperator.Text <> "" Then


    Select Case cboPagelevel.Text

    Case "On Success"
    oOutcomeLevel = 1
    Case "On Failure"
    oOutcomeLevel = 2
    Case "On Completion"
    oOutcomeLevel = 3
    End Select
```

```
oServer.JobServer.Jobs(strJobName).BeginAlter
    oServer.JobServer.Jobs(strJobName).OperatorToPage = cboPageOperator.Text
    oServer.JobServer.Jobs(strJobName).PageLevel = oOutcomeLevel
oServer.JobServer.Jobs(strJobName).DoAlter
```

```
End If
```

The following code listing shows you how to set an operator to be notified by net send:

```
If chkNetSend.Value = vbChecked And cboNetSendLevel.Text <> "" And
cboNetSendOperator.Text <> "" Then


    Select Case cboNetSendLevel.Text

    Case "On Success"
    oOutcomeLevel = 1
    Case "On Failure"
    oOutcomeLevel = 2
    Case "On Completion"
    oOutcomeLevel = 3
    End Select

    oServer.JobServer.Jobs(strJobName).BeginAlter
        oServer.JobServer.Jobs _
(strJobName).OperatorToNetSend = _
cboNetSendOperator.Text
        oServer.JobServer.Jobs(strJobName).NetSendLevel = oOutcomeLevel
    oServer.JobServer.Jobs(strJobName).DoAlter

End If
End Sub
```

Creating an Alert

Finally, we're going to take you through the process of creating an alert.

Creating an Alert in Enterprise Manager

In Enterprise Manager, if you look in the same tree group that you found Jobs in, you'll see an Alerts icon. If you right-click the icon and select New Alert, you'll see the screen shown in Figure 5-21.

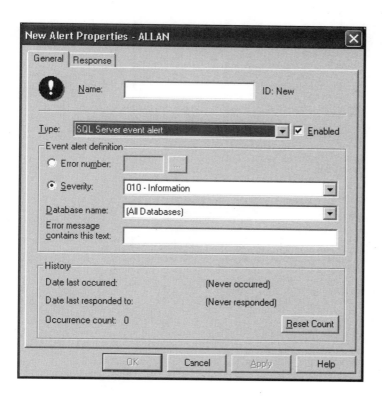

Figure 5-21. Defining an alert in Enterprise Manager

The options available are lengthy, and we'd have to fill a good many pages to list them here. Basically, there are two types of alerts: the SQL Server event alert and the SQL Server performance condition alert. You can specify error numbers to look for, severity numbers, or errors that contain a certain message.

Figure 5-22 shows you how to tell an operator that an alert has fired. Remember earlier when we wrote about the tokens that get replaced at runtime in a job and that we use them when we fire an alert? Well, the screen in 5-22 is where we do this.

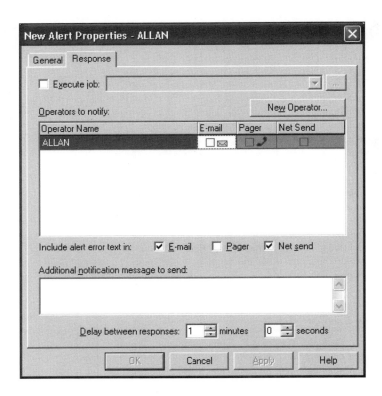

Figure 5-22. Informing an operator of an alert

Creating an Alert in T-SQL

In the following code listing (taken from SQL Server Books Online), you can see how to create an alert using T-SQL:

```
sp_add_alert [ @name = ] 'name'
    [ , [ @message_id = ] message_id ]
    [ , [ @severity = ] severity ]
    [ , [ @enabled = ] enabled ]
    [ , [ @delay_between_responses = ] delay_between_responses ]
    [ , [ @notification_message = ] 'notification_message' ]
    [ , [ @include_event_description_in = ] include_event_description_in ]
    [ , [ @database_name = ] 'database' ]
    [ , [ @event_description_keyword = ] 'event_description_keyword_pattern' ]
    [ , { [ @job_id = ] job_id | [ @job_name = ] 'job_name' } ]
    [ , [ @raise_snmp_trap = ] raise_snmp_trap ]
    [ , [ @performance_condition = ] 'performance_condition' ]
    [ , [ @category_name = ] 'category' ]
```

Here's an example of alert creation. In this case, you want to be notified when the Pubs database log is more than 75% full. You also want to inform an operator by e-mail when this happens.

```
exec msdb..sp_add_alert
@name = N'MyAlert',
@performance_condition = N'SQLServer:Databases|Percent Log Used|Pubs|>|75'
```

```
sp_add_notification [ @alert_name = ] 'alert' ,
    [ @operator_name = ] 'operator' ,
    [ @notification_method = ] notification_method
```

Table 5-22 lists the possible methods of notification.

Table 5-22. Alert Notification Types

Value	Description
1	E-mail
2	Pager
4	Net send

The following line of code shows you how to alert the operator Allan via e-mail when the alert MyAlert fires:

```
exec msdb..sp_add_notification N'MyAlert', N'ALLAN', 1
```

Creating an Alert in SQL-DMO

Probably the best way to illustrate creating an alert in SQL-DMO is to actually create an alert, so you're going to imitate what you did in T-SQL using SQL-DMO.

```
Dim oserver As SQLDMO.SQLServer
Dim oalert As SQLDMO.Alert

Set oserver = New SQLDMO.SQLServer
```

```
oserver.LoginSecure = True
oserver.Connect "ALLAN"

Set oalert = New SQLDMO.Alert

oalert.Name = "MyAlert"
oalert.PerformanceCondition = "SQLServer:Databases|Percent Log Used|Pubs|>|75"

oserver.JobServer.Alerts.Add oalert

oalert.BeginAlter
oalert.AddNotification "ALLAN", SQLDMONotify_Email
oalert.DoAlter
```

Summary

As you learned in this chapter, a lot of thinking goes into creating a job. SQL Server Books Online recommends that you use Enterprise Manager to create jobs, but once you get over the number of options available to you, you can quite easily create your own jobs in T-SQL and SQL-DMO. Jobs can be very powerful, and they're supremely useful in automating many of the tasks you do. If you've managed to follow along in this chapter, then hopefully you have a better understanding of how SQL Server creates jobs. When you get stuck with syntax, you should be able to refer back to this chapter and find the information you need in one of the tables.

In the next chapter we'll show you how to manipulate server-wide options on your SQL Server.

CHAPTER 6

Viewing and Setting Server-wide Options

LARGE CORPORATIONS OFTEN HAVE vast server rooms packed full of servers, as you will find if you work with them. We've encountered corporations with 20–50 SQL Servers running, all of which must be managed properly. SQL-DMO really helps in these vast environments to automate your work so that you can sit back and do the interesting stuff instead of fighting fires most of the day. For example, you can script out your server properties for all SQL Servers in the enterprise. In the event of disaster recovery, you know exactly how your server was set up because you've scripted it all out using your nifty SQL-DMO VBScript, Visual Basic, or C# program (or whatever you want to use).

To illustrate the power of SQL-DMO in large, multiserver environments, we've opted to use the tool that we're most familiar with: Visual Basic (VB) 6.0. You can accomplish very similar things with your favorite language.

In this chapter you're going to write a very simple VB program that will script out to a text file all the options that you find in Enterprise Manager when you right-click a server and select Properties. We're going to go through each tab on the SQL Server Properties dialog box in turn and explain how to query the information through SQL-DMO and send it to a text file. The output could quite easily be sent to an Active Server Pages (ASP) Web page and formatted nicely to be shared in a secured area on your company intranet if you so desire.

We're just going to concentrate on getting the data out and you can do the fancy stuff. As you'll soon see, the information on the SQL Server Properties dialog box in Enterprise Manager comes from all sorts of places, including the registry, direct queries on the database, and properties in the SQL-DMO library. You're going to query the database and the registry directly and do everything through SQL-DMO.

This chapter covers the following topics:

- Viewing server options

- Extracting Enterprise Manager server properties

- Creating your own Enterprise Manager tabs

- Setting server-wide options

Once you've looked at how to view the server properties, you'll write a small application to set options on individual servers or multiple servers. This could be very useful if you have a standard build and want to bring all your servers to the same settings.

Viewing Server Options

In this section, you'll go through the SQL Server Properties dialog box tab by tab in Enterprise Manager and dump the information into a text file. Then you'll take advantage of SQL-DMO's power by looking at server options not found on Enterprise Manager's SQL Server Properties dialog box. You'll query every server you've registered in Enterprise Manager. You could also look at the ListAvailableSQLServers method of the Application object, but we've found that this can't enumerate servers on a different network segment than you're on (i.e., across routers). You're only usually interested in SQL Servers that have been registered in Enterprise Manager anyway. Let's first construct a loop so that you can investigate every server in Enterprise Manager.

 NOTE   Full source code for the program is available from the Downloads area of the Apress Web site (http://www.apress.com). This source code will only work on SQL Server 2000 (tested on RTM and SP2) as it uses the extended objects in the SQL Server 2000 SQL-DMO library version 8.

The Main() Procedure

The Main() procedure is where the program starts—there's no user interface to this program. The next piece of code iterates through all server groups in Enterprise Manager and also through subserver groups within server groups.

```
Sub Main()
  ' iterate through all server groups in Enterprise Manager
  For Each oServerGroup In oApp.ServerGroups
  ' find subgroups within this group
  GetServerGroupsInGroups oServerGroup
  Next oServerGroup
End Sub
```

The GetServerGroupsInGroups Procedure

The GetServerGroupsInGroups procedure iterates through each subgroup in each group so that you can find out information about servers that are more than one level deep in Enterprise Manager. The following code iterates through the ServerGroups collection recursively to enumerate all servers registered in Enterprise Manager:

```
Private Sub GetServerGroupsInGroups(oGroup As SQLDMO.ServerGroup)
  ' find all registered servers in this group
  GetRegisteredServers oGroup
  ' iterate through subgroups of this group
  For Each oServerGroup In oGroup.ServerGroups
  ' recursively repeat until all groups and servers have been done
  GetServerGroupsInGroups oServerGroup
  Next
End Sub
```

The GetRegisteredServers Procedure

The GetRegisteredServers procedure iterates through each server in a group and calls the GetServerInfo procedure to actually get the information you're after for every server.

During the iteration through your registered servers in your server groups, you can go through each one by calling the GetServerInfo function. This function accepts four parameters, with the last two being optional: group name, server name, login, and password. If the server has been registered in Enterprise Manager using Windows Authentication, then the login and password parameters will be blank.

Extracting Enterprise Management Server Properties

We'll now go through this function in detail, showing how to extract the information displayed on the SQL Server Properties dialog box of Enterprise Manager. The following code iterates through the RegisteredServers collection, and for each RegisteredServer, it calls the procedure GetServerInfo. GetServerInfo performs most of the work of extracting server properties.

```
Private Sub GetRegisteredServers(oGroup As SQLDMO.ServerGroup)
' go through each registered server in the group
  For Each oRegServer In oGroup.RegisteredServers
' call the function to actually do the work of extracting information
  GetServerInfo oGroup.Name, oRegServer.Name, oRegServer.Login,
oRegServer.Password
  Next
End Sub
```

In the following sections we discuss each tab in the SQL Server Properties dialog box.

General Tab

The General tab, shown in Figure 6-1, is easy to extract using SQL-DMO. You simply connect to and query the SQLServer and SQLServer2 objects.

 NOTE The SQLServer2 object was added in SQL Server 2000 to extend the functionality of the SQLServer object with 10 new properties and 11 new methods. Have a look in SQL Server Books Online for more information on this.

Connecting to SQL Server

You connect to SQL Server using the Connect method of the SQLServer and SQLServer2 objects. Here's the code to connect to SQL Server:

```
Dim oServer as New SQLDMO.SQLServer  ' define the SQLServer object
If sLogin = "" Then
   oServer.LoginSecure = True
   oServer2.LoginSecure = True
   oServer.Connect sServerName
   oServer2.Connect sServerName
Else
   oServer.LoginSecure = False
   oServer2.LoginSecure = False
   oServer.Connect sServerName, sLogin, sPassword
   oServer2.Connect sServerName, sLogin, sPassword
End If
```

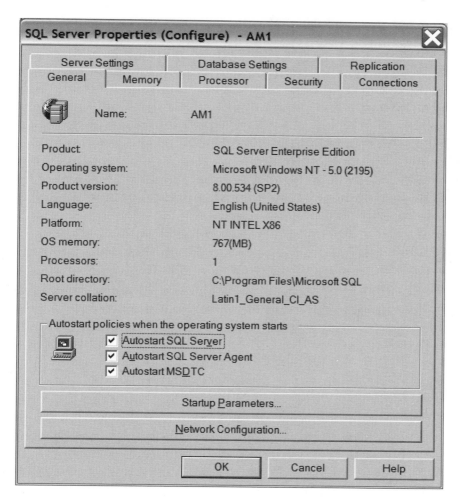

Figure 6-1. The General tab

Querying the Server

Now that you've connected to the server and logged in, you can start querying it. The first item in the list is the easy one: the name of the server. There are three different names that you can query in the SQLServer object: Name, NetName, and TrueName. We've opted to query TrueName here, as this matches the one displayed using

```
select convert(sysname, serverproperty(N'servername'))
```

in T-SQL, which in turn matches what's stored in the sysservers system table. You can amend this table using sp_addserver and sp_dropserver. NetName is the name of the server as it appears on the network, and Name is what's used to connect to SQL Server and identify the machine name. We'll use the TrueName property of the SQLServer object, as this usually returns the correct information:

```
Debug.Print "Server name: " & oServer.TrueName
```

T-SQL (Version 2000)

```
select convert(sysname, serverproperty(N'servername'))
```

T-SQL (Prior to Version 2000)

```
select @@servername
```

TIP When you want to query the server name using T-SQL, it's always best to use `select convert(sysname, serverproperty(N'servername'))` because this always reflects the name if it's changed. `select @@servername` requires you to restart the SQL Server service to reflect the change, and it's still provided for backward compatibility.

Finding the Product Name

The next item in the list (product) isn't available via a property in SQL-DMO, so you'll have to submit a query to the database. The way we discovered this was that we ran a profiler trace to see what Enterprise Manager did to get the information. It turns out that in order to find the product name of SQL Server, Enterprise Manager issues this statement:

```
select 'ServerSKU'=
SUBSTRING(@@version,PATINDEX(N'%Corporation%',@@version)+DATALENGTH
('Corporation')+2,PATINDEX(N'% on %',@@version)-
(PATINDEX(N'%Corporation%',@@version)+DATALENGTH('Corporation')+2))
```

Perhaps Enterprise Manager is doing this to maintain compatibility with SQL Server 7.0. You can issue a very simple query to a SQL Server 2000 database as follows and store the results in a QueryResults object:

```
Dim oResults as QueryResults
Set oResults = oServer.Databases("Master").ExecuteWithResults
("select SERVERPROPERTY ('Edition')")
Debug.Print "Product: SQL Server " & oResults.GetColumnString(1, 1)
```

Various properties and methods are available to enable you to query the results. As you're only getting one row back, you can just display the first column of the first row using the GetColumnString method of the QueryResults object. On our Enterprise Edition of SQL Server, this produces the following in the debug window:

```
Product: SQL Server Enterprise Edition
```

The next two items require you to issue direct queries also, as they aren't available via the SQL-DMO object library. Here's how you find out the operating system and SQL Server product version:

```
Set oResults = oServer.Databases("Master").ExecuteWithResults
("xp_msver N'ProductVersion', N'Language', N'Platform', N'WindowsVersion',
 N'ProcessorCount', N'PhysicalMemory'")
Debug.Print "Operating System: " & oResults.GetColumnString(4, 4)
Debug.Print "Product Version: " & oResults.GetColumnString(1, 4) & "
(" & oServer2.ProductLevel & ")"
```

The rest of the items on the General tab are easier to get to, as you can simply use the SQL-DMO library to get the information. You need to make use of the SQLServer2 object to retrieve collation information because this is specific to SQL Server 2000. The rest of the information is available through the SQLServer object. Here's the code to get the rest of the information:

```
Debug.Print "Server Language: " & oServer.Language
Debug.Print "Physical Memory: " & oServer.Registry.PhysicalMemory & "MB"
Debug.Print "Number of Processors: " & oServer.Registry.NumberOfProcessors
Debug.Print "Root directory: '" & oServer.Registry.SQLRootPath & "'"
Debug.Print "Server collation: " & oServer2.Collation
Debug.Print "Autostart SQLServer: " & oServer.Registry.AutostartServer
Debug.Print "Autostart SQLAgent: " & oServer.JobServer.AutoStart
Debug.Print "Autostart MSDTC: " & oServer.Registry.AutostartDTC
```

Extracting Enterprise Manager Server Properties Information with T-SQL

Here's how you get the information using good old T-SQL:

```
-- for Language, Physical Memory, Number of Processors
EXEC Xp_msver N'ProductVersion', N'Language', N'Platform',
N'WindowsVersion', N'ProcessorCount', N'PhysicalMemory'
```

```
EXEC master..xp_regread
    @rootkey='HKEY_LOCAL_MACHINE',
    @key='SOFTWARE\Microsoft\MSSQLServer\Setup',
    @value_name='SQLDataRoot'

EXEC master..xp_regread
    @rootkey='HKEY_LOCAL_MACHINE',
    @key='SOFTWARE\Microsoft\MSSQLServer\Setup',
    @value_name='SQLDataRoot'

select SERVERPROPERTY ('Collation') as 'Server Collation'
EXEC xp_regread
    @rootkey='HKEY_LOCAL_MACHINE',
    @key='SYSTEM\CurrentControlSet\Services\MSSQLServer',
    @value_name='Start'

EXEC msdb..sp_get_sqlagent_properties

EXEC xp _regread
    @rootkey='HKEY_LOCAL_MACHINE',
    @key='SYSTEM\CurrentControlSet\Services\MSDTC',
    @value_name='Start'
```

WARNING   Notice that you have to resort to using an undocumented and unsupported extended stored procedure when you go down the T-SQL route. However, you can get the information you need using documented and supported commands using SQL-DMO. This information will prove very useful if you can wrap the preceding code into a VB function and then call it for every server in the enterprise and add it to your disaster recovery logs.

Memory Tab

The Memory tab shown in Figure 6-2 is very easy to script out.

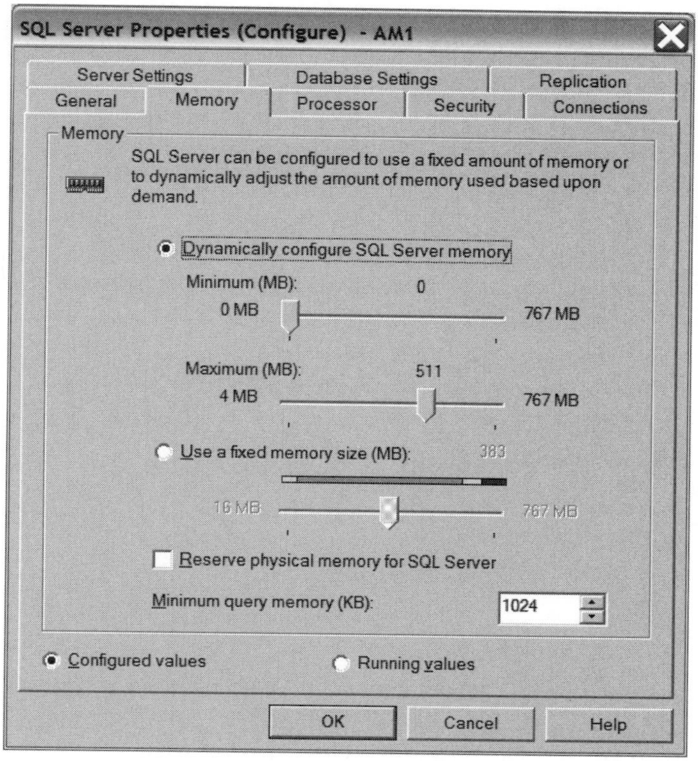

Figure 6-2. The Memory tab

All you need to do is look at the SQLServer.Configuration object and iterate through the ConfigValues collection. You can script out all SQL Server's configuration options with just three lines of code, but here you want to script out selected ones, in a specific order, so you need to script them individually. Here's how to script out all configured and runtime values with three lines of code (well, four if you include the Dim statement):

```
Dim oConfiguration as SQLDMO.ConfigValue
For Each oConfiguration In oServer.Configuration.ConfigValues
    Debug.Print oConfiguration.Name & ": " & oConfiguration.CurrentValue _
    & ", " & oConfiguration.RunningValue
Next
```

The equivalent code in T-SQL is more concise:

```
Exec sp_configure
```

What you really want to do is script out only "maximum RAM," "minimum RAM," "reserve physical memory for SQL Server," and "minimum query memory." You can accomplish this with four lines of code:

```
    Debug.Print "max server memory (MB): " & oServer.Configuration.ConfigValues
("max server memory (MB)").CurrentValue
    Debug.Print "min server memory (MB): " & oServer.Configuration.ConfigValues
("min server memory (MB)").CurrentValue
    Debug.Print "set working set size: " & oServer.Configuration.ConfigValues
("set working set size").CurrentValue
    Debug.Print "min memory per query (KB): " &
oServer.Configuration.ConfigValues("min memory per query (KB)").CurrentValue
```

This is what you get in the debug window:

```
max server memory (MB): 511
min server memory (MB): 0
set working set size: 0
min memory per query (KB): 1024
```

If the max server memory is equal to the min server memory, then you know that the option "Use a fixed memory size" has been checked. On an initial installation of SQL Server, the max server memory is usually set to the maximum. You may get a false value if the max server memory is set to its maximum; we recommend you reduce this anyway.

 TIP On a dedicated SQL Server with no third-party or in-house applications installed, we recommend that you allocate *at least* 128MB of RAM to the operating system if you have 512MB physical RAM or more installed.

Here's how to script this out in T-SQL.

T-SQL

```
exec sp_configure 'max server memory (MB)'
exec sp_configure 'min server memory (MB)'
exec sp_configure 'set working set size'
exec sp_configure 'min memory per query (KB)'
```

Processor Tab

The first item in the Processor tab shown in Figure 6-3 is the *affinity mask* in configuration options. It is labeled "Processor control" in Enterprise Manager, but it's referred to as "affinity mask" internally and in T-SQL.

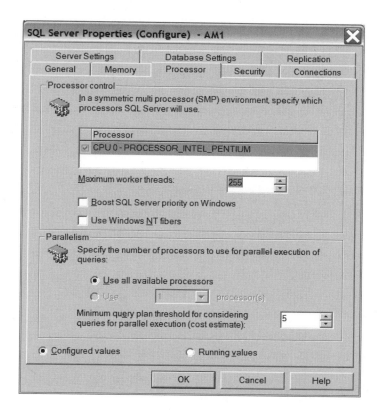

Figure 6-3. The Processor tab

This is an advanced option and it's normally set to 0 (the default) in most environments. It's recommended that you only change this option if your SQL Server is under heavy load and your users are suffering from performance problems. We never change this option from the default if we have fewer than four processors. Keep in mind that Windows NT 4 and Windows 2000 assign deferred process call (DPC) activity associated with network interface cards (NICs) to the highest numbered processor in the system. If you have more than one NIC, the next NIC is assigned to the next highest numbered processor. See SQL Server Books Online for more detailed information on this.

The affinity mask is stored in SQL Server as a bit mask. Table 6-1, which is taken from SQL Server Books Online, contains the affinity mask values.

Table 6-1. Affinity Mask Values

Decimal Value	Binary Bit Mask	Allow SQL Server Threads on Processors
1	00000001	0
3	00000011	0 and 1
7	00000111	0, 1, and 2
15	00001111	0, 1, 2, and 3
31	00011111	0, 1, 2, 3, and 4
63	00111111	0, 1, 2, 3, 4, and 5
127	01111111	0, 1, 2, 3, 4, 5, and 6 (isolates SQL Server activity from DPC processor only)

You can display this information using the Configuration object once more:

```
Debug.Print "Affinity mask: " & oServer.Configuration.ConfigValues
("affinity mask").CurrentValue
```

With T-SQL you could display it like this:

```
Exec sp_configure 'affinity mask'
```

You can retrieve the rest of the information on this tab using the Configuration object either in a loop as shown previously or individually as shown here:

```
    Debug.Print "Max worker threads: " & oServer.Configuration.ConfigValues
("max worker threads").CurrentValue
    Debug.Print "Boost SQL Priority on Windows: " &
oServer.Configuration.ConfigValues("priority boost").CurrentValue
    Debug.Print "Use Windows NT fibers: " &
oServer.Configuration.ConfigValues("lightweight pooling").CurrentValue
    Debug.Print "Num processors for parallelism (0=All): " &
 oServer.Configuration.ConfigValues("max degree of parallelism").CurrentValue
    Debug.Print "Cost threshold for parallelism: " &
oServer.Configuration.ConfigValues("cost threshold for
parallelism").CurrentValue
```

You can retrieve the rest of the information on this tab with T-SQL as follows.

T-SQL

```
exec sp_configure 'max worker threads'
exec sp_configure 'priority boost'
exec sp_configure 'lightweight pooling'
exec sp_configure 'max degree of parallelism'
exec sp_configure 'cost threshold for parallelism'
```

Using Profiler to Discover Under-the-Hood Information

We were curious to see how Enterprise Manager retrieved information for the processor tab using SQL-DMO, so we applied a profiler trace to the server. We were surprised to find that SQL-DMO uses the older-style non-ANSI join syntax to issue direct queries on the system tables. When you query the Configuration object, SQL-DMO issues this query:

```
select
        v.number,
        v.name,
        minimum = v.low,
        maximum = v.high,
        dynamic = c.status & 1,
        config_value = c.value,
        run_value = r.value
from master.dbo.sysconfigures c,
        master..spt_values v,
        master.dbo.syscurconfigs r
where
        v.type = 'C'
and v.number = c.config
and v.number >= 0
and v.number = r.config
and (c.status & 2 = 0
or exists
        (select * from master.dbo.syscurconfigs
        where config = 518 and value = 1))
order by v.name
```

Microsoft has recommended that people move to the ANSI join syntax—perhaps this has just been overlooked on their part, or they've applied the philosophy of "If it ain't broke, don't fix it."

Let's move on to the Security tab.

Security Tab

You can gather information from the Security tab in Figure 6-4 using the IntegratedSecurity object.

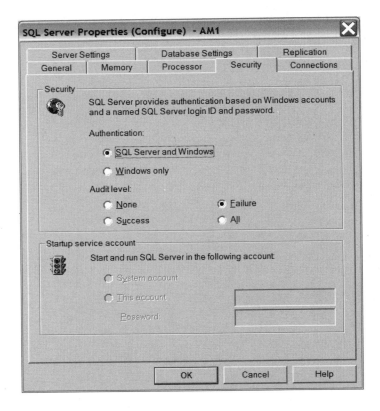

Figure 6-4. The Security tab

The Authentication and Audit levels are stored as integers. You'll need to look them up in a table to find out what they mean. Table 6-2 lists the Security modes.

Table 6-2. Security Modes

Security Mode	Description
1	Integrated
2	Mixed
0	SQL Server only
9	Unknown

This is how we queried the Security mode:

```
Dim sSecurityMode as String
Select Case oServer.IntegratedSecurity.SecurityMode
    Case 1
    sSecurityMode = "Integrated."
    Case 2
    sSecurityMode = "Mixed."
    Case 0
    sSecurityMode = "SQL Server only."
    Case 9
    sSecurityMode = "Unknown."
End Select
Debug.Print "SQL Security Authentication mode: " & sSecurityMode
```

This is what we got in the debug window:

```
SQL Security Authentication mode: Mixed.
```

In T-SQL, you can issue this query on SQL Server 2000:

```
select SERVERPROPERTY('IsIntegratedSecurityOnly')
```

or

```
exec master..xp_loginconfig 'login mode'
```

You can do a similar thing with the Audit level:

```
Dim sAuditLevel as String
Select Case oServer.IntegratedSecurity.AuditLevel
    Case 0
    sAuditLevel = "None."
    Case 1
    sAuditLevel = "Success only."
    Case 2
    sAuditLevel = "Failure only."
    Case 3
    sAuditLevel = "Success and failure."
End Select
Debug.Print, "Audit level: " & sAuditLevel
```

You get this in the debug window:

```
Audit level: Failure only.
```

In T-SQL, you query the Audit level like this:

```
exec master..xp_loginconfig 'audit level'
```

Connections Tab

Again, you use the Configuration object to get most of the information from the Connections tab (see Figure 6-5).

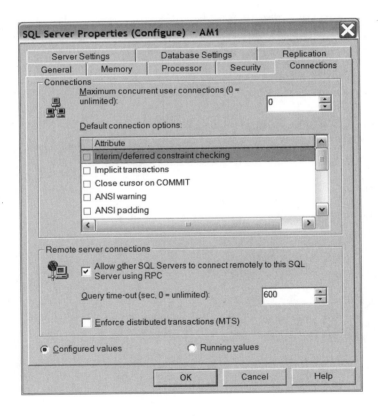

Figure 6-5. The Connections tab

For the maximum concurrent user connections, you use the following code:

```
Debug.Print "Max User connections (0=unlimited): " &
oServer.Configuration.ConfigValues("user connections").CurrentValue
```

In T-SQL, you use this:

```
exec sp_configure 'user connections'
```

The default connections information is stored as a bit mask field. You query the Configuration object again and use a ConfigValue of "user options" to retrieve the bit mask. Each value can be logically ANDed according to Table 6-3 (taken from SQL Server Books Online) to find out the value.

Table 6-3. Default Values of SET Options

Value	Configuration	Description
1	DISABLE_DEF_CNST_CHK	Controls interim or deferred constraint checking.
2	IMPLICIT_TRANSACTIONS	Controls if a transaction is started implicitly when a statement is executed.
4	CURSOR_CLOSE_ON_COMMIT	Controls the behavior of cursors after a commit operation has been performed.
8	ANSI_WARNINGS	Controls truncation and NULL in aggregate warnings.
16	ANSI_PADDING	Controls padding of fixed-length variables.
32	ANSI_NULLS	Controls NULL handling when using equality operators.
64	ARITHABORT	Terminates a query when an overflow or divide-by-zero error occurs during query execution.
128	ARITHIGNORE	Returns NULL when an overflow or divide-by-zero error occurs during a query.

Table 6-3. Default Values of SET Options (Continued)

Value	Configuration	Description
256	QUOTED_IDENTIFIER	Differentiates between single and double quotation marks when evaluating an expression.
512	NOCOUNT	Turns off the message returned at the end of each statement that states how many rows were affected.
1024	ANSI_NULL_DFLT_ON	Alters the session's behavior to use ANSI compatibility for nullability. New columns defined without explicit nullability are defined to allow nulls.
2048	ANSI_NULL_DFLT_OFF	Alters the session's behavior not to use ANSI compatibility for nullability. New columns defined without explicit nullability are defined not to allow nulls.
4096	CONCAT_NULL_YIELDS_NULL	Returns NULL when concatenating a NULL value with a string.
8192	NUMERIC_ROUNDABORT	Generates an error when a loss of precision occurs in an expression.
16384	XACT_ABORT	Rolls back a transaction if a Transact-SQL statement raises a runtime error.

It's important to note here that server-level user options are often overwritten by ODBC and OLE DB drivers, and also by SET statements in stored procedures. The server-level options provide a default value if it isn't provided when a user connects. In the following paragraphs, we won't go through the entire list. Say, however, that you want to find out the server-level ANSI_NULLs setting. You do it like this:

```
Dim iCurOptions as Integer
iCurOptions = oServer.Configuration.ConfigValues("user options").CurrentValue
If (iCurOptions And 32) Then Debug.Print "ANSI nulls: ON"
Else Print #FileNum, "ANSI nulls: OFF"
```

Here, you're logically ANDing the current user options value with 32 to find out if bit position 32 is on or off. This code produces the following in the debug window:

```
ANSI nulls: OFF
```

Here's the equivalent code in T-SQL.

T-SQL

```
select case
    when value & 32 = 32 then 'ON'
    else 'OFF'
    end as ANSI_NULLS
from sysconfigures
where comment = 'user options'
```

You can find all the options in the "Remote server connections" frame in the Configuration object also. You can discover those options using the following code:

```
Debug.Print "Allow other SQL Servers to connect remotely to this SQL Server
using RPC: " & oServer.Configuration.ConfigValues("remote access").CurrentValue
    Debug.Print "Remote server query time-out: " &
oServer.Configuration.ConfigValues("remote query timeout (s)").CurrentValue
    Debug.Print "Enforce distributed transactions (MTS): " &
oServer.Configuration.ConfigValues("remote proc trans").CurrentValue
```

This is the output:

```
Allow other SQL Servers to connect remotely to this SQL Server using RPC: 1
Remote server query time-out: 600
Enforce distributed transactions (MTS): 0
```

You can script this in T-SQL as shown here.

T-SQL

```
exec sp_configure 'remote access'
exec sp_configure 'remote query timeout (s)'
exec sp_configure 'remote proc trans'
```

Let's move on now to the Server Settings tab.

Server Settings Tab

You can get all the options from the Server Settings tab shown in Figure 6-6 from the Configuration object once again, except for the SQL Mail login, which you can find in the Registry object.

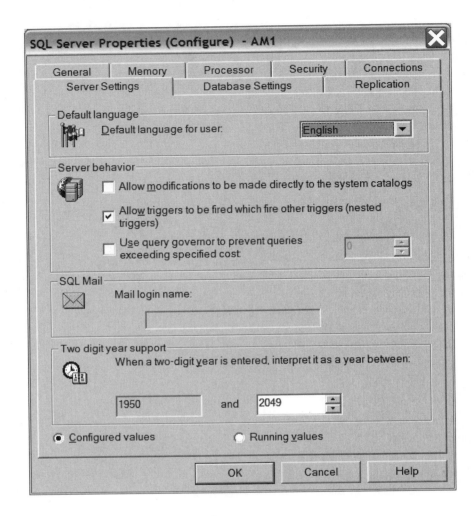

Figure 6-6. The Server Settings tab

We won't go through each option, as we expect you've gotten the idea now with the Configuration object. Here's the code to query all the information on the Server Settings tab:

```
Debug.Print "Default language (ID): " &
oServer.Configuration.ConfigValues("default language").CurrentValue
    Debug.Print "Allow updates to system catalogs: " &
oServer.Configuration.ConfigValues("allow updates").CurrentValue
    Debug.Print "Nested triggers: " & oServer.Configuration.ConfigValues
("nested triggers").CurrentValue
    Debug.Print "Query governor cost limit: " &
```

```
oServer.Configuration.ConfigValues("query governor cost limit").CurrentValue
    Debug.Print "Mail session profile: " & oServer.Registry.MailAccountName
    Debug.Print "If a two digit year is entered interpret it as a year between" &
oServer.Configuration.ConfigValues("two digit year cutoff").CurrentValue-99 &
" and " & oServer.Configuration.ConfigValues("two digit year cutoff")
.CurrentValue
```

This is what you get in the debug window:

```
Default language (ID): 0
Allow updates to system catalogs: 0
Nested triggers: 1
Query governor cost limit: 0
Mail session profile:
If a two digit year is entered interpret it as a year between 1950 and 2049
```

This is how you query all the information on the Server Settings tab in T-SQL.

T-SQL

```
exec sp_configure 'default language'
exec sp_configure 'allow updates'
exec sp_configure 'query governor cost limit'
exec sp_configure 'two digit year cutoff'
EXEC master..xp_regread
    @rootkey='HKEY_LOCAL_MACHINE',
    @key='SOFTWARE\Microsoft\MSSQLServer\MSSQLServer',
    @value_name='MailAccountName'
```

We'll now move on to a trickier tab to query: the Database Settings tab.

Database Settings Tab

Everything from the Database Settings tab shown in Figure 6-7 comes from the Configuration object except for the backup/restore time-out period and the new database default locations.

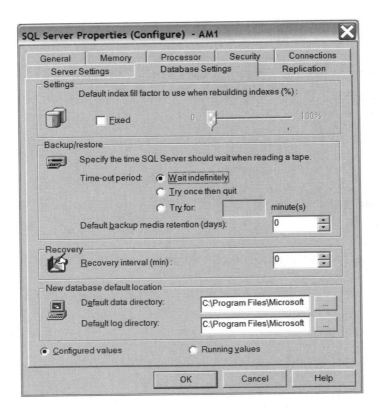

Figure 6-7. The Database Settings tab

We'll focus on the latter as we're sure you've got the hang of the Configuration object by now. The backup/restore tape time-out period is stored in the TapeLoadWaitTime property of the Registry object as an integer value. Table 6-4 shows what the values mean.

Table 6-4. Backup/Restore Tape Time-Out Period

Value	Description
–1	This is the default. A backup or restore operation will not time out.
0	A backup or restore operation will attempt to access the tape device exactly one time.
Any positive integer	This is the number of minutes during which the backup or restore operation will attempt to access the tape device.

The new database data and log default locations are stored in the registry, and you must access them using xp_regread and xp_regwrite. You can't access this information using SQL-DMO. Here's the code to produce the information in the Database Settings tab:

```
Debug.Print "Default fill factor: " & oServer.Configuration.ConfigValues
("fill factor (%)").CurrentValue
Dim iWaitTime As Integer
Dim sTapeLoadWaitTime As String
iWaitTime = oServer.Registry.TapeLoadWaitTime
Select Case iWaitTime
    Case -1
    sTapeLoadWaitTime = "Default (will not time-out)."
    Case 0
    sTapeLoadWaitTime = "Backup or restore operation will attempt to
access the tape device exactly one time."
    Case Is > 0
    sTapeLoadWaitTime = iWaitTime & " mins"
End Select
Debug.Print "Time SQL Server should wait when reading from tape: " &
sTapeLoadWaitTime
Debug.Print "Media retention (days): " & oServer.Configuration.ConfigValues
("media retention").CurrentValue
Debug.Print "Recovery interval (min): " &
oServer.Configuration.ConfigValues("recovery interval (min)").CurrentValue
Debug.Print "Default data directory: " & oServer.Registry.SQLDataRoot
```

Here's the code in T-SQL.

T-SQL

```
exec sp_configure 'fill factor (%)'
exec sp_configure 'media retention'
exec sp_configure 'recovery interval'

EXEC master..xp_regread
    @rootkey='HKEY_LOCAL_MACHINE',
    @key='SOFTWARE\Microsoft\MSSQLServer\MSSQLServer',
    @value_name='TapeLoadWaitTime'

EXEC master..xp_regread
    @rootkey='HKEY_LOCAL_MACHINE',
    @key='SOFTWARE\Microsoft\MSSQLServer\Setup',
    @value_name='SQLDataRoot'
```

So there you have it. It's all very easy stuff once you get into it, and the real power of SQL-DMO comes when you're operating in corporations with large numbers of servers. In this scenario, scripting out information for all the servers in Enterprise Manager becomes an easy task indeed. You could create it as a VBScript and you wouldn't even need to compile any code.

Creating Your Own Enterprise Manager Tabs

Now for an added bonus, you can add to what Enterprise Manager displays to you and create your own Enterprise Manager tabs by digging through the SQL-DMO library to find information that you're particularly interested in. This way, you can create a filter and only display the stuff you want.

Information Not Included in Enterprise Manager

Table 6-5 presents a list of information you won't find in Enterprise Manager.

Table 6-5. Information Not Found in Enterprise Manager

Item	SQL-DMO Code	Description
Autostart Mail	oServer.Registry.AutostartMail	Exposes the SQL Mail startup behavior
Mail password	oServer.Registry.MailPassword	Microsoft Exchange client account password
SQL error log path	oServer.Registry.ErrorLogPath	Path and file name of the SQL Server error log
Master database path	oServer.Registry.MasterDBPath	Path and file name of the master database
NT event logging	oServer.Registry.NTEventLogging	Sends results to the event log if true
Perfmon mode	oServer.Registry.PerfMonMode	Controls performance monitor polling behavior
Registered owner	oServer.Registry.RegisteredOwner	Returns the name of the installer when a SQL Server instance was installed

Table 6-5. Information Not Found in Enterprise Manager (Continued)

Item	SQL-DMO Code	Description
Password	oRegisteredServer.Password	Exposes the mail server password registered in Enterprise Manager in plain text

NOTE oServer.Registry.RegisteredOrganization doesn't exist. Microsoft has confirmed this to be an error in SQL Server Books Online. This is left over from SQL Server 6.5.

Here's the code in T-SQL to display the information described in Table 6-5.

T-SQL

```
Exec xp_instance_regread N'HKEY_LOCAL_MACHINE',
N'SOFTWARE\Microsoft\MSSQLServer\MSSQLServer', N'StartupHandlers'
Exec xp_instance_regread N'HKEY_LOCAL_MACHINE',
N'SOFTWARE\Microsoft\MSSQLServer\MSSQLServer', N'MailAccountName'
Exec xp_instance_regread N'HKEY_LOCAL_MACHINE',
N'SOFTWARE\Microsoft\MSSQLServer\MSSQLServer', N'MailPassword'
Exec xp_instance_regenumvalues N'HKEY_LOCAL_MACHINE',
N'SOFTWARE\Microsoft\MSSQLServer\MSSQLServer\Parameters'
Exec xp_instance_regread N'HKEY_LOCAL_MACHINE',
N'SOFTWARE\Microsoft\MSSQLServer\MSSQLServer\CurrentVersion', N'RegisteredOwner'
Exec xp_instance_regread N'HKEY_LOCAL_MACHINE',
N'SYSTEM\CurrentControlSet\Services\MSSQLServer\Performance'
```

WARNING These extended stored procedures are undocumented and unsupported.

The NameList Object

In this section we'll show you how to use an object we haven't come across yet: the NameList object. If you want to query the server to see what instances of SQL Server are installed, you can use the ListInstalledInstances() method of the SQLServer2 object. You first need to declare the NameList object and then populate it using the ListInstalledInstances() method. Next, you simply iterate through the NameList object to get a list of instance names. Here's the code:

```
Dim nlInstalledInstances As SQLDMO.NameList
Dim i As Integer
Set nlInstalledInstances = oServer2.ListInstalledInstances()
Debug.Print "Number of SQL Server instances: " & nlInstalledInstances.Count
For i = 1 To nlInstalledInstances.Count
    Debug.Print vbTab & "Instance " & i & ": " & nlInstalledInstances.Item(i)
Next i
```

This code produces the following in your debug window:

```
Number of SQL Server instances: 2
    Instance 1: (local)
    Instance 2: KEYMOO\SERVER2
```

It isn't possible to script out this information using T-SQL.

Setting Server-wide Options

Now comes the fun bit: actually setting some options via SQL-DMO. It goes without saying that you can only modify object properties that are read/write. Some SQL-DMO properties are read-only, such as the Registry.ReplicationInstalled property. If you try and set these properties, you'll get an error similar to the one shown in Figure 6-8.

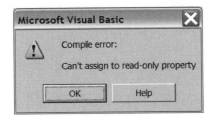

Figure 6-8. The error you receive when you try to set read-only properties

We've written a small application, which you can download from the Downloads area of the Apress Web site (http://www.apress.com), to demonstrate how to display and set server-wide properties. We'll show you how to display and set properties that are displayed on the Enterprise Manager SQL Server Properties dialog box and also how to display and set properties that don't appear on the dialog box.

Setting Properties in the Registry

The Registry and Registry2 objects expose a lot of read/write properties that you can set programmatically. Common ones that you'll use are the Autostart properties. Figure 6-9 shows a duplication of the Enterprise Manager General tab that we put together in Visual Basic 6.0.

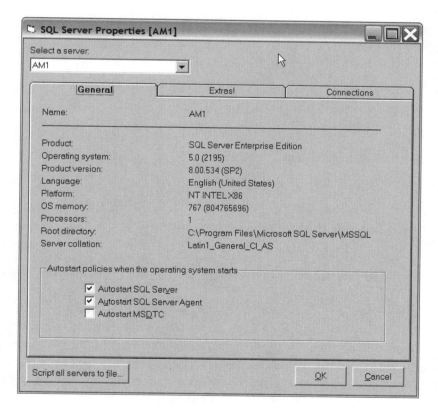

Figure 6-9. The SQL Server Properties dialog box's General tab

When the form loads, you populate the labels and the check boxes with their current running values. If a user changes the value of any of the check boxes, these changes will be saved if the user clicks the OK button. The changes won't be saved if the user clicks the Cancel button. Here's the code to populate the check boxes:

```
If (oServer.Registry.AutostartServer) Then chkAutostartSQLServer.Value = 1
If (oServer.JobServer.AutoStart) Then chkAutoStartSQLAgent.Value = 1
If (oServer.Registry.AutostartDTC) Then chkAutostartMSDTC.Value = 1
```

When the user clicks OK, you update the registry with the values in the check boxes:

```
If chkAutostartSQLServer.Value = 1 Then
    oServer.Registry.AutostartServer = True
Else
    oServer.Registry.AutostartServer = False
End If
If chkAutostartMSDTC.Value = 1 Then
    oServer.Registry.AutostartDTC = True
Else
    oServer.Registry.AutostartDTC = False
End If
If chkAutoStartSQLAgent.Value = 1 Then
    oServer.JobServer.AutoStart = True
Else
    oServer.JobServer.AutoStart = False
End If
```

There's no supported way to write this information to the registry using T-SQL. You could possibly have a go at using xp_regwrite:

```
xp_regwrite [@rootkey=]'rootkey', [@key=]'key', [@value_name=]'value_name',
[@type=]'type', [@value=]'value'
```

We're not very happy about manipulating the registry in an unsupported way. We don't have a problem reading the registry using undocumented procedures because we can't do any damage. However, you could possibly damage your system using this extended stored procedure. Make sure you back up your registry and don't use it on a production machine. If you must edit the registry, make sure it has been thoroughly tested in a dedicated test environment first.

Setting Properties Using Registry2 Object

A trickier object to query and manipulate is the Registry2 object. It isn't available intuitively like the Registry object. You would think you would be able to query it like this:

```
Dim oServer2 as New SQLDMO.SQLServer2
Debug.Print oServer2.Registry.SQLAgentLogFile
```

That doesn't work. How about this:

```
Dim oServer as New SQLDMO.SQLServer
Debug.Print oServer.Registry2.SQLAgentLogFile
```

No joy there either. Let's try this:

```
Dim oServer2 as New SQLDMO.SQLServer2
Debug.Print oServer2.Registry2.SQLAgentLogFile
```

That doesn't work either. The only way to query and set this object's properties is to first declare it as a SQLDMO.Registry2 object and then set the SQLServer object's Registry object to point to the Registry2 object. Confused? Perhaps this code will clear it up for you:

```
Dim oServer as New SQLDMO.SQLServer
Dim oRegistry2 as SQLDMO.Registry2
Set oRegistry2 = oServer.Registry
Debug.Print oRegistry2.SQLAgentLogFile
```

This is just one of a few quirks you'll need to get used to when working with SQL-DMO. Not all of it works according to SQL Server Books Online. Sometimes you have to play around with it for a while until you can get it to work, or you can take the easy option and read this book (as you're doing right now). To set the SQLAgentLogFile property, use this code:

```
Dim oServer as New SQLDMO.SQLServer
Dim oRegistry2 as SQLDMO.Registry2
Set oRegistry2 = oServer.Registry
oRegistry2.SQLAgentLogFile = "D:\Logs\SQLAgent.out"
```

Discovering Sysadmin Passwords Using SQL-DMO

It's rather startling to discover that all registered servers, along with their logins and passwords, can be scripted out to a plain text file or displayed on a VB form in plain text very easily. Someone could easily write a malicious VBScript and e-mail it to an inexperienced DBA. If the DBA executes this script, it could script out all passwords and e-mail them to the script author. The script author now has all the logins and passwords of servers of his target organization. The chances of this happening obviously depend on the wit of the person that the script author has sent the script to, and most intelligent people would not execute a VBScript on their machine if they didn't know what it contained, especially if that script was from an anonymous source. Windows Authenticated SQL Servers aren't affected by this security hole, as you cannot easily script out a domain password—another good argument for using Windows Authentication.

Also, do you lock your workstation when you go to the bathroom? We usually do, but not *every* time. We notice that a lot of coworkers don't lock their workstations either. We could quickly run to a coworker's machine while he or she is in the bathroom, run a VBScript to get all the sysadmin (sa) passwords, and then send it to a share on our machine. Our coworker would be none the wiser, and we would have all the sa passwords! We're not sure whether this is an oversight on Microsoft's part or whether it's by design. The only thing we know is that you must consider your security practices and educate your coworkers about the dangers of potentially malicious scripts.

Extras Tab

Consider the Extras tab (see Figure 6-10) from the SQL-DMO application we wrote.

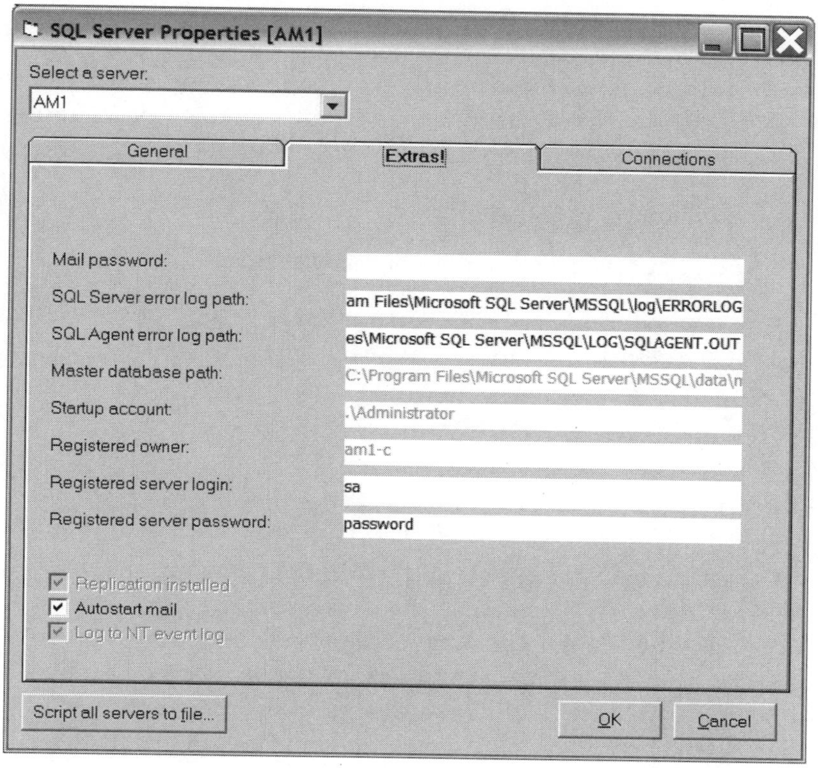

Figure 6-10. The Extras tab

Here, we can see the password of our registered server. We can see all the passwords very easily here by just selecting the server from the drop-down box. The application will show the corresponding registered login and password. The text in black is read/write, and the text in gray is read-only and locked by the application. We've made this information easily available by including a "Script all servers to file" button. When this button is clicked, all properties on the Enterprise Manager SQL Server Properties dialog box are scripted out, along with the properties shown on the Extras tab. This gives us all of Enterprise Manager's information and some extra stuff conveniently scripted into a text file. The code to show the login and password is as follows:

```
Dim oApp as SQLDMO.Application
txtLogin.Text = oApp.SQLServers("Home").RegisteredServers("AM1").Login
txtLogin.Password = oApp.SQLServers("Home").RegisteredServers("AM1").Password
```

Also notice that on this tab we have other useful information, such the SQL Mail password. This isn't displayed on this machine as we don't have an Exchange Server set up. We're using Internet mail on this machine. If, however, you use SQL Server with Exchange, as most corporations do, then you would see the Microsoft Exchange client account password for SQL Mail, displayed using the Registry object:

```
txtMailAccountPassword.Text = oServer.Registry.MailPassword
```

To set these properties, you just flip them around like this:

```
oApp.ServerGroups(.GroupName).RegisteredServers(.ServerName).Login = txtLogin.Text
oApp.ServerGroups(.GroupName).RegisteredServers(.ServerName).Password =
txtPassword.Text
oServer.Registry.MailPassword = txtMailPassword.Text
```

The ReconfigureWithOverride Property

You use the ReconfigureWithOverride property of the Configuration object to persist any changes to the Configuration object. This disables value checking and forces some options to be set even if they may cause a fatal error. You could use the Reconfigure property instead if you prefer these values to be checked.

Some options may need a SQL Server service restart in order for them to take effect. To check that an option has taken effect, you should make sure that the CurrentValue is equal to the RunningValue in the ConfigValues collection. You can check to see if the option you're changing needs a restart by looking at the DynamicReconfigure property before you change it. If this value is True, then you could prompt your user to stop and start the SQL Server service, or you could ask the user if it's OK to stop and start the SQL Server service and do it yourself using SQL-DMO in code. You could use some code like this:

```
Dim bNeedRestart as Boolean
bNeedRestart = False
With oServer.Configuration.ConfigValues("user options")
    .CurrentValue = iCurinfo
    If .DynamicReconfigure = True Then bNeedRestart = True
End With
oServer.Configuration.ReconfigureWithOverride
... set some more options here and check .DynamicReconfigure
If bNeedRestart = True Then
    oSQLServer.Stop
Do While oSQLServer.Status <> SQLDMOSvc_Stopped
    ' do nothing - just loop
Loop
oSQLServer.Start
End If
```

Setting Bit Mask Properties

You saw earlier how to query bit mask properties by looking at the user options configuration option. This value is stored as a bit mask. You may want to set some of these bits within the bit mask, and you do this by using logical AND. Let's have a look at a replica of the Connections tab in Enterprise Manager shown in Figure 6-11, and you'll set the user options configuration option using SQL-DMO.

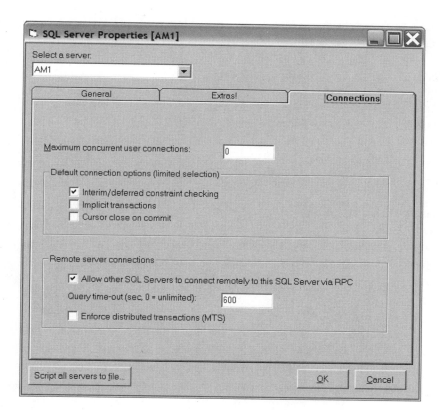

Figure 6-11. The Connections tab in our SQL-DMO application

Let's look at the "Interim/deferred constraint checking" option as an example. When the user clicks the OK button, you need to check the status of the check box. If the check box is checked, you need to look at the current value of the option. To do this, you need to logically AND the value of the user option with 1. Recall from Table 6-3 earlier in the chapter on user options that the "Interim/deferred constraint checking" option is bit position 1 in the bit mask. If the user option is already set, then you don't need to do anything. If the user option isn't already set, then you need to add 1 to the current value in order to "switch" that option on. Try and think of it as a bit mask.

Likewise, if the user has removed the check mark from the "Interim/deferred constraint checking" option, you need to check to see if the current value is 1. If it is, then you need to subtract 1 from the user option in order to switch that bit position off. This is probably better illustrated with some code:

```
Dim iCurinfo As Integer
iCurinfo = oServer.Configuration.ConfigValues("user options").CurrentValue
If chkInterim.Value = 1 Then    ' check box has been ticked
    If (iCurinfo And 1) = 0 Then iCurinfo = iCurinfo + 1 'current value is 0
Else
    If (iCurinfo And 1) Then iCurinfo = iCurinfo - 1
End If
oServer.Configuration.ConfigValues("user options").CurrentValue = iCurinfo
oServer.Configuration.ReconfigureWithOverride
```

Summary

You've learned in this chapter how to query and configure your servers through SQL-DMO. In a lot of areas, it may seem more concise to do the operation in T-SQL, however, with T-SQL it's not as easy to perform operations on large numbers of servers as it is with SQL-DMO. If you download the source code mentioned earlier in the chapter from the Downloads area of the Apress Web site (http://www.apress.com), you'll see that the program will show you server options for all servers that you've registered in Enterprise Manager. You can also apply changes to groups of servers very easily by looping through the RegisteredServers collection. You can't do some operations in T-SQL or Enterprise Manager, such as viewing the registered server login and password. Enterprise Manager stores these values in the registry as an encrypted hexadecimal number, and therefore you can't read it using the xp_regread extended stored procedure. SQL-DMO makes it easy to script these out, but this could be a potential security risk and you need to use SQL-DMO carefully, so as not to expose yourself to a security hole.

In the next chapter, you'll take a deep breath as we look at how to harness SQL-DMO to manage replication.

CHAPTER 7

Replication and SQL-DMO

WHEN WE WERE DECIDING which topics to cover in this book, we came to a point where we wanted to try something a little adventurous. Mark suggested that maybe we should include replication. After I got my breath back, we both agreed that replication would be in the book.

Replication is one of those subjects that most people shy away from because they think it's hard. Replication should be regarded as a specialty. There are people out there who know replication very well: Microsoft SQL Server MVPs Mike Hotek, Hilary Cotter, and Ron Talmage, to name a few. (You'll note the omissions of two names from that list: Mark Allison and Allan Mitchell. With all due humility, we'll stand on the proverbial shoulders of the giants.)

With all this in mind, then, we wanted to present replication without the fire and brimstone, devoid of all the mysticism. Now, we won't even try to dispel those replication fears (illusions?), but we hope that by looking at replication through the eyes of SQL-DMO you'll better understand how everything fits together—and how you can exercise more granular control over the process. The application we've built is very simple, but it does what it says on the package.

In this chapter, we cover the following topics:

- Types of replication

- Installing merge replication using SQL-DMO and Enterprise Manager

- Generating replication scripts using SQL-DMO

Types of Replication

Although you're going to be building a merge replication scenario in this chapter, it's worth looking at the other types of replication available to you.

- *Snapshot:* This type of replication pushes the whole publication to the subscriber at given intervals. This in general minimizes the number of times you send the data, but it increases the amount of data you send because you have to send all of the data each time.

- *Transactional:* Whenever a change is made to a table that's part of the publication, it's communicated to the subscriber. This, again in general, causes you to send data to the subscriber more often, but you send much less data each time. Transactional replication is designed for well-connected servers—in other words, servers where the network/Internet connection is up the majority of the time.

- *Merge:* In this type of replication, subscribers and publishers make changes to their copies of the publication independent of each other, and when they synchronize, the data is merged. Any conflicts encountered are resolved based on preset parameters. Merge replication is designed for servers and clients that aren't always online—for instance, sales agents who get a portion of their data on their laptop, and then go out in the field and hourly/nightly/weekly synchronize their changes with the publication. Unlike transactional replication, where each bit of data goes across the ether to the subscribers, in merge replication only the net changes go across the wire.

Transactional Replication Example

The following transactional replication example comes from Microsoft SQL Server MVP Hilary Cotter.

An article showing the Oracle stock price in transactional replication would look like this:

- At 9:00 A.M. Update StockPrice values ("Oracle",$50.00)
- At 12:00 P.M. Update StockPrice values ("Oracle",$43.00)
- At 2:30 P.M. Update StockPrice values ("Oracle",$23.00)
- At 3:30 P.M. Update StockPrice values ("Oracle",$12.00)

If you were disconnected from the server between 9:00 A.M. and 4:00 P.M., all of these transactions would flow across the ether.

In merge replication, if you were disconnected from 9:00 A.M. to 4:00 P.M., only a single transaction would flow across the ether: the net change showing the price drop of Oracle to $12.00.

- Update StockPrice values ("Oracle",$12.00)

Our application sets out to do the following:

1. Create a distributor.

2. Create a publisher.

3. Create a publication.

4. Create an article.

5. Create a subscriber.

6. Subscribe the subscriber to our publication.

As you can see, we're not trying to do anything too sexy or difficult. If you're new to replication or you just want our version in English of what each of these points means, then here goes using the good old magazine subscriptions analogy that everyone, including Microsoft, uses:

- *Distributor:* The distributor can be likened to the newsagent. The distributor handles getting the publication to the people who want to read it.

- *Publisher:* The publisher is the person who produces the publication, so in our analogy, the publisher is the publication house.

- *Publication:* The publication is the thing the publisher is sending you. It's the whole package, not the things that make up the package. So in our analogy, the publication could be a magazine or a newspaper.

- *Article:* The article is the thing that goes in a publication. There can be more than one article in a publication. You don't subscribe to an article, much the same way as you don't buy page 10 of the *Financial Times*. Instead, you subscribe to the whole newspaper, the publication.

- *Subscriber:* This is the person who ultimately wants to read the magazine or newspaper.

In this chapter, we'll show you three ways of building this setup: first with SQL-DMO, then with Enterprise Manager, and finally by using the supplied stored procedures. (Enterprise Manager uses the stored procedures but provides you with a usable, friendly GUI to use.) We'll start with SQL-DMO.

Installing Merge Replication Using SQL-DMO

Our application consists of one button that does what we need. In this section, we take you through the steps in our application and explain a few things along the way.

First, you set up a few variables at the top of the form that define the objects you're going to be using later in the code:

```
Dim bConnected As Boolean

Dim objSrv1 As New SQLDMO.SQLServer
Dim objSrv2 As New SQLDMO.SQLServer

Dim objReplication As New SQLDMO.Replication
Dim objDistribDB As New SQLDMO.DistributionDatabase
Dim objPublisher As New SQLDMO.DistributionPublisher
Dim mpsMergesubscription As SQLDMO.MergeSubscription
Dim subSubscriber As SQLDMO.RegisteredSubscriber
Dim bMergeExists As Boolean
```

```
Private Sub cmdGo_Click()
```

Then you check that you have a publisher, as you want to make sure somebody is publishing something:

```
    bConnected = False
    bMergeExists = False
```

Next, you log onto the server with the following code:

```
    With objSrv1
        .LoginSecure = True
        .Connect "ALLAN" ' The publisher and distributor
    End With
```

```
    bConnected = True
```

With the following code, you carry out a check to see if the distributor is already available, and if it is, you can jump ahead:

```
If objSrv1.Replication.Distributor.DistributorAvailable = False Then
```

Now you set the distribution database name:

```
objDistribDB.Name = "distribution"
```

Then you add the distribution database to the Distribution Databases collection. Here's the code:

```
objSrv1.Replication.Distributor.DistributionDatabases.Add objDistribDB
With objSrv1.Replication.Distributor
```

You set the distribution server to the true name of the local server. You want to have a distributor in this case local to the publisher.

```
    .DistributionServer = objSrv1.TrueName
    .Install
End With
End If
```

Now you add a publisher, checking if it already is one first:

```
If objSrv1.Replication.Distributor.IsDistributionPublisher = False Then
```

Then you set the publisher to be the local server:

```
objPublisher.Name = objSrv1.TrueName
objPublisher.DistributionDatabase = "distribution"
objPublisher.DistributionWorkingDirectory = App.Path & "\ReplWorkingDir"
objSrv1.Replication.Distributor.DistributionPublishers.Add objPublisher
objPublisher.ThirdParty = True

End If
```

Once you've added the publisher and the distributor, you need to create a publication. This is where you set it to be a merge publication. You also need to set up the publisher's database for merge publishing.

```
Dim objReplicationDB As SQLDMO.ReplicationDatabase
Dim objMergeReplication As New SQLDMO.MergePublication
Dim objMergeArticle1 As New SQLDMO.MergeArticle
```

```
        If objSrv1.Replication.ReplicationDatabases _
("Northwind").EnableMergePublishing = False Then
            objSrv1.Replication.ReplicationDatabases _
("Northwind").EnableMergePublishing = True
        End If
```

Now you check to see if a publication with your chosen name already exists in the replication database. If the name already exists, it will return an error. Here's how:

```
        For Each objMergeReplication In objSrv1.Replication.ReplicationDatabases _
("Northwind").MergePublications
            If objMergeReplication.Name = _
"NewMergeReplication" Then
                bMergeExists = True
            End If
        Next


        If bMergeExists = False Then
        objMergeReplication.Name = _
"NewMergeReplication"
objMergeReplication.PublicationAttributes = _
SQLDMOPubAttrib_AllowPull + SQLDMOPubAttrib_AllowPush
        objSrv1.Replication.ReplicationDatabases _
("Northwind").MergePublications.Add objMergeReplication
```

Add an article to your new publication as follows:

```
        objMergeArticle1.Name = "Customers"
        objMergeArticle1.SourceObjectName = "Customers"
        objMergeArticle1.SourceObjectOwner = "dbo"
```

Set column tracking on to improve accuracy, and add your article to the Publication object's MergeArticles collection:

```
objMergeArticle1.ColumnTracking = True
objMergeArticle1.Status = SQLDMOArtStat_Active
objMergeReplication.MergeArticles.Add objMergeArticle1

End If
```

Next, register a subscriber at the publisher—but you aren't subscribing the subscriber to anything yet.

```
Set subSubscriber = New SQLDMO.RegisteredSubscriber

subSubscriber.Name = "ALLAN\Am3"

objSrv1.Replication.Publisher.RegisteredSubscribers.Add subSubscriber
```

Here's where you associate the previous subscriber with a publication. The Subscriber property of MergeSubscription has to be a registered subscriber.

```
Set mpsMergesubscription = New SQLDMO.MergeSubscription

With mpsMergesubscription

.Subscriber = "ALLAN\Am3"
.SubscriptionDB = "Northwind"


End With
```

Add the subscriber to the subscriptions of the publication with this code:

```
objSrv1.Replication.ReplicationDatabases("Northwind").MergePublications _
("NewMergeReplication").MergeSubscriptions.Add mpsMergesubscription

End Sub
```

There you go. That wasn't too painful, was it? To run the code itself, all you need to do is click one button. You can obviously extend this to add more buttons for a function and show publications in a graphical way on the server. The point of this chapter, though, is to get you thinking about replication and hopefully using it through SQL-DMO. We think that replication has a lot to do with understanding the logical process of things. If you know what needs to go where and in what order, then it makes your job so much easier. We hope this application has shown you a little of how that applies.

TIP   The GUI in Enterprise Manager will do checks for you, but when you're using code to build up your replication scenario, always have checks at each significant stage so you can trap any errors. You then avoid little errors such as –2147207430 "The Server 'ALLAN' is already listed as a Publisher."

Installing Merge Replication Using Enterprise Manager

We'll now show you what we think are the relevant screens in Enterprise Manager to install merge replication on your SQL Server. We don't include everything—if we did, this chapter would look like a coloring book. Figure 7-1 shows where to find the main Replication menu in Enterprise Manager.

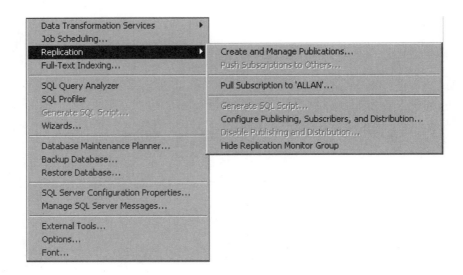

Figure 7-1. Where to find the main Replication menu

You can get to this menu by selecting Tools from the Enterprise Manager toolbar. If you select the option Configure Publishing, Subscribers, and Distribution, you start to work through the Configure Publishing and Distribution Wizard to put together all the pieces that make up replication. Figure 7-2 shows the welcome screen that appears when you start to configure replication using the wizard.

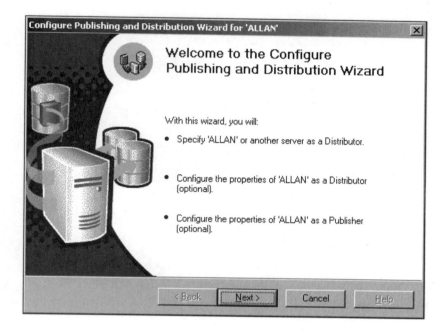

Figure 7-2. The Configure Publishing and Distribution Wizard welcome screen

Click the Next button and the screen shown in Figure 7-3 appears. On this screen, you determine which server the distributor will be. In SQL Server, you can have a local distributor or you can offload the workload to another server. In Figure 7-3, we chose to leave it on the local server.

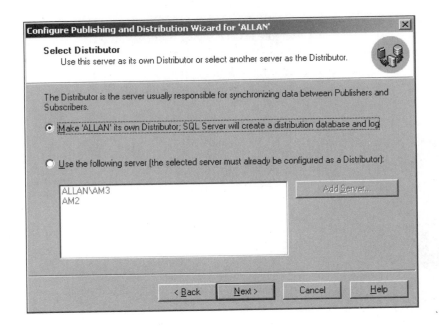

Figure 7-3. Determining where to place the distributor

After you click through a few screens, you come to a screen where you set up your server as a distributor. Figure 7-4 shows the steps that SQL Server goes through to do this.

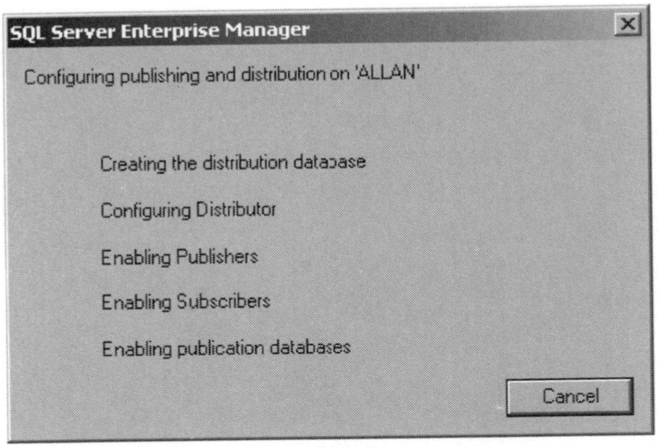

Figure 7-4. Configuring the distributor

If all went well, you should see the screen in Figure 7-5 informing you that everything went well.

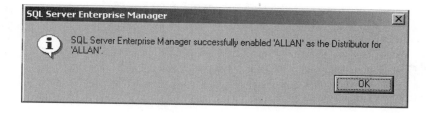

Figure 7-5. Success!

If you now go to your Databases collection, you'll find another database has been added by replication. In the majority of cases (i.e., if you haven't explicitly changed it), its name will be "distribution."

Another interesting point is that you'll only go through the Configure Publishing and Distribution Wizard the first time you select the option and need to set up your distributor, as you can see in Figure 7-6.

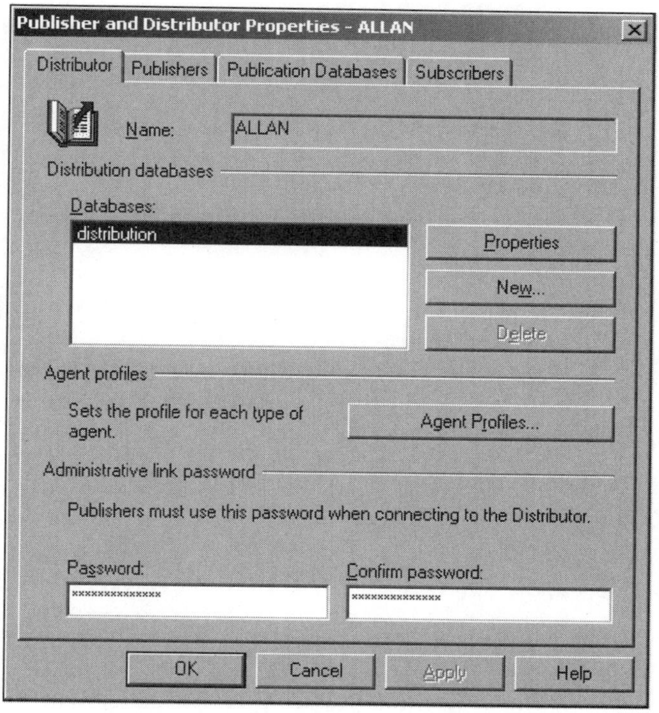

Figure 7-6. The new look

As you can see from the Publishers tab shown in Figure 7-7, "ALLAN" has been enabled as a distributor (newsagent).

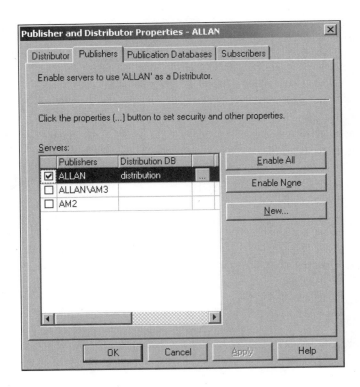

Figure 7-7. The Publishers tab

On the next tab, Publication Databases, you're able to specify which databases on your publisher you want to allow to create publications. Figure 7-8 shows what we saw when we did it on our server, and you can clearly see that Northwind is enabled as a database that's allowed to publish articles in a publication.

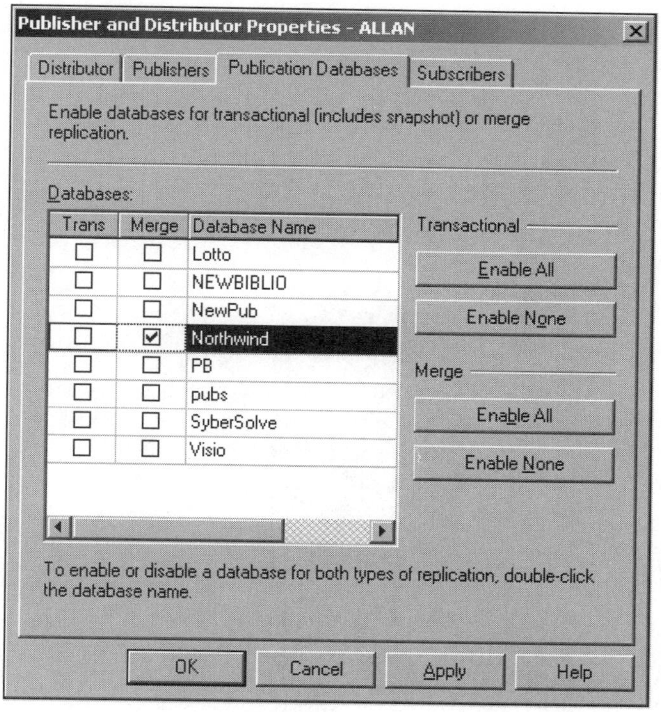

Figure 7-8. The Publication Databases tab

The next tab brings relates to your subscribers. There seems to be little point in going to all the trouble of putting something into print if nobody is going to buy it, so you decide on your subscriber base here. You can see in Figure 7-9 that we've enabled two servers as subscribers.

OK, so now you have a distributor, a publisher, and a subscriber. Unfortunately, at the moment they have nothing to do and are twiddling their thumbs. Let's create your publication and add an article to it. For this, you're going to go back to the Tools menu and select the option Create and Manage Publications. Figure 7-10 shows the resulting screen.

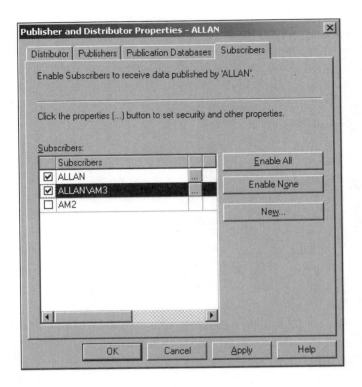

Figure 7-9. The Subscribers tab

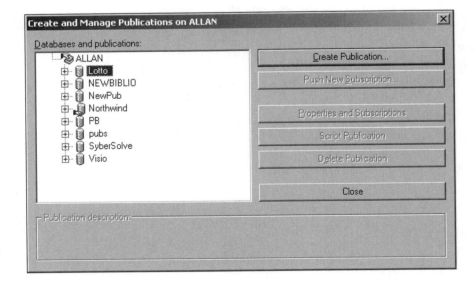

Figure 7-10. Creating a publication

Click the Create Publication button to step through the Create Publication Wizard. Figure 7-11 shows the welcome screen for the wizard.

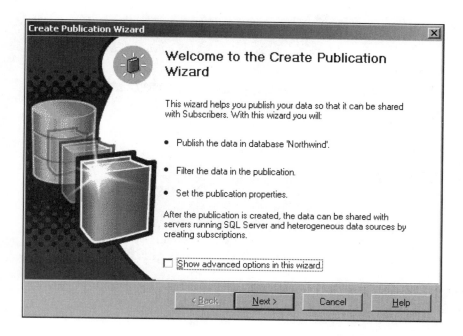

Figure 7-11. The Create Publication Wizard welcome screen

After you've had a look at the welcome screen, click Next to move on.

The screen in Figure 7-12 allows you to choose the database that has the data you want to publish.

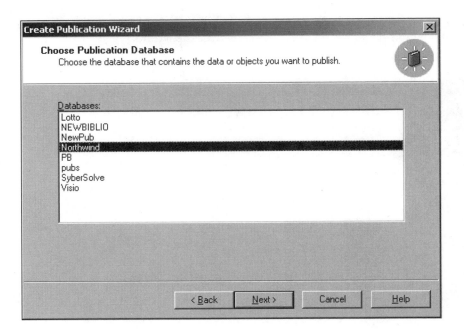

Figure 7-12. Selecting a database

In the screen in Figure 7-13, you get to choose what type of publication you want to create. Here's a quick recap of the publication types:

- *Snapshot:* This type pushes the whole publication to the subscriber at given intervals. This in general minimizes the number of times you send the data, but it increases the amount of data you send each time.

- *Transactional:* Whenever a change is made to a table that's part of the publication; it's communicated to the subscriber. This, again in general, causes you to send data to the subscriber more often, but when you do, the amount of data is a lot smaller.

- *Merge:* This is where the subscribers and publishers make changes to their copies of the publication independent of each other, and when they synchronize, the data is merged. Any conflicts encountered are resolved based on preset parameters.

You're creating a merge publication, so click the radio button next to the "Merge publication" option on the screen shown in Figure 7-13.

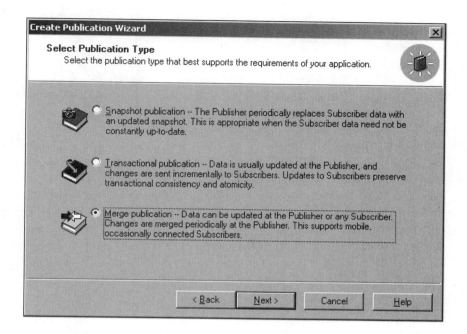

Figure 7-13. Selecting the publication type

Because you can have different types of subscribers to a SQL Server publication, you need to tell the wizard what to expect in the screen in Figure 7-14.

Using our analogy, you can think of the publication itself as the pieces of paper that make up the newspaper or magazine. Articles are what you actually read in a newspaper, and that's why in Figure 7-15 you need to add some to the publication. Articles can be stored procedures, tables, views, or a combination of those things.

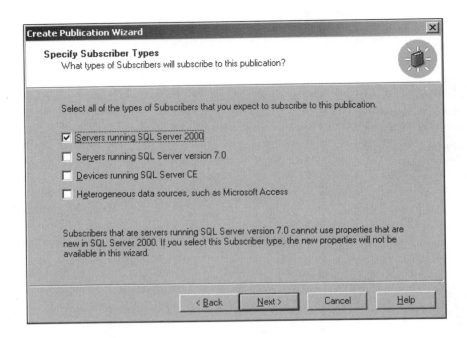

Figure 7-14. Choosing the subscriber type

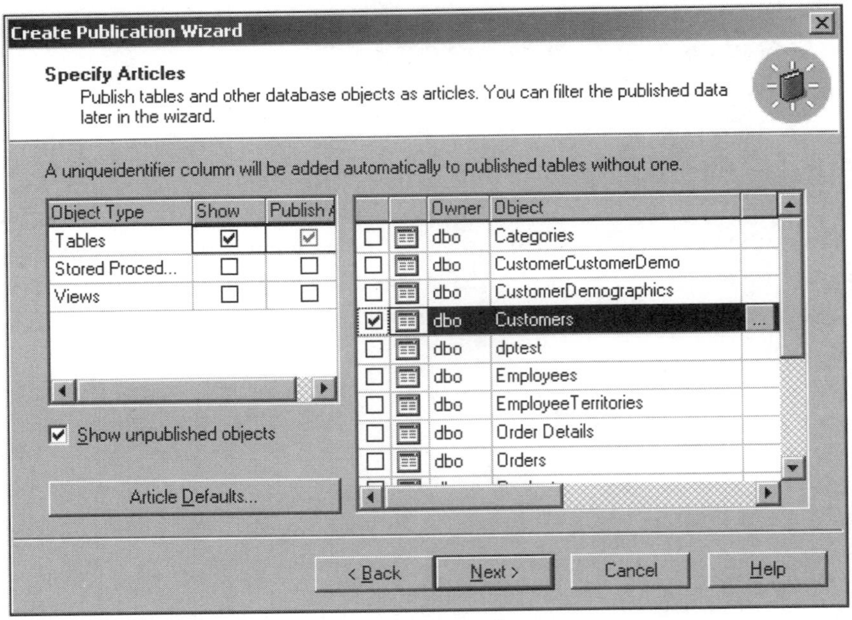

Figure 7-15. Adding articles

As with everything, you give the publication a name so you can at least recognize it later on. Figure 7-16 shows you where to do that.

Finally, you come to the end of the Create Publication Wizard. Figure 7-17 shows that milestone.

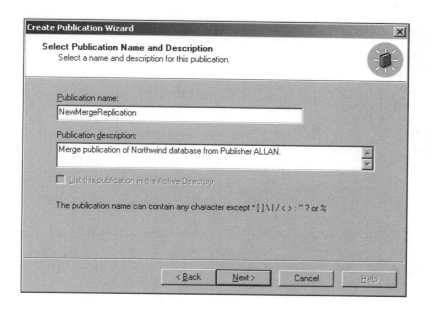

Figure 7-16. Assigning the publication a name

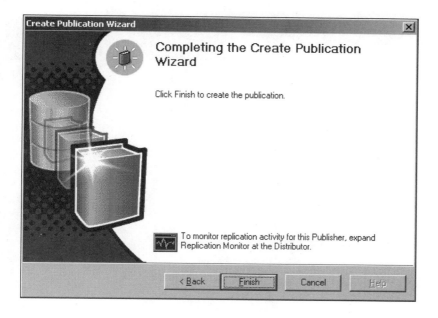

Figure 7-17. Finishing the Create Publication Wizard

After all that effort, let's flick over to Enterprise Manager in Figure 7-18 to see what you've created.

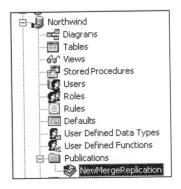

Figure 7-18. Publication in the database

Now you need to add a subscriber to your publication and you're finished. For this, you can right-click the publication and choose Properties. The screen in Figure 7-19 appears, and you select the Subscriptions tab.

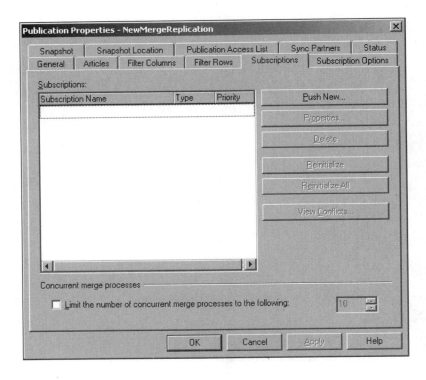

Figure 7-19. Configuring subscriptions

The screen in Figure 7-19 shows a blank list of subscriptions being pushed to subscribers. Let's change that and create a new push subscription. Click the Push New button.

Yet another wizard opens. Figure 7-20 shows the welcome screen of the Push Subscription Wizard.

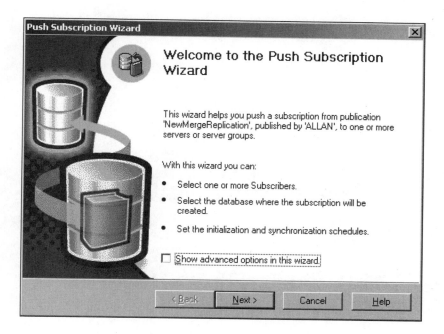

Figure 7-20. The Push Subscription Wizard welcome screen

Click Next to move on from the first screen of the wizard, and the screen shown in Figure 7-21 appears. This is where you choose who the subscribers to your publication will be.

The subscriber has to have somewhere to put the data that's contained in the publication. Figure 7-22 shows you where you choose this subscriber database.

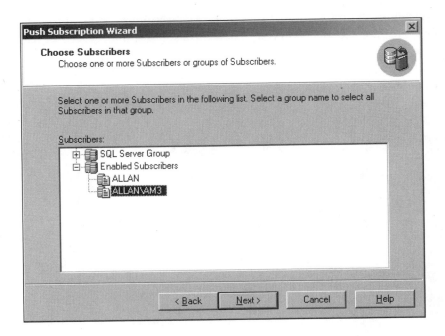

Figure 7-21. Choosing subscribers to your publication

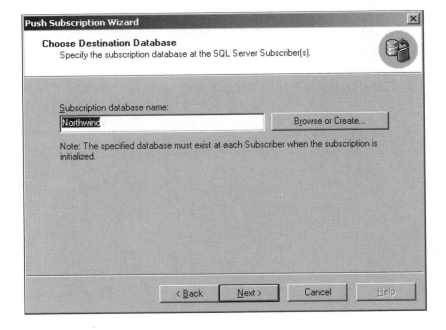

Figure 7-22. Choosing a subscription database

In all likelihood, you're going to want to update the data in the subscription database on a schedule. The screen in Figure 7-23 shows you how to arrange that schedule.

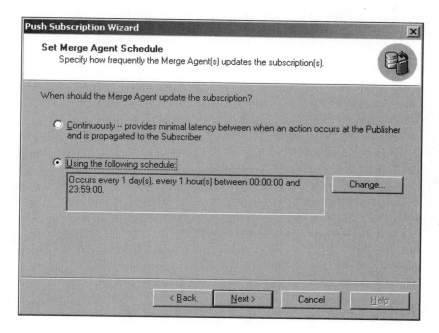

Figure 7-23. Creating a schedule

In the screen in Figure 7-24, you tell SQL Server if your subscriber has the schema and data already or if once you've finished this wizard you should send over the publication as it stands now ready for future use.

The thing about merge replication is that you get conflicts. This is where data has changed on two of the parties in replication, and the data values need to be resolved. Figure 7-25 shows you where you can decide how to resolve these conflicts.

NOTE SQL Server has a built-in default resolver, and it also has a couple of custom resolvers that you can use.

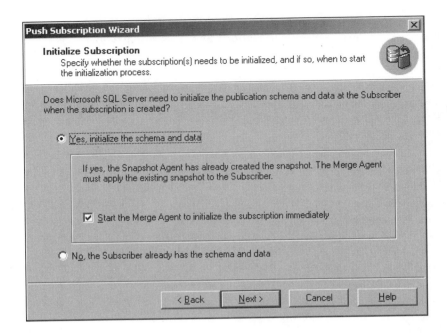

Figure 7-24. Initializing the subscriber

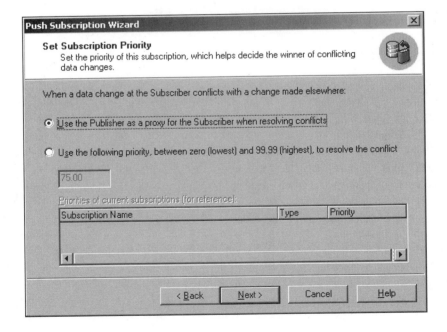

Figure 7-25. Resolving conflicts

Click the Next button a few times to move to the end of the wizard (see Figure 7-26).

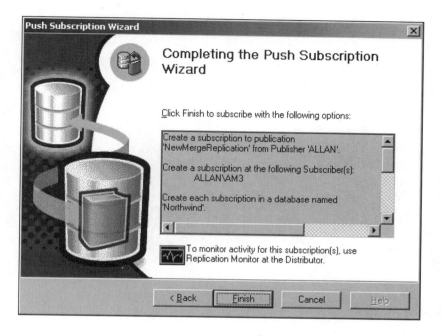

Figure 7-26. Finishing the Push Subscription Wizard

As you can see, there's quite a lot to setting replication up, and if you're new to it or you aren't overly confident with it, then using Enterprise Manager is definitely the way to go. This isn't a book about replication, so we don't go into any more detail about it than we have in this chapter.

NOTE   There are a couple of great sites out there on the Web where you can get more information on replication. The first is SQL Server MVP Hilary Cotter's site, http://www.replicationfaq.com. The second is from another SQL Server MVP, Mike Hotek, which you can find at http://www.mssqlserver.com. Mike's site includes a great primer section.

Generating Replication Scripts Using SQL-DMO

Remember how we said earlier that wizards are a great way for you to get a feel for things that you aren't comfortable with? Well here's another. SQL Server has an option to generate scripts for a few of its features, and luckily for us, replication is one of those features. How do you access this great option? Well, after you've created a replication scenario that you're happy with, you go back to your favorite menu (see Figure 7-27) and click the Generate SQL Script option.

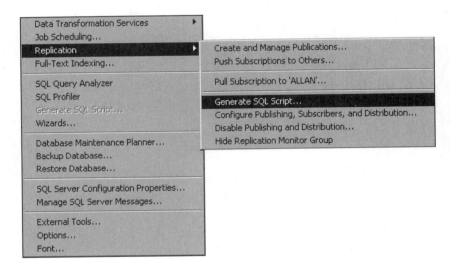

Figure 7-27. Where to find the Generate SQL Script option

NOTE All Enterprise Manager is doing with the Generate SQL Script option is calling the replication stored procedures. We don't recommend that you use stored procedures as your first port of call if you're trying to learn replication. When you feel more comfortable with the order in which the steps for creating the scenario should be executed, then by all means look at them. A great way to do this would be to do exactly what we do in this section and get Enterprise Manager to script it out. Once you have a printed copy, you can then refer to SQL Server Books Online for a full discussion of the individual stored procedures.

After you select the Generate SQL Script option, you're greeted by a two-tab screen (see Figure 7-28). The only tab of any relevance to you here is the General tab.

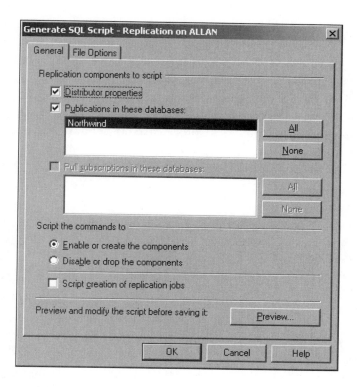

Figure 7-28. Generating the script

When you click the Preview button, Enterprise Manager will generate reams of data for you to look at, which is all very wonderful and does what you think it would. We're not going to show you all this data, but instead we're going to show you how to script out replication using SQL-DMO.

NOTE An interesting point here: When you create the publication, it will create a few jobs as well. Even though the jobs are there in the system tables of msdb, unless you refresh the jobs icon under SQL Server Agent, when you script out replication you'll have the error "Either the job does not exist or you do not have permission to view it" in the script. All you have to do is refresh the jobs and all will be fine.

Scripting Replication Using SQL-DMO

This is really quick, and there's very little to it. A quick search in SQL Server Books Online reveals that the Replication object has a Script method that takes two arguments. Here's how to script replication:

```
Object.Script ([Script Type],[ScriptFilePath]) as String
```

The only part that is a little strange here is the ScriptType argument, but we guess that it would enable you to define what about replication it is that you want to script. Luckily, SQL Server Books Online again provides a very handy table with all the values that you could ever need. If you do a search in the index under "Replication, Scripting" you'll find it.

Summary

As we've said all along, replication is a tricky and specialized subject, but it isn't impossible. We hope that what we've shown you in this chapter will give you ideas about experimenting with it in development and perhaps expanding upon it. Don't forget about the scripting capability in Enterprise Manager. It's a very useful learning tool as well as a backup for when you need to reinstall replication but don't want to go through all the screens in Enterprise Manager. The SQL-DMO option is also a very good option for disaster recovery. Although we don't have any war stories to tell of replication gone wrong, we're sure you can speak to people who do. Our motto is, "You can never be overprepared for a disaster," and let's face it, a flat text file takes up very little room. You could have buttons that install each publication and the publisher, distributor, and subscribers as well.

Chapter 9 deals with another type of scripting in SQL-DMO that we consider essential: your server. Meanwhile, in the next chapter, you're going to build a really cool and easy-to-use query tool using nothing but SQL-DMO.

CHAPTER 8

QALite

EARLIER IN THE BOOK we mentioned that we don't think the SQL-DMO library is best at data querying and manipulation. Microsoft has a raft of data-access techniques to perform data querying and manipulation, and in the main you should use these techniques. Users of MSDE don't get any front-end tools to manipulate their databases, so we thought we'd be kind to them and give them something to play with. In this chapter, we develop a simple query tool using SQL-DMO.

This chapter is all about building a very small, very simple replica of SQL Server's Query Analyzer, hence the application's name, "QALite." You could give this application to your users of MSDE who don't necessarily need anything too powerful—just something they can quickly query a SQL Server database with.

NOTE Other QA look-alike tools are available. An interesting one is Query Express, which is available at `http://www.albahari.com/query%20express.html`. It was written using C#, which is really kind of cool. William (Bill) Vaughn offers a tool as well, and you can find it at `http://www.betav.com/Files/Content/code/SampleCode.htm`.

In this chapter, we cover the following topics:

- The code for the QALite application

- The logon form for the QALite application

- The combo box in the QALite application

The QALite Application

As we said in the introduction, we're going to build a "lite" version of one of the tools that Microsoft gives you with SQL Server Personal Edition and above. Query Analyzer is a powerful tool you use to query your SQL Server data sources. It's easily configurable and, with the version supplied with SQL Server 2000, it's intuitive and can be used to quickly navigate the servers. Figure 8-1 shows a typical view of Query Analyzer in SQL Server 2000 with the object browser displayed.

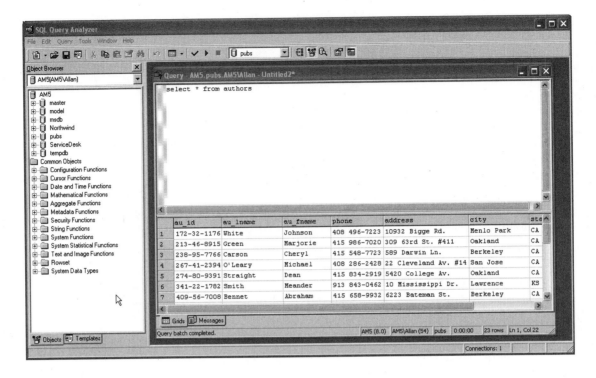

Figure 8-1. Query Analyzer and object browser

Figure 8-2 gives you an idea of the application you're going to build. It isn't as elaborate as Query Analyzer, but it *does* get the job done. It's also something you can legally use for accessing MSDE.

Now that you've had a look at the front screen of the application, let's take a few minutes to look at what happens when you click each button.

- *Connect button:* The Connect button is the largest button on the form, and it does just what its label says: It connects you to one of your SQL Servers so you can start to query it.

- *Hand button:* Clicking the Hand button does the same in the QALite application as pressing Ctrl-F5 or clicking the check mark does in Query Analyzer. It parses the statement you're about to run.

- *Lightning Bolt button:* If you click the button with the lightning bolt graphic on it, you execute the query. You do this by clicking the green play button or by pressing F5 in Query Analyzer.

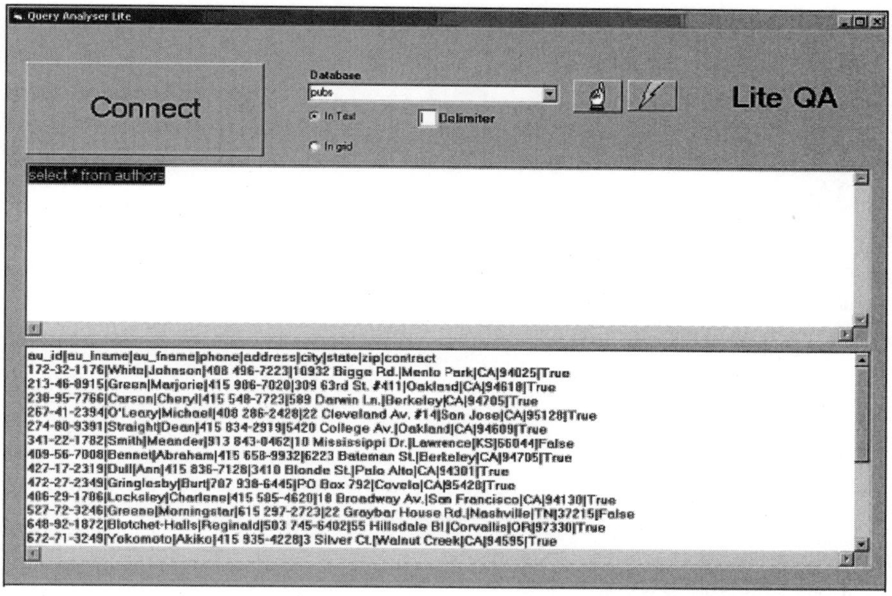

Figure 8-2. QALite

The QALite application's screen is split into two just like Query Analyzer. The top half is where you type in your query and the bottom half is where you get the results. Just above the top pane, you can specify whether your results should be returned to you in a grid or as text. If you want the results to come back as text, then you can also specify what delimiter you would like, with the default being a comma (,). The results in Figure 8-2 were formatted to be returned with a pipe (|) as the delimiter.

The Code

OK, you've looked at the graphical part of the application and you've seen the competition. Now it's time to get underneath the bonnet and see how to use SQL-DMO to build your offering, so hold on and enjoy the ride. Here are the steps you perform.

The first thing you should do is log on. When you click the Connect button, you're greeted by the screen shown in Figure 8-3, which is self-explanatory.

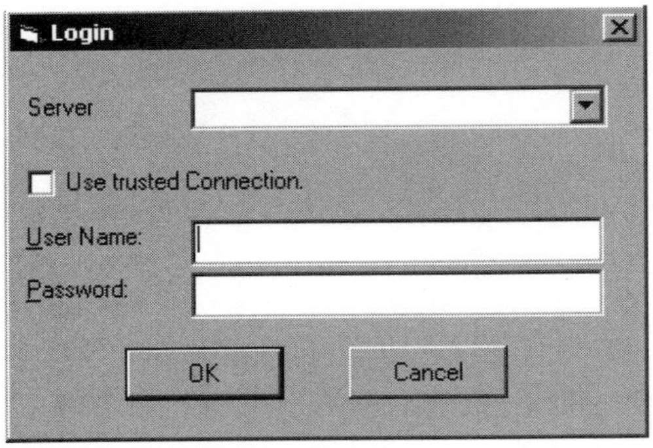

Figure 8-3. Login prompt

The code behind the button is short and to the point. You've seen similar snippets elsewhere, but here's the code we've used in this instance:

```
Private Sub cmdLogon_Click()
    frmLogin.Show 1, Me
    If b_IsConnected = True Then
        MsgBox "Connected to " & glb_Server
        ShowDatabases
    End If
End Sub
```

This code doesn't tell you much other than you call the logon form itself. This is where you do the bulk of the logon code.

The Logon Form

On the form you fill a combo box with a list of your servers:

```
Set oApp = New SQLDMO.Application
Set oGroup = New SQLDMO.ServerGroup

For Each oGroup In oApp.ServerGroups

    For Each oRserver In oGroup.RegisteredServers

        cboServer.AddItem oRserver.Name

    Next oRserver

Next oGroup
```

When you click the OK button, you call the logon procedure:

```
Private Sub Logon(servername, Integrated As Integer)

    On Error GoTo err_handler

    Set oServer = New SQLDMO.SQLServer

    'check whether we require trusted connection or not

    If Integrated = 1 Then

        oServer.LoginSecure = True
        oServer.Connect servername

    Else

        oServer.Connect servername, txtUserName.Text, txtPassword.Text

    End If

    b_IsConnected = True
    glb_Server = oServer.Name
    Me.Visible = False

    Exit Sub

err_handler:
    MsgBox Err.Description, vbCritical, "Incorrect Login"
    Exit Sub

End Sub
```

In the procedure, you set a global variable, glb_Server, to the name of the server that you've connected to. You then close this form and return to the original front screen.

Populating the Combo Box

Once you return to your form, you need to populate the combo box in the middle of the form with a list of all the databases on the server you've just connected to. The following sections describe how you do it.

Showing the Databases

You need to populate the list of databases for the server first because you need something to issue a query against.

```
cboDatabases.Clear

    If glb_Server <> "" Then

        For Each oDatabase In oServer.Databases

            cboDatabases.AddItem oDatabase.Name

        Next oDatabase

    End If
```

Choosing to Execute or Parse a Query

So now you're connected to a server and you have a list of databases to choose from. The next logical step is to type a query into the top half of the form and either execute it or parse it. Here are the steps you need to perform to parse the query.

NOTE   *Parsing* means that you want to see whether the query you're about to send is syntactically correct. It doesn't check to see if the objects that you're querying for actually exist.

You need to check for two things when the user clicks the Parse button:

1. Is there anything to execute?

2. If the user has highlighted text, then you need only parse that particular code. If the user hasn't highlighted anything, then you pass the whole window.

The next code section tests to see what code the user wants to execute:

```
If txtQuery.Text = "" Then
```

```
        txtResults.Text = "Command Completed Successfully - No Query Offered"

    ElseIf txtQuery.SelLength > 0 Then

        ExecuteQuery cboDatabases.Text, txtQuery.SelText, 1, 1

    Else

        ExecuteQuery cboDatabases.Text, txtQuery.Text, 1, 1

    End If
```

You pass the relevant parameters to a subroutine, which handles not only parsing but also executing the query.

Running the Query

If the user doesn't enter a query, then you want to return a polite message to him or her indicating that you've done what you were asked but nothing came back for the user as a result of it.

```
    If txtQuery.Text = "" Then

    txtResults.Visible = True

    txtResults.Text = "Command Completed Successfully - No Query Offered"
```

In the following code, you find out what the user has chosen to execute and how the user wants it returned.

Actively Selected Text in the Query Pane and Output Returned As Text

```
    ElseIf txtQuery.SelLength > 0 And optText.Value = True Then

        ExecuteQuery cboDatabases.Text, txtQuery.SelText, 2, 1, txtDelimiter.Text
```

Actively Selected Text and Return Results in a Grid

```
ElseIf  txtQuery.SelLength > 0 And _
 optText.Value = False Then

ExecuteQuery cboDatabases.Text, txtQuery.SelText, 2, _
2, txtDelimiter.Text
```

Execute the Contents of the Query Pane and Output the Results As Text

```
ElseIf optText.Value = True Then

    ExecuteQuery cboDatabases.Text, txtQuery.Text, 2, _
1, txtDelimiter.Text
```

Execute the Contents of the Query Pane and Return Results in a Grid

```
ElseIf optText.Value = False Then

    ExecuteQuery cboDatabases.Text, txtQuery.Text, 2, 2, txtDelimiter.Text

End If
```

Note how we always call the same routine but the parameters we pass are different. We like to do this because it keeps things nice and simple and we have one place to look if things aren't going as well as they should be.

```
If i_IsGridOrText = 1 Then

    Debug.Print "To Text Output"

Else

    Debug.Print "To Grid Output"

End If

Dim str_OutputText As String
Dim oQryresults As SQLDMO.QueryResults
Dim i As Integer
Dim j As Integer
Dim txt_Results As String

txt_Results = ""
txtResults.Text = ""
```

Remember what we said earlier: If the user doesn't pass in a delimiter, you're going to choose one for him or her.

```
    If str_delimiter = "" Then

        str_delimiter = ","

    End If

    On Error GoTo err_handler

    Select Case EXECType
```

This is where you need to translate the parameters passed into your routines into something meaningful.

You need to see what kind of execution you'll be performing:

```
    Case 1

        msf_grid.Visible = False
        txtResults.Visible = True
```

The following code only parses the code, and the thing that makes it do this is the final parameter SQLDMOExec_ParseOnly. Here's the method without anything filled in:

```
object.ExecuteImmediate( Command , [ ExecutionType ] , [ Length ] )
```

The object it applies to is either the SQLServer object or the Database object. The command is, as its name suggests, the command you want to execute or parse:

```
 oServer.Databases(DatabaseName).ExecuteImmediate Query,  _ SQLDMOExec_ParseOnly
txtResults.Text = "Parse of query Completed successfully"
```

The following piece of code will actually execute the query you pass. The method we use is slightly different, though, and requires a little explanation.

```
object.ExecuteWithResultsAndMessages( Command , Length , Messages )
as QueryResults
```

In addition to this method applying to the Database and SQLServer objects, it applies to the RemoteServer and LinkedServer objects. The command parameter is exactly what you would expect, but here you see a new parameter: messages. The documentation says that this parameter returns any informational messages to you. In our experience, it's a pretty hit and miss affair. Try it and see what mileage you get from it.

```
        Case 2

Set oQryresults =  oServer.Databases(DatabaseName). _
ExecuteWithResultsAndMessages(Query,
Len(Query), str_OutputText)
```

Regardless of selection, if the rows returned are 0, then you return the results as text:

```
    If oQryresults.Rows = 0 Then

        txtResults.Text = "No Row(s) affected"

    Else


        If i_IsGridOrText = 1 Then 'Text

            msf_grid.Visible = False
            txtResults.Visible = True
```

You want to output column names, so you need to loop through them and read them one by one:

```
  For j = 1 To oQryresults.Columns

      txt_Results = txt_Results &
oQryresults.ColumnName(j) & str_delimiter

            Next j

            txt_Results = Left(txt_Results, Len(txt_Results) - 1) & vbCrLf
```

After you have the column headers, you're going to need the data:

```
        For i = 1 To oQryresults.Rows

            For j = 1 To oQryresults.Columns

    txt_Results = txt_Results &
oQryresults.GetColumnString(i, j) &
str_delimiter

    Next j
```

```
        txt_Results = _
Left(txt_Results, Len(txt_Results) - 1) & vbCrLf

                Next i

                txtResults.Text = txt_Results

        Else
```

Now you need to be able to do the same thing as when you showed the results as text, except you output the results to a grid:

```
                txtResults.Visible = False

                msf_grid.Visible = True

                msf_grid.Rows = 0
                msf_grid.Cols = oQryresults.Columns
                msf_grid.FixedCols = 0
```

In the first run-through, you want the column names:

```
For j = 1 To oQryresults.Columns

    txt_Results = txt_Results &
oQryresults.ColumnName(j) & vbTab
```

Now you'll check the column widths and resize them. We've defined a constant that does a basic conversion to try and resize the columns of the grid. In this case, we chose the nominal value of 110:

```
If msf_grid.ColWidth(j - 1) < _
(Len(oQryresults.ColumnName(j)) * TWIPS_PER_CHAR) Then

        msf_grid.ColWidth(j - 1) = _
Len(oQryresults.ColumnName(j)) * TWIPS_PER_CHAR

                End If

        Next j

        msf_grid.AddItem txt_Results

        txt_Results = ""
```

Now you want the data:

```
For i = 1 To oQryresults.Rows

    For j = 1 To oQryresults.Columns

        txt_Results = txt_Results & _
oQryresults.GetColumnString(i, j) & vbTab
```

Finally, you check the column widths and resize them:

```
If msf_grid.ColWidth(j - 1) < _ (Len(oQryresults.GetColumnString(i, j)) * _
TWIPS_PER_CHAR) Then

msf_grid.ColWidth(j - 1) = Len(oQryresults.GetColumnString(i, j)) * TWIPS_PER_CHAR

            End If

        Next j

        msf_grid.AddItem txt_Results

        txt_Results = ""

    Next i

            End If

        End If

End Select

If str_OutputText <> "" Then

    txtResults.Text = txtResults.Text & vbCrLf & str_OutputText

End If
```

Cool Trick in Query Analyzer

You can instantiate Query Analyzer by using the command line. No groaning, please—there's a reason we bring this up. If you go to a command prompt and type in **isqlw /?**, you get a list of the possible options available to you. Most are available in both SQL Server 7.0 and SQL Server 2000 but others aren't. One of those options that's only available in version 2000 is –C.

You know when you're working in Query Analyzer and you change your fonts to your liking and everything is fine, but when you close down Query Analyzer and start it again it reverts to the old settings? Well, this trick puts an end to all that nonsense. If you head over to Tools ? Options, you'll notice on the General tab a Load button and a Save button. After you've made your changes to fonts and s o forth, you can click Save and save the configuration—yes, that's the –C we mentioned. When you want to reuse that setup again (say, for a presentation), you can create a command line shortcut on your desktop with the options already entered:

```
Isqlw.exe –Cf:\MyConfigs\Presentation.sqc –SmyServer –E –dNorthwind
```

This command opens Query Analyzer with a trusted connection to MyServer in the database Pubs with the configuration file of Presentation.sqc. Brilliant. We can't claim credit for finding this out, though—thanks go to Tom Moreau and Pinnacle Publishing for allowing us to reprint this trick from the *SQL Server Professional* July 2002 article, "Configuring Query Analyzer" (http://www.pinnaclepublishing.com/sq).

Summary

We hope you've had a bit of fun building this application. You could expand on it by including buttons that do general housekeeping tasks, such as running DBCC checks on your databases, or you could build export routines into it so you can take your results out to a csv file. This application could be the start of something a lot bigger, and hopefully it will. The ExecuteWithResultsAndMessages method is a little tricky, and we see many instances of problems with it on SQL Server newsgroups. We would be interested in hearing about your experiences and examples of when you've found it to work and not work. Contact us at info@allisonmitchell.com.

In the final chapter you're going to look at a really useful application called Scripter that scripts out all your database objects.

Using SQL-DMO to Script an Entire Server

IN THE EVENT of a disaster, we prefer to have as many options to recover our data as possible. We may replicate all data off-site in real time using a mirrored storage area network (SAN) (but this can be expensive), using a third-party replication tool (see Table 9-1), or perhaps using log shipping (see Table 9-2). Of course, backups and transaction log dumps are taken frequently and shipped off-site. We also like to include sqldiag.exe in our plan to provide some extra, detailed information about our servers.

Table 9-1. Examples of Third-Party Replication Tools

Tool	Description
DataMirror	Replicates many RDBMS systems, including SQL Server, using block checksum. Block checksum looks at the bytes on the physical disk and monitors them for changes. Any changes at the physical-disk level are replicated to the target machine.
DoubleTake	Similar to DataMirror in that it replicates at the physical-disk, block-checksum level.
Legato RepliStor	Formerly known as Octopus. Also writes at the disk level (i.e., it doesn't replicate data), but it replicates actions made on the disk system.

Table 9-2. Some Log Shipping Resources on the Internet

URL	Description
http://msdn.microsoft.com/library/default.asp?url=/library/en-us/adminsql/ad_1_server_8elj.asp	Microsoft article on log shipping
http://www.sql-server-performance.com/sql_server_log_shipping.asp	Very detailed article on log shipping
http://www.sql-server-performance.com/dt_log_shipping.asp	Covers log shipping with Visual Basic
http://msdn.microsoft.com/library/default.asp?url=/library/en-us/dnsqlmag02/html/LogShippinginSQLServer2000Part2.asp	Covers log shipping in SQL Server 2000

This chapter walks you through a real-world application called Scripter that we developed using Visual Basic 6.0 and use in production on a day-to-day basis.

The Scripter command-line application scripts out an entire server to text files to give you extra comfort if you have to recover a server. As a DBA, you can't afford to make mistakes, especially with your clients' data, and it's nice to have the luxury to choose which method of recovery to use in a disaster.

A few months back, we had a junior DBA download a script from the Internet that dropped all permissions on all objects in the database. After his face had gone red and beads of perspiration appeared on his forehead, we asked him what the problem was. Luckily for him, we managed to undo the problem by simply applying a script generated from Scripter the night before. We managed to apply the correct permissions to all tables, views, and stored procedures in about 2 minutes flat, before the help desk telephone started ringing.

This problem would have been difficult to remedy if we didn't have a script to go from. Of course, most environments should have a test environment that's a replica of production, in which case some of you could recover quite easily. In my experience, very few companies have the budget to afford the luxury of a replica production environment, so most organizations would therefore find it difficult to recover without incurring some downtime and experiencing a potential loss of data.

This chapter covers the following topics:

- Describing what Scripter does

- Describing what Scripter *doesn't* do

- Explaining Scripter's structure

Let's begin with an overview of what Scripter does.

What Scripter Does

Scripter will script out the following data from a server for you:

Logins	Stored procedures
Alerts	Rules
Operators	User-defined functions
Replication	Views
Local DTS packages (not password protected)	Foreign key constraints
Jobs	Check constraints
Backup devices	Indexes
Databases	Permissions
Database roles	Full-text indexes
Database users	Database object permissions
Defaults	System data in native BCP format
Tables	User data in native BCP format (optional)
Triggers	

In this chapter, you're going to examine each area in the preceding list to learn how to harness SQL-DMO in your applications. You can download the full source code for Scripter from the Downloads section of the Apress Web site (http://www.apress.com).

Scripter will detect what version of SQL Server you're using, and it's been tested successfully on versions 7.0 and 2000. It doesn't work on SQL Server 6.5 or earlier, although you could adapt it to work with earlier versions. SQL Server 6.5 supports SQL-DMO within a library called SQL-OLE. As support for SQL Server 6.5 is now very limited and few places still run it, we didn't think there was enough demand to provide support for versions prior to 7.0.

Scripter has also been successfully tested on Microsoft Data Engine (MSDE). MSDE is essentially a limited version of the SQL Server engine. Some features are limited in MSDE, such as limited concurrent connections, no replication capability, a maximum database size of 2GB, and so forth. Check Microsoft's Web site for further information about MSDE.

What Scripter Doesn't Do

Scripter is heavily dependent on SQL-DMO, and as such, it's limited by the SQL-DMO library much like Enterprise Manager is. SQL-DMO can't script out certain areas:

- Analysis Services and online analytical processing (OLAP) cubes

- Microsoft English Query projects

- Repository DTS packages

Scripter's Parameters

Scripter is a command-line application; it has no GUI. We decided not to use a GUI because Scripter will be called from a batch file periodically and run as a SQL Agent job. It accepts the following command-line parameters, which Table 9-3 lists and describes:

```
Scripter.exe /sserver_name /foutput_path [/ulogin /ppassword] [/b] [/v]
[/dnum_log_days]
```

Table 9-3. Scripter Command-Line Parameters

Argument	Function
/sserver_name	The name of the server to script from.
/foutput_path	The path for output files. This path must already exist.
[/ulogin]	Login to use to connect to the server. Leave empty for trusted connection.
[/ppassword]	Password to use to connect to the server. Leave empty for trusted connection.
[/b]	BCPs all user data from all tables in native format. System tables are always BCP'd. Omit this parameter to only BCP system tables.
[/v]	Verbose logging. Adds detailed information to the log file. Every database object is logged but creates a much larger log file. Omit to create a smaller log file with less detailed information.
[/dnum_log_days]	Number of days to keep log files. Log files are written to the application path with the format Scripter_yyyymmdd.log. If a log file from today already exists, the new one is appended to it. If a log file doesn't already exist, then a new one is created. Old log files are automatically deleted. If /d is omitted, then the default (30 days) is applied.

We describe some example command-line ways to use Scripter in the following sections.

Scripter Example 1

In this example, we connect to SERVER1 using trusted (NT) security and script out all database objects to C:\Scripts. We want to BCP out all data and have verbose logging switched on. We want Scripter log files to be deleted after 30 days (the default).

```
Scripter.exe /fc:\Scripts /sSERVER1 /b /v
```

Scripter Example 2

In this example, we want to connect to SERVER2 using standard SQL security with a username of scripter_user and a password of scr1pt3r. We don't want verbose logging and we only want system tables BCP'd out. We want log files to be deleted after 14 days.

```
Scripter.exe /f"H:\Disaster Recovery\Scripts" /sSERVER2 /uscripter_user
/pscr1pt3r /d14
```

Using Scripter in a Batch File

If you want to script out a large group of servers, then you can list them in a batch file one after the other. A sample batch file called script_all_my_servers.bat might appear like this:

```
Start /wait scripter.exe /fC:\Scripts\DR /sSERVER1 /b /d7
Start /wait scripter.exe /fC:\Scripts\DR /sSERVER2 /b /d7 /udbadmin /pyouW1sh
Start /wait scripter.exe /fC:\Scripts\DR /sSERVER3 /d7
Start /wait scripter.exe /fC:\Scripts\DR /sSERVER4 /d7
Start /wait scripter.exe /fC:\Scripts\DR /sSERVER5 /d7
```

We like to use start with the /wait switch because it tells the operating system to wait until the Scripter program has finished executing before going on to the next line. You can find more information on start in the Windows NT/2000 help files. SQL Server Books Online demonstrates the use of start when performing an unattended installation.

Overview of Scripter's Structure

Throughout this chapter, we concentrate on areas of the program concerned with SQL-DMO because that's what interests us. The rest of the Scripter program is fairly well commented, so you should be able to understand what's going on.

NOTE   We'd like to point out at this stage that we're not full-time Visual Basic programmers. We are DBAs working in production and development environments and we write Visual Basic programs to help us be more efficient and to automate routine tasks.

Scripter is one Visual Basic module split into five procedures:

1. *Main:* Where the program starts

2. *GenerateDBScripts:* Where most of the scripting work is done

3. *GenerateDTSPackages:* Where DTS packages are saved to DTS files in the file system

NOTE   Local DTS packages aren't strictly scripted out; rather, they're saved as DTS structured storage files into the file system in a subdirectory called DTS Packages.

4. *HouseKeepLogs:* Procedure to delete old log files

5. *LogScripting:* Procedure to write lines to the error log

Let's take a look at Main to start with.

Main

The Main procedure begins by starting the program, examining which parameters have been passed, and initializing the appropriate variables. It then creates output directories and starts writing a header to the error log. Next, it calls the GenerateDBScripts procedure, followed by the GenerateDTSPackages procedure, followed by HouseKeepLogs. That's it really—you wouldn't expect much else from Main(), would you?

GenerateDBScripts

This is what we're really concerned with and where the action starts. This procedure performs the scripting of all our database objects except for DTS packages, which are handled by a separate procedure.

Setting Constants and Connecting to SQL Server

We first of all set some constants for the SQL-DMO scripting options as defined by the Script method of the various database objects we're going to script out:

```
Const cScriptOptions = SQLDMOScript_Default Or SQLDMOScript_IncludeHeaders Or
SQLDMOScript_OwnerQualify Or SQLDMOScript_Drops Or
SQLDMOScript2_FullTextCat

Const cTableScriptOptions = cScriptOptions Or SQLDMOScript_Indexes Or
SQLDMOScript_Triggers Or SQLDMOScript_DRI_PrimaryKey Or
SQLDMOScript_DRI_UniqueKeys Or SQLDMOScript_Drops

Const cScriptReplicationOptions = SQLDMORepScript_Creation Or
SQLDMORepScript_Default Or SQLDMORepScript_InstallPublisher Or
SQLDMORepScript_InstallReplication Or SQLDMORepScript_PublicationCreation Or
SQLDMORepScript_SubscriptionCreation
```

These options are described in detail in SQL Server Books Online, so there's little point in duplicating that information here. Briefly, we're interested in

- Scripting headers (SQLDMOScript_IncludeHeaders)

- Prefixing object names by their owner (SQLDMOScript_OwnerQualify)

- Prefixing each scripted statement with a drop statement (SQLDMOScript_Drops)

- Scripting full-text catalogs (SQLDMOScript_FullTextCat)

The Script method of the Table object has additional options that we're interested in:

- Indexes (SQLDMOScript_Indexes)

- Triggers (SQLDMOScript_Triggers)

- Primary keys (SQLDMOScript_DRI_Primary_Key)

- Unique keys (SQLDMOScript_DRI_UniqueKeys)

- Drop statements (SQLDMOScript_Drops)

Notice that we haven't included foreign keys here (SQLDMOScript_DRI_ForeignKeys). This is for good reason: When SQL Server scripts out all the tables, if we include SQLDMOScript_DRI_ForeignKeys in the table script options, the output file will have all the foreign keys together with the table creation statements. This isn't a problem in itself, but SQL Server doesn't order the tables hierarchically; it creates the tables in alphabetical order. When disaster strikes and you need to run this script, it would fail because child tables would get created before parent tables. We therefore need to create the foreign key constraints separately and run this script after the table script in the event of a disaster.

Finally, we've created a constant for replication scripting options. We want to script the following:

- Creation of replication objects (SQLDMORepScript_Creation)

- Creation of the distributor (SQLDMORepScript_Default)

- Installation of the publisher (SQLDMORepScript_InstallPublisher)

- Installation of the replication (SQLDMORepScript_InstallReplication)

- Creation of publications (SQLDMORepScript_PublicationCreation)

- Creation of subscriptions (SQLDMORepScript_SubscriptionCreation)

We then declare objects to be used (refer to the source code) and set options for the BulkCopy object for when we BCP out system and/or user tables.

```
Set DMO_BCP = New SQLDMO.BulkCopy
DMO_BCP.DataFileType = SQLDMODataFile_NativeFormat
```

Now that we have our objects defined, we attempt to connect to the SQL Server that was passed in with the /s parameter. We connect to the SQLServer object and the SQLServer2 object so that we can use SQL Server 2000's scripting options (if we're scripting a SQL Server 2000 server).

```
With objServer
    If Trusted = True Then
        .Name = Servername
        .LoginSecure = True
        .Connect Servername
    Else
        .Name = Servername
        .Login = UserName
        .Password = Password
        .Connect Servername
    End If
End With

With objServer2
    If Trusted = True Then
        .Name = Servername
        .LoginSecure = True
        .Connect Servername
    Else
        .Name = Servername
        .Login = UserName
        .Password = Password
        .Connect Servername
    End If
End With
```

We should now have successfully connected to our desired SQL Server. The next section of code creates a FileSystemObject and output folders and files for us. We won't describe this process in detail, as it's all documented in the MSDN library and beyond the scope of this book.

Scripting Logins

We create a file called logins.sql and place it in the root of the server directory that we're scripting out using the FileSystemObject. We then need to loop through the Logins collection of the SQLServer object and script out each login, one by one.

```
strFile = foldServerLogins & "\Logins.sql"
Open strFile For Output As #iFileNumber
i = 0

Print #iFileNumber, strHeader

For Each objLogin In objServer.Logins
    i = i + 1
    strScript = objLogin.Script(ScriptType:=cScriptOptions,
Script2Type:=SQLDMOScript2_LoginSID)
    If VerboseLogging = True Then
        LogScripting "--Scripting " & objLogin.Name
    End If

    Print #iFileNumber, strScript

Next objLogin
LogScripting "-Scripted " & CStr(i) & " logins."
Close #iFileNumber
```

We use the For Each…Next construct to loop through each login. We use the constant cScriptOptions that we defined earlier in the module to set the scripting options. Notice that we also add an extra scripting option, SQLDMOScript2_LoginSID. This option includes security identifiers (SIDs) for each login that's scripted. This can be useful when moving logins between servers, for instance.

Alerts and Operators

We can script out alerts and operators very quickly because the collections have Script methods. We therefore don't need to create a For Each…Next construct; SQL-DMO does this for us.

```
If objServer.JobServer.Status = SQLDMOSvc_Running Then ' check SQLAgent
strScript = objServer.JobServer.Operators.Script(ScriptType:=cScriptOptions)

    strScript2 = objServer.JobServer.Alerts.Script(ScriptType:=cScriptOptions,
Script2Type:=SQLDMOScript2_AgentNotify)
End If
```

Notice that we need to use the JobServer object and this information requires SQL Agent to be running. We use the Operators and Alerts collections of the JobServer object. We supply two additional options when scripting alerts:

SQLDMOScript2_AgentNotify to include any notifications that may be present and SQLDMOScript2_AgentAlertJob in case the alert needs to run a job.

SQL Agent Jobs

Again, this is very simple to do. We just use the Script method of the JobServer.Jobs collection. This will script out all the SQL Agent jobs for us. Note that SQL Agent must be running for this command to work.

```
If objServer.JobServer.Status = SQLDMOSvc_Running Then
    strScript = objServer.JobServer.Jobs.Script(ScriptType:=cScriptOptions)
End If
```

That's it! One line of SQL-DMO code will script out all of our SQL Agent jobs. It can't get much easier than that.

Backup Devices

Backup devices allow you to specify a logical mapping, such as an alias, to a physical medium (usually tape, although many people use backup devices to map to a physical disk location). To script these backup devices out, we need to go through the SQLServer.BackupDevices collection.

```
For Each objBackupDevice In objServer.BackupDevices
        i = i + 1
        If VerboseLogging = True Then
            LogScripting "--Scripting backup device " & CStr(i) & ": " &
objBackupDevice.Name
        End If
        strScript = objBackupDevice.Script(ScriptType:=cScriptOptions)

        Print #iFileNumber, strScript
        DoEvents
    Next objBackupDevice
    Close #iFileNumber
```

Replication

Replication is my favorite part of SQL-DMO. You can script out the entire replication setup with one line of SQL-DMO. Actually, that's not strictly true—you need to specify which replication options you want scripted with another line of code. So, that's two lines of code to script out replication. We specified the replication options earlier on, if you recall. We've reproduced them here for easy reference:

```
Const cScriptReplicationOptions = SQLDMORepScript_Creation Or
SQLDMORepScript_Default Or SQLDMORepScript_InstallPublisher Or
SQLDMORepScript_InstallReplication Or
SQLDMORepScript_PublicationCreation Or
SQLDMORepScript_SubscriptionCreation

strScript = objServer.Replication.Script(ScriptType:=cScriptReplicationOptions)
```

We have a few more lines of code to handle the FileSystemObject, but that's essentially it. Amazed? We certainly were when we started using it in our disaster recovery procedures.

NOTE When the distributor is separate from the publisher, scripting the distributor server won't give you all the information. This is also true of the publisher.

Databases

There are many depedent database objects that must be scripted out when scripting a database. We start by scripting out the database creation statement along with the database options. Then we look at scripting out all the objects within a database such as users, tables, views, stored procedures, and so forth.

We script out the database creation statement by using the Script method of the SQLServer.Database object. We've summarized the code from the full program for brevity:

```
For Each objDatabase In objServer.Databases
strScript = objDatabase.Script(ScriptType:=cScriptOptions,
Script2Type:= SQLDMOScript2_FullTextCat)
' all other database objects are scripted here
Next objDatabase
```

Here we're using the standard scripting options we specified earlier and full-text catalogs. Don't worry if you don't have full text installed—SQL Server will ignore the SQLDMOScript2_FullTextCat option if you don't have full text. This For

Each...Next loop can be quite large, as we need to include all the database objects contained within each database. We go through all of these objects in the sections that follow. Just bear in mind that they're contained within the Database object that's contained within the SQLServer object.

Database Users

When you script users, you have an additional step of checking to see whether the user is a system object or not by using the SystemObject method. This prevents scripting out system users.

```
For Each objUser In objDatabase.Users
        If Not objUser.SystemObject Then
    strScript = objUser.Script(ScriptType:=cScriptOptions)
Next objUser
```

Database Roles

This is more involved. If you only use the Script method of the DatabaseRole object, you will find that SQL-DMO only scripts out the database roles and won't script out role members or role permissions. We believe these pieces of information to be vital in disaster recovery, and we're puzzled as to why these aren't scripted out. We have to do it ourselves by using the EnumDatabaseRoleMember() method of the DatabaseRole object to place the database role members into a QueryResults object. We then iterate through the QueryResults object and build up the T-SQL ourselves for each member using the GetColumnString method of the QueryResults object.

```
For Each objRole In objDatabase.DatabaseRoles
        If Not objRole.IsFixedRole Then
            strScript = objRole.Script(ScriptType:=cScriptOptions)
            Print #iFileNumber, strScript

            Set qryDBRoleMembers = objRole.EnumDatabaseRoleMember()
            For i = 1 To qryDBRoleMembers.Rows
                Print #iFileNumber, "exec sp_addrolemember '" & objRole.Name
& "', '" & Trim(qryDBRoleMembers.GetColumnString(i, 1)) & "'"
            Next I
```

Within the same For Each objRole loop, we then script out the permissions for each database role. We accomplish this by using the ListObjectPermissions method of the DatabaseRole object and placing the results into a SQLObjectList object. This object is similar to a collection but with one important difference: All objects within the container aren't guaranteed to be of the same type. To get around this, you can use the TypeOf property of an object contained within the SQLObjectlist container. Try and use collections whenever they're available and only use the SQLObjectList object when necessary. In our case, the SQLObjectList object stores a collection of Permission objects for the DatabaseRole we're currently looking at. We then simply loop through the SQLObjectList and examine the Permission object for each permission to discover the permissions for each database role. With each iteration, we build up a T-SQL GRANT/DENY command to grant or deny permissions.

```
Set qryDBRoleMembers = objRole.EnumDatabaseRoleMember()
For i = 1 To qryDBRoleMembers.Rows
    Print #iFileNumber, "exec sp_addrolemember '" & objRole.Name &
"', '" & Trim(qryDBRoleMembers.GetColumnString(i, 1)) & "'"
Next i
Set olRolePermissions = objRole.ListObjectPermissions
For Each objPermission In objRole.ListObjectPermissions
    Dim sPermission As String
    If (objPermission.Granted = True) Then
        sPermission = "GRANT "
    Else
        sPermission = "DENY "
    End If
    If (objPermission.PrivilegeType And SQLDMOPriv_Select) = 1 Then
sPermission = sPermission & objPermission.PrivilegeTypeName '& "SELECT"
    If (objPermission.PrivilegeType And SQLDMOPriv_Insert) = 2 Then
sPermission = sPermission & objPermission.PrivilegeTypeName
    If (objPermission.PrivilegeType And SQLDMOPriv_Update) = 4 Then
sPermission = sPermission & objPermission.PrivilegeTypeName
    If (objPermission.PrivilegeType And SQLDMOPriv_Delete) = 8 Then
sPermission = sPermission & objPermission.PrivilegeTypeName
    If (objPermission.PrivilegeType And SQLDMOPriv_Execute) = 16 Then
sPermission = sPermission & objPermission.PrivilegeTypeName
    If (objPermission.PrivilegeType And SQLDMOPriv_References) = 32 Then
sPermission = sPermission & objPermission.PrivilegeTypeName
    If (objPermission.PrivilegeType And SQLDMOPriv_AllObjectPrivs) = 63 Then
sPermission = sPermission & objPermission.PrivilegeTypeName
    If (objPermission.PrivilegeType And SQLDMOPriv_CreateTable) = 128 Then
sPermission = sPermission & objPermission.PrivilegeTypeName
    If (objPermission.PrivilegeType And SQLDMOPriv_CreateDatabase) = 256 Then
sPermission = sPermission & objPermission.PrivilegeTypeName
```

```
      If (objPermission.PrivilegeType And SQLDMOPriv_CreateView) = 512 Then
   sPermission = sPermission & objPermission.PrivilegeTypeName
      If (objPermission.PrivilegeType And SQLDMOPriv_CreateProcedure) = 1024 Then
   sPermission = sPermission & objPermission.PrivilegeTypeName
      If (objPermission.PrivilegeType And SQLDMOPriv_DumpDatabase) = 2048 Then
   sPermission = sPermission & objPermission.PrivilegeTypeName
      If (objPermission.PrivilegeType And SQLDMOPriv_CreateDefault) = 4096 Then
   sPermission = sPermission & objPermission.PrivilegeTypeName
      If (objPermission.PrivilegeType And SQLDMOPriv_DumpTransaction) = 8192 Then
   sPermission = sPermission & objPermission.PrivilegeTypeName
      If (objPermission.PrivilegeType And SQLDMOPriv_CreateRule) = 16384 Then
   sPermission = sPermission & objPermission.PrivilegeTypeName
      If (objPermission.PrivilegeType And SQLDMOPriv_AllDatabasePrivs) = 65408
   Then sPermission = sPermission & objPermission.PrivilegeTypeName

      sPermission = sPermission & " ON " & objPermission.ObjectOwner & "." &
      objPermission.ObjectName & " TO " & objRole.Name
      Print #iFileNumber, sPermission
   Next objPermission


   End If
   Next objRole
```

As you can see, the permission information is stored as a bitmap in the Privilege property of the Permission object. We therefore need to do some bit math to discover the permissions. You should be very familiar with bit arithmetic if you've read the preceding chapters. To find out whether the permission is "granted" or "denied", we need to evaluate the Granted property of the Permission object when we build our T-SQL statement.

Tables

The Table object has a special Script method created for it called the Script (Table) method. This method exposes much more functionality and many more scripting options than the Script method used for all other objects. Take a quick look at SQL Server Books Online now, and in the index type **Script method** and select "Script (Table Object)." This shows you all the table scripting options available to you. There are quite a lot of them, aren't there? We won't look at all of them, as that would be a chapter in itself. You can experiment with these options yourself. We're only concerned with the options defined at the beginning of the chapter. You might find it useful to flip back to the beginning of this chapter to refresh your memory about the scripting options that we're going to use.

```
For Each objTab In objDatabase.Tables
    If objTab.SystemObject = False Then
        strScript = objTab.Script(cTableScriptOptions, , ,
IIf(objServer.FullTextService.IsFullTextInstalled, SQLDMOScript2_FullTextIndex,
SQLDMOScript2_Default))
    End If
```

Notice that we check to see if full-text service is installed by using the IsFullTextInstalled method of the FullTextService object with this line of code:

```
IIf(objServer.FullTextService.IsFullTextInstalled, SQLDMOScript2_FullTextIndex,
SQLDMOScript2_Default)
```

If full-text service is installed, then we script out full-text indexing. If full-text service isn't installed, then we use the default scripting options.

As we're looping through the Tables collection, we check to see if the /b parameter was specified on the command line, and if it was, then we need to BCP out all user tables and all system tables. We achieve this using the BulkCopy object. We also need to check that the table name doesn't begin with "SYSREMOTE," as SYSREMOTE tables are virtual tables owned by Microsoft that aren't caught by the SystemObject property. Normally, the SystemObject property of a database object is sufficient, but we've found that not to be true for tables. To BCP out the data, we set the DataFileType to native (SQLDMODataFile_NativeFormat). There are seven types in all that you can play with. We then set the datafile path using the DataFilePath property and use the ExportData method of the Table object to initiate the BCP operation.

```
    If BCP = True And Left(objTab.Name, 9) <> "SYSREMOTE" Then
        DMO_BCP.DataFilePath = foldDatabase & "\_" & objTab.Name & ".BCP"
        objTab.ExportData DMO_BCP
    End If

    If (BCP = False And objTab.SystemObject = True And Left(objTab.Name, 9)
<> "SYSREMOTE") Then
        DMO_BCP.DataFilePath = foldDatabase & "\_" & objTab.Name & ".BCP"
        If VerboseLogging = True Then
            LogScripting "--BCPing data from " & objTab.Name
        End If
        objTab.ExportData DMO_BCP
    End If

Next objTab
```

Table Permissions

We like to keep our permissions separate from our tables in case we need to run the script on its own as described in the beginning of this chapter.

We script table permissions by looping through the Tables collection and using the Script method of the Table object as we did before, but this time we use different scripting options. We set only one scripting option, SQLDMOScript_ObjectPermissions.

```
For Each objTab In objDatabase.Tables
    If objTab.SystemObject = False Then
        strScript =
objTab.Script(ScriptType:=SQLDMOScript_ObjectPermissions)
    End If
Next objTab
```

We need to make another pass of the Tables collection, this time to script out the foreign key constraints. We do realize that we could script out the tables, permissions, and foreign keys in one scan of the Tables collection, but we've separated them out in the book to try and make the code clearer. The program runs much faster when it's scripted out together in one loop of the Tables collection. Download the program from the Downloads section of the Apress Web site (http://www.apress.com) to view the entire code.

As mentioned earlier in the chapter, we can't include the foreign key option when we script the tables because this creates dependency problems when we try to run the ouput file back into SQL Server. We therefore create a separate foreign keys file and run this in after we've created our tables.

```
For Each objTab In objDatabase.Tables
    If objTab.SystemObject = False Then
        strScript = objTab.Script(ScriptType:=SQLDMOScript_DRI_ForeignKeys)
    End If
Next objTab
```

Triggers

Scripting out triggers is the coolest thing in SQL-DMO. All you do is add the option SQLDMOScript_Triggers, and Hey Presto! Triggers get scripted out with your tables. So, in other words, you don't have to write any additional code to get your triggers scripted out. How easy is *that*?

Views

We script out views in a similar manner to tables in that we script out the views first, and then we script out the permissions. We won't reproduce the code for views here, as it's very similar to the code for tables. Refer to the application source code if you need to view it, or cut and paste it out.

Stored Procedures, Rules, and Defaults

Again, these objects use the same method as tables and views, and we won't repeat the code here. Use the Script method of the StoredProcedure, Rule, and Default objects within the StoredProcedures, Rules, and Defaults collections, respectively. The scripting options remain the same as the ones we used for views.

User-Defined Functions

First of all, we check the version of SQL Server, and if it's greater than 7.0, then we continue. SQL Server 7.0 doesn't support user-defined functions (UDFs), so we need to skip them in this case. We then iterate through the UserDefinedFunctions collection of the Database2 object. Note that you can only access this collection through the Database2 object. We then script out the UDFs using the same method we used with the previous database objects. This brings us to the end of scripting database objects, and we now move on to saving DTS packages out to DTS files.

GenerateDTSPackages

In this section, we walk you through the procedure that "scripts" out local DTS packages.

 CAUTION You may have problems scripting out SQL Server 7.0 Service Pack 2 or earlier DTS packages when you run this program with the SQL Server 2000 version of SQL-DMO (i.e., on a machine with SQL Server 2000 client utilities installed). Microsoft has fixed this in SQL Server 7.0 Service Pack 3 and later.

We can't script DTS packages—we can only save them as structured files that can be loaded back into SQL Server should they get accidentally deleted or become corrupted. In SQL Server 2000, we can't script them into Visual Basic storage files using the Package2 object methods because they're COM objects and saving to a VB bas file is implemented internally of SQL Server and isn't exposed. We only look at scripting them into structured storage files because DTS is a vast subject that could fill a book on its own. Scripting into Visual Basic files is a very similar process to scripting storage files, and you could probably work it out on your own. If you have problems, we're more than happy to help—just visit our help forum at www.allisonmitchell.com.

 NOTE   You can't script out SQL Server 2000 DTS packages using SQL-DMO version 7.0. You must have SQL-DMO version 8.0 (2000) on your client machine. It's rare that SQL-DMO gets installed on its own, so making sure you have the 2000 client tools is sufficient.

Let's dive into the code now. First, we create a subdirectory to save the packages into. We then create an ADO Connection object and an ADO RecordSet object. This is the first time we've been forced to use ADO; we haven't found any other way of querying the server for a list of packages.

SQL-DMO doesn't have a Packages or Packages2 collection. If you find a way to script the packages using SQL-DMO, please let us know.

```
Set cnSQL = New ADODB.Connection
Set rsPackages = New ADODB.Recordset
```

Setting ADO Connection Object Properties

We now need to set the properties of our ADO Connection object:

```
With cnSQL
    .Provider = "sqloledb"
    .Properties("Data Source").Value = strServerName
    .Properties("Initial Catalog").Value = "msdb"
    If Trusted = True Then
        .Properties("Integrated Security").Value = "SSPI"
    Else
        .Properties("User ID").Value = strUserName
        .Properties("Password").Value = strPassword
    End If
    .Open
End With
```

We set the Provider property to "sqloledb," and then delve into the Properties collection to set properties specific to our provider. Here, we've chosen to use sqloledb, and we therefore set the "Data Source" to be the server that we're interested in and the "Initial Catalog" (database) to msdb. A check is made to see what connection type we want to make. If we're using trusted security, then we set the "Integrated Security" property to "SSPI." If we're using standard security, then we set the "User ID" and "Password" properties.

We establish a connection with the database by opening the connection using the Open method of the Connection object. Once our connection is established, we submit a query to the database to get a list of DTS packages. We need to do something that we're not fond of: query the system tables.

```
strSQLquery = "SELECT DISTINCT id,name FROM sysdtspackages"
rsPackages.Open strSQLquery, cnSQL
```

If you're wondering what happened to SQL-DMO, fear not, we'll employ it again shortly. We loop through our recordset and use the LoadFromSQLServer method of the Package object to extract the package information from SQL Server. At this stage we should point out that password-protected DTS packages can't be saved from SQL Server using SQL-DMO. We therefore set up an error handler to trap error –2147220454, which means that the package is password protected. If this happens, we log the event to the Scripter log and move on to the next package.

```
ErrorHandler:   If Err.Number = -2147220454 Then ' password protected package
        LogScripting "** Package '" & rsPackages.Fields("name") & "' is password
protected and cannot be scripted out."
    Else
        LogScripting "** Error: " & Err.Number & ", Description: " &
Err.Description
    End If
    ErrEncountered = 1
    Resume Next
```

Once we've extracted the information from SQL Server into memory, we need to dump it into a file. We do this using the SaveToStorageFile method of the Package object. Next, we need to uninitialize the package using the Uninitialize method; this clears all state information, which allows the package object to be reused for the next package in our Packages recordset.

```
While Not rsPackages.EOF

    Set oPackage = New DTS.Package
    If Trusted = True Then
        oPackage.LoadFromSQLServer strServerName, "", "",
DTSSQLStgFlag_UseTrustedConnection, "", rsPackages.Fields("id")
    Else
        oPackage.LoadFromSQLServer strServerName, strUserName, strPassword,
DTSSQLStgFlag_Default, "", rsPackages.Fields("id")
    End If
    If ErrEncountered = 0 Then ' we successfully loaded the DTS package

        DoEvents
        strPackageFileName = strDumpLocation & "\" & strServerName &
"\DTS Packages\" & oPackage.Name & ".dts"
        ' delete the existing package before saving new one
        If FSO.FileExists(strPackageFileName) Then
            FSO.DeleteFile (strPackageFileName)
        End If

        oPackage.SaveToStorageFile strPackageFileName
        DoEvents
        If VerboseLogging = True Then
            LogScripting "--Scripting '" & oPackage.Name & "'"
        End If
        oPackage.UnInitialize
        DoEvents
    End If
    ErrEncountered = 0
    rsPackages.MoveNext
Wend
```

Finally, we close the recordset and the ADO connection and exit the procedure.

```
    rsPackages.Close
    Set rsPackages = Nothing
    cnSQL.Close
    Set cnSQL = Nothing
Exit Sub
```

HouseKeepLogs

This procedure doesn't employ SQL-DMO and it's used to delete old log files so that we don't run out of space. We simply use the FileSystemObject and check for files older than our /d parameter. If any exist, we delete them.

LogScripting

You may have noticed us calling a LogScripting procedure throughout the code. All this does is write a line to a text file, optionally adding a date, for use in debugging and reporting. We can tell how many database objects we've scripted out, along with any errors that occurred along the way. There isn't any SQL-DMO code in this procedure, so we won't show you any code here. You can, however, have a look at the source code.

Summary

We've been able to script out our server very easily using SQL-DMO, and we can place this program into a batch file so that all of the servers in our enterprise can be scripted out as part of our disaster recovery procedures. We've been able to achieve things in SQL-DMO that we couldn't achieve using T-SQL or Enterprise Manager in a supported way. There are known workarounds for most SQL Server problems, but many aren't supported by Microsoft if you happen to get in trouble and need to raise a support call.

SQL-DMO Object Library Quick Reference

THIS IS NOT INTENDED to be a complete reference—rather, it includes the most common objects and their properties. Methods and events are listed along with their usage syntaxes. At the end of the appendix is the SQL-DMO object library diagram

SQLServers Collection

The SQLServers collection contains SQLServer objects created by the SQL-DMO application.

.Count: number of SQL Servers in the collection

SQLServer Object

This SQLServer object exposes the attributes of an instance of SQL Server.

.Hostname: network name of the client; object.**HostName** [= value]

.Login: username for connecting to a SQL Server; object.**Login** [= value]

.Password: password for the login used above; object.**Password** [= value]

.LoginSecure: authentication mode (true = NT, false = standard) when connecting using the Connect method; object.**LoginSecure** [= value]

.Status: status of the SQL Server service (Running, stopped, and so on); object.**Status**

.Truename: returns the output of select @@servername; object.**TrueName**

.VersionString: returns the output of select @@version; object.**VersionString**

.AddStartParameter: adds a startup parameter; object.**AddStartParameter** (str)

.AttachDB: attaches a database and makes it visible to SQL Server; object.**AttachDB** (DBName, DataFiles) as String

.BeginTransaction: begins a unit of work (transaction); object.**BeginTransaction** ([TransactionName])

.CommitTransaction: commits a unit of work (transaction); object.**CommitTransaction** ([TransactionName])

.Connect: connects to a SQL Server; object.**Connect** ([ServerName], [Login], [Password])

.DetachDB: detaches a database and makes it invisible to SQL Server; object.**DetachDB** (DBName, [DBCheck]) as String

.Disconnect: disconnects from a SQL Server; object.**DisConnect** ( )

.ExecuteImmediate: submits a T-SQL batch using SQL-DMO using the current connection; object.**ExecuteImmediate** (Command, [ExecutionType], [Length])

.RollbackTransaction: discards changes in a unit of work corresponding to .BeginTransaction; object.**RollbackTransaction** ([SavePoint])

SQLServer2 Object

The SQLServer2 object extends the functionality of the SQLServer object for SQL Server 2000. Inherits all properties and methods from the SQLServer object.

.Collation: returns the server collation; object.**Collation**

.InstanceName: returns the name of a SQL Server instance; object.**InstanceName**

.ServerLoginMode: returns the default login mode for the server; object.**ServerLoginMode** (ServerName) as SQLDMO_SECURITY_TYPE

Configuration Object

The Configuration object represents SQL Server engine-configurable parameters and values.

.ShowAdvancedOptions: shows advanced configuration options; object.**ShowAdvancedOptions** [= value]

.ReconfigureWithOverride: applies changes to configuration options; object.**ReconfigureWithOverride** ( )

ConfigValue Object

The ConfigValue object represents the attributes of a single configuration option.

.CurrentValue: use this to set the value of a configuration option; object.**CurrentValue** [= value]

.DynamicReconfigure: indicates whether changes take effect without restarting the service; object.**DynamicReconfigure**

.Name: character string identifying the Configuration; object.**Name** [= value]

.RunningValue: returns the current value of a configuration; object.**RunningValue**

IntegratedSecurity Object

The IntegratedSecurity object exposes configurable parameters that affect all logins to SQL Server regardless of the login authentication type.

.AuditLevel: exposes SQL Server Authentication logging behavior; object.**AuditLevel** [= value]

.SecurityMode: sets/reads the authentication mode; object.**SecurityMode** [= value]

Databases Collection

The Databases collection contains Database objects that expose databases.

.Count: number of databases in the collection

Database Object

The Database object represents properties of a single SQL Server database.

.Name: name of the database; object.**Name** [= value]

.IsFullTextEnabled: true when full-text is enabled for the database; object.**IsFullTextEnabled**

.IndexSpaceUsage: returns the number of kilobytes assigned to index storage within all data files; object.**IndexSpaceUsage**

.Owner: exposes the owner of the database; object.**Owner**

.Size: total size (MB); object.**Size** [= value]

.SpaceAvailableInMB: returns the amount of disk resource (MB) allocated and unused; object.**SpaceAvailableInMB**

.Status: shows current state of the DB; object.**Status**

.SystemObject: returns true for database objects whose implementation is owned by Microsoft; object.**SystemObject**

.CheckTables: tests the integrity of database pages for all tables and indexes; object.**CheckTables** ([RepairType]) as String

.EnableFullTextCatalogs: enables Microsoft Search full-text indexing on the referenced database; object.**EnableFullTextCatalogs** ( )

.ListDatabasePermissions: returns a **SQLObjectList** object that enumerates database maintenance privilege for one or more SQL Server security accounts; object.**ListDatabasePermissions** ([Privilege]) as SQLObjectList

.ListObjectPermissions: returns a **SQLObjectList** object that enumerates object access privilege for one or more SQL Server security accounts; object.**ListObjectPermissions** ([Privilege]) as SQLObjectList

.Script: generates a T-SQL command batch; object.**Script** ([ScriptType] [,ScriptFilePath] [,Script2Type]) as String

.Shrink: attempts to reduce the size of all operating system files maintaining the referenced database; object.**Shrink** (NewSize, Truncate)

.Transfer: copies database schema and/or data from one database to another; object.**Transfer** (Transfer)

Database2 Object

The Database2 object extends the functionality of the Database object. Inherits all properties and methods from the Database object.

.Collation: default collation for the current database; object.**Collation**

.CurrentCompatibility: specifies the current database compatibility level; object.**CurrentCompatibility** [= value]

DatabaseRoles Collection

The DatabaseRoles collection contains DatabaseRole objects that expose security privilege roles defined within a database.

.Count: number of DatabaseRoles in the collection

DatabaseRole Object

The DatabaseRole object represents the properties of a single database role.

.AppRole: exposes the security context for a database role; object.**AppRole** [= value]

.AddMember: assigns database or server role membership to the specified user, database role, or login; object.**AddMember** (User)

.DropMember: removes the specified user, database role, or login from the role referenced; object.**DropMember** (User)

.EnumDatabaseRoleMember: a **QueryResults** object that enumerates the database users granted role membership; object.**EnumDatabaseRoleMember** ( ) as QueryResults

.IsFixedRole: returns true when the database role referenced is system-defined; object.**IsFixedRole** ()

DBOption Object

The DBOption object represents the settings for database options for a specific SQL Server database. For example, **.ReadOnly**, **.AutoUpdateStat**, and so on.

FileGroups Collection

The FileGroups collection contains FileGroup objects that reference the file groups of a database.

FileGroup Object

The FileGroup object exposes the attributes of a file group.

.Name: character string identifying a FileGroup; object.**Name** [= value]

.Size: exposes the total size, in megabytes, of a FileGroup; object.**Size** [= value]

.EnumFiles: returns a QueryResults object that enumerates the operating system files used to implement a database; object.**EnumFiles** ( ) as QueryResults

DBFiles Collection

The DBFiles collection contains DBFile objects that expose operating system files used by SQL Server for table and index data storage.

.Count: number of DBFiles in the collection; object.**Count**

DBFile Object

The DBFile object represents the properties of an operating system file used by SQL Server for table and index data storage.

.FileGrowth: specified the growth increment of the data file; object.**FileGrowth** [= value]

.FileGrowthType: specifies the method of incremental allocation applied (MB or %); object.**FileGrowthType** [= value]

.MaximumSize: specifies an upper limit for the size of a data file; object.**MaximumSize** [= value]

.PhysicalName: specifies the path and file name of the data file; object.**PhysicalName** [= value]

.Size: exposes the total size, in megabytes, of the data file; object.**Size** [= value]

FullTextService Object

The FullTextService object exposes attributes of the Microsoft Search full-text indexing service.

.IsFullTextInstalled: returns true if full-text service is installed; object.**IsFullTextInstalled**

FullTextCatalogs Collection

The FullTextCatalogs collection contains FullTextCatalog objects that reference Microsoft Search data organized in full-text catalogs.

> .Count: number of FullTextCatalogs in the collection; object.**Count**

FullTextCatalog Object

The FullTextCatalog object exposes the properties of a single Microsoft Search data store.

> .PopulateStatus: returns the population state of a full-text catalog; object.**PopulateStatus**
>
> .UniqueKeyCount: returns an approximate number of words uniquely addressable in a catalog; object.**UniqueKeyCount**
>
> .Rebuild: re-creates the full-text catalog; object.**Rebuild** ( )
>
> .Start: launches full-text catalog population by building the full-text index; object.**Start** (StartType)
>
> .Stop: halts building the full-text catalog; object.**Stop** ( )

StoredProcedures Collection

The StoredProcedures collection contains StoredProcedure objects that reference stored procedures of a database.

StoredProcedure Object

.Name: character string identifying stored procedure; object.**Name** [= value]

.Owner: exposes the owner of the stored procedure; object.**Owner** [= value]

.Startup: is true when the stored procedure is executed automatically when the SQL Server services starts; object.**Startup** [= value]

.SystemObject: returns true for stored procedures owned by Microsoft; object.**SystemObject**

.Text: the text of the stored procedure; object.**Text** [= value]

.EnumParameters: returns a **QueryResults** object that enumerates the parameters of a stored procedure: object.**EnumParameters( )** as **QueryResults**

.Grant: assigns a stored procedure permission or a list of permissions to users or roles; object.**Grant** (Privilege, GranteeNames, [GrantGrant], [AsRole])

SystemDataType Object

The SystemDataType object exposes the attributes of a SQL Server base data type.

Tables Collection

The Tables collection contains Table objects that reference system and user-defined tables in a database.

.Count: number of tables in a database; object.**Count**

Table Object

The Table object exposes the attributes of a single table.

.Attributes: exposes various properties of a referenced table; object.**Attributes**

.DataSpaceUsed: reports the storage space, in kilobytes, used by a table; object.**DataSpaceUsed**

.FakeSystemTable: returns true when the Table object references a system-defined table that is not real, such as sysprocesses, syslocks; object.**FakeSystemTable**

.FullTextIndex: returns true when the table participates in full-text queries; object.**FullTextIndex** [= value]

.FullTextCatalogName: returns the name of the full-text catalog that this table participates in; object.**FullTextCatalogName** [= value]

.HasClusteredIndex: returns true if the table has a clustered index; object.**HasClusteredIndex**

.HasIndex: returns true if the table has at least one clustered or non-clustered index; object.**HasIndex**

.IndexSpaceUsed: reports the storage space, in kilobytes, used by an index; object.**IndexSpaceUsed**

.Name: name of the table; object.**Name** [= value]

.Owner: owner of the table; object.**Owner** [= value]

.CheckTable: tests the integrity of database pages that the table is defined on; object.**CheckTable** ( ) as String

.CheckIdentityValues: equivalent to DBCC CHECKIDENT; object.**CheckIdentityValues** ( )

.ExportData: uses the indicated BulkCopy object to copy data from database to the data file specified by the BulkCopy object; object.**ExportData** (BulkCopy) as Long

.ImportData: implements the bulk insert of data specified by the controlling BulkCopy object; object.**ImportData** (BulkCopy) as Long

.InsertColumn: adds a column to the Columns collection of a Table object; object.**InsertColumn** (Column , InsertBeforeColumn)

.RebuildIndexes: re-creates all indexes on the table; object.**RebuildIndexes** ([IndexType], [FillFactor])

.TruncateData: equivalent to T-SQL, TRUNCATE TABLE; object.**TruncateData** ( )

.UpdateStatistics: forces data distribution statistics update on the table; object.**UpdateStatistics** ()

Table2 Object

The Table2 object extends the functionality of the Table object. Inherits all properties and methods of the Table object.

.FullTextPopulateStatus: returns the population state of a full-text table; object.**FullTextPopulateStatus**

.TableFullTextChangeTrackingOn: specifies whether to enable the tracking and propagation of changes to a full-text table; object.**TableFullTextChangeTrackingOn** [= value]

.TableFullTextUpdateIndexOn: specifies whether to start or stop propagating tracked changes to the Microsoft Search service automatically; object.**TableFulltextUpdateIndexOn** [= value]

Columns Collection

The Columns collection contains Column objects that expose the columns of a table.

Column Object

The Column object represents the properties of a single column in a table.

.AllowNulls: exposes ability of the datatype to allow nulls; object.**AllowNulls** [= value]

.DataType: datatype name for the column; object.**Datatype** [= value]

.Default: identifies a default bound to the referenced column; object.**Default** [= value]

.FullTextIndex: identifies whether the referenced column participates in full-text queries; object.**FullTextIndex** [= value]

.Identity: indicates whether this column is an identity property; object.**Identity** [= value]

.IdentityIncrement: the stepping increment; object.**IdentityIncrement** [= value]

.IdentitySeed: exposes the initial value for an identity column; object.**IdentitySeed** [= value]

.InPrimaryKey: exposes primary key participation; object.**InPrimaryKey**

.IsComputed: when true, the column is computed; object.**IsComputed** [= value]

.Length: specifies the maximum number of characters or bytes accepted by the referenced column; object.**Length** [= value]

.Name: character string identifying the column; object.**Name** [= value]

.ListKeys: returns a SQLObjectList object that enumerates the PRIMARY KEY and FOREIGN KEY constraints in which a column participates; object.**ListKeys** ( ) as SQLObjectList

Column2 Object

Extends the functionality of the Column object. Inherits all properties and methods of the Column object.

.SetFullTextIndexWithOptions: creates or removes a full-text index on the current column; object.**SetFullTextIndexWithOptions** (Index, [LanguageID], [ColumnType])

TransactionLog Object

The TransactionLog object exposes the attributes of the transaction log of a database.

.LastBackup: the most recent date and time that a transaction log backup was performed; object.**LastBackup**

.SpaceAvailableinMb: returns amount of disk space allocated and unused in log files for the transaction log; object.**SpaceAvailableInMB**

.Truncate: archive-marks transaction log records; object.**Truncate** ( )

LogFile Object

Exposes the attributes of an operating system file used to maintain transaction log records for a database. See "DBFile Object" for properties and methods.

Users Collection

The Users collection contains User objects that reference database users.

User Object

Exposes the attributes of a single database user.

.HasDBAccess: returns true if a user has access to the database; object.**HasDBAccess**

.Login: associates the user with a login; object.**Login** [= value]

.Role: identifies the initial security role assigned to the user; object.**Role** [= value]

.Name: character string identifying the user name; object.**Name** [= value]

.ListOwnedObjects: returns a **SQLObjectList** object that enumerates the user-defined objects owned by the user; object.**ListOwnedObjects** ([ObjectType], [SortBy]) as SQLObjectList

.IsMember: returns true when the user is a member of the role identified in the Role argument; object.**IsMember** (Role)

Views Collection

The Views collection contains View objects that reference the view tables defined in a database.

View Object

The View object exposes the attributes of a view.

.Name: character string identifying the name of the view; object.**Name** [= value]

.ListColumns: returns a SQLObjectList object that enumerates the columns view; object.**ListColumns** ( ) as SQLObjectList

.ExportData: uses the indicated BulkCopy object to copy data from a view to the data file specified by the BulkCopy object; object.**ExportData** (BulkCopy) as Long

View2 Object

The View2 object extends the functionality of the View object. Inherits all properties and methods of the View object.

Triggers Collection

The Triggers collection contains Trigger objects that reference the triggers defined on a table or view.

Trigger Object

The Trigger object exposes the attributes of a single trigger.

.Text: exposes the Transact-SQL text defining the trigger; object.**Text** [= value]

.Name: character string identifying the name of the trigger; object.**Name** [= value]

.Type: exposes whether the trigger is Insert, Update, Delete, All, and so on; object.**Type**

Trigger2 Object

The Trigger2 object extends the functionality of the Trigger object.

.AfterTrigger: indicates whether a trigger is an AFTER trigger; object.**AfterTrigger**

.InsteadOfTrigger: indicates whether a trigger is an INSTEAD OF trigger; object.**InsteadOfTrigger**

.Encrypted: indicates whether the referenced stored procedure was created with encryption; object.**Encrypted**

JobServer Object

The JobServer object exposes attributes associated with SQL Server Agent.

.Autostart: does SQLAgent auto start with an OS start; object.**AutoStart** [= value]

.Status: status of the SQLAgent service (Running, stopped, and so on); object.**Status**

.Type: master (MSX) or target (TSX) server; object.**Type**

.EnumJobHistory: enumerates history of all jobs; object.**EnumJobHistory** ([JobHistoryFilter]) as QueryResults

.EnumJobs: enumerates all jobs; object.**EnumJobs** ([JobFilter]) as QueryResults

.Start: starts SQLAgent service; object.**Start** ( )

.Stop: stops SQLAgent service; object.**Stop** ( )

Alerts Collection

The Alerts collection contains Alert objects that reference SQL Server Agent alerts.

.Script: scripts out all alerts; object.**Script** ([ScriptType], [ScriptFilePath] [,Script2Type]) as String

JobFilter Object

The JobFilter object is used to constrain the output of the EnumJobs method of the JobServer object.

Jobs Collection

The Jobs collection contains Job objects that reference all SQL Server Agent jobs

.Script: scripts all SQLAgent jobs into a T-SQL batch file; object.**Script** ([ScriptType], [ScriptFilePath], [Script2Type]) as String

Job Object

The Job object exposes the attributes of a single SQL Server Agent job.

.CurrentRunStatus: returns the executing state of a SQL Server Agent job; object.**CurrentRunStatus**

.CurrentRunStep: reports the currently executing step of a SQL Server Agent job; object.**CurrentRunStep**

.EmailLevel: specifies the job completion status that causes an e-mail notification to a specified operator; object.**EmailLevel** [= value]

.Enabled: represents the enabled/disabled state of a job; object.**Enabled** [= value]

.HasSchedule: reports whether a schedule exists for a SQL Server Agent job; object.**HasSchedule**

.LastRunDate: reports the last run date that the job was executed; object.**LastRunDate**

.LastRunOutcome: returns the most recent execution completion status of the job; object.**LastRunOutcome**

.OperatorToEmail: specifies the SQL Server Agent operator receiving e-mail notification of job completion; object.**OperatorToEmail** [= value]

.Owner: exposes the owner of the job; object.**Owner** [= value]

.EnumHistory: returns a QueryResults object that enumerates the execution history of the job; object.**EnumHistory** ([JobHistoryFilter]) as QueryResults

.Invoke: executes the SQL Agent job from step 1; object.**Invoke** ()

.Start: executes the SQL Agent job starting at a specified job step; object.**Start** ([Val])

.Stop: stops the SQL Agent job; object.**Stop** ( )

JobSchedules Collection

The JobSchedules collection contains JobSchedule objects, each referencing one execution schedule for a SQL Server Agent job.

JobSchedule Object

The JobSchedule object exposes the attributes of a single SQL Server Agent executable job schedule.

> .Enabled: returns true if enabled; object.**Enabled** [= value]

Schedule Object

The Schedule object exposes the attributes of a timetable for automated SQL Server tasks.

> .ActiveEndDate: indicates the last effective date for a schedule; object.**ActiveEndDate** [= value]
>
> .ActiveStartDate: indicates the first effective date for a schedule; object.**ActiveStartDate** [= value]
>
> .FrequencyInterval: defines the most significant portion of a schedule for daily, weekly, or monthly schedules; object.**FrequencyInterval** [= value]
>
> .FrequencyType: specifies the unit for the most significant portion of a **Schedule** object; object.**FrequencyType** [= value]

JobSteps Collection

The JobSteps collection contains JobStep objects defining the administrative tasks automated by a SQL Server Agent job.

JobStep Object

The JobStep object exposes the attributes of a single SQL Server Agent executable job step.

> .Command: specifies the task of a job step; object.**Command** [= value]
>
> .Name: name of the job step; object.**Name** [= value]
>
> .OnFailAction: controls the behavior of a job when the referenced step fails execution; object.**OnFailAction** [= value]
>
> .OnSuccessAction: controls the behavior of a job when the referenced step succeeds; object.**OnSuccessAction** [= value]
>
> .SubSystem: specifies the execution subsystem used to interpret job step task-defining text, such as TSQL, CmdExec; object.**SubSystem** [= value]

Operators Collection

The Operators collection contains Operator objects referencing SQL Server Agent operators.

Operator Object

The Operator object represents a single SQL Server operator. SQL Server operators receive alert and job status notification in response to events generated by the server.

.EmailAddress: specifies an operator's e-mail address; object.**EmailAddress** [= value]

.Enabled: represents the enabled/disabled state of an operator; object.**Enabled** [= value]

.PagerAddress: specifies an e-mail address used to route operator notification; object.**PagerAddress** [= value]

.PagerDays: specifies the days of the week on which SQL Agent attempts to notify the referenced operator by page; object.**PagerDays** [= value]

Logins Collection

The Logins collection contains Login objects that reference login records that form one part of Microsoft SQL Server security.

Login Object

The Login object exposes the attributes of a single SQL Server Authentication record.

.Database: identifies the default database; object.**Database** [= value]

.DenyNTLogin: when true, any Windows NT authenticated connection attempt that specifies the user or group name, fails authentication; object.**DenyNTLogin** [= value]

.Name: character string identifying the login name; object.**Name** [= value]

.SystemObject: returns true for objects whose implementation is owned by Microsoft, such as 'sa'; object.**SystemObject**

.Type: exposes whether the login is standard, NT User or NT Group; object.**Type** [= value]

.ListMembers: returns a **NameList** object that enumerates the server roles in which a login has membership; object.**ListMembers** ( ) as NameList

Registry Object

The Registry object exposes the Windows registry settings that maintain an instance of SQL Server and run-time parameters.

.AutoStartMail: exposes the SQL Mail startup behavior; object.**AutostartMail** [= value]

.CaseSensitive: indicates the comparison method for multibyte character data on an instance of SQL Server; object.**CaseSensitive**

.CharacterSet: identifies the code page used by an instance of SQL Server; object.**CharacterSet**

.NumberOfProcessors: returns the number of CPUs available to SQL Server on the server; object.**NumberOfProcessors**

.PhysicalMemory: returns the total physical RAM installed, in megabytes; object.**PhysicalMemory**

.ReplicationInstalled: returns true when components supporting replication are installed; object.**ReplicationInstalled**

.SortOrder: returns a string describing the character set used and ordering applied to an instance of SQL Server; object.**SortOrder**

Registry2 Object

The Registry2 object extends the functionality of the Registry object for SQL Server 2000.

.BackupDirectory: specify a location other than the default directory location when running multiple instances of SQL Server; object.**BackupDirectory** [= value]

.SuperSocketEncrypt: specifies whether Super Sockets Net-Library encryption (SSL) is enabled on an instance of SQL Server; object.**SuperSocketEncrypt** [= value]

BulkCopy Object

Represents the parameters of a single bulk copy command issued against a database.

.DataFilePath: indicates the target or source for a bulk copy operation; object.**DataFilePath** [= value]

.LogFilePath: specifies the full operating system path and file name for the bulk copy log file; object.**LogFilePath** [= value]

`.DataFileType`: indicates the format type of the file desired or in use. Can be one of the following:

Constant	Value	Description
SQLDMODataFile_CommaDelimitedChar	1	Columns are delimited using a comma character. Each data row is delimited by a carriage return/linefeed character pair.
SQLDMODataFile_Default	1	SQLDMODataFile_CommaDelimitedChar.
SQLDMODataFile_NativeFormat	4	SQL Server bulk copy native format.
SQLDMODataFile_SpecialDelimitedChar	3	User-defined by the **ColumnDelimiter** and **RowDelimiter** properties of the **BulkCopy** object.
SQLDMODataFile_TabDelimitedChar	2	Columns are delimited using a tab character. Each data row is delimited by a carriage return/linefeed character pair.
SQLDMODataFile_UseFormatFile	5	Bulk copy uses the file identified in the **FormatFilePath** property of the **BulkCopy** object.

SQLObjectList Object

The SQLObjectList object is a fixed-membership container for *objects* enumerated by an object listing method. SQLObjectList does not guarantee that all objects contained have the same type.

QueryResults Object

The QueryResults object presents tabular data to the SQL-DMO application.

SQL-DMO enumeration methods, such as the EnumLocks method of the Database object, return a QueryResults object to report their data. SQL-DMO statement execution methods, such as the ExecuteWithResults method of Database and SQLServer objects, also return a QueryResults object.

.GetColumnString: returns a QueryResults object result set member converted to a String; object.**GetColumnString**(Row , Column) as String

.GetRangeString: returns a single string that contains a block of rows and columns from the current result set of the QueryResults object; object.**GetRangeString**([Top] , [Left] , [Bottom] , [Right] , [RowDelimiter] , [ColDelimiter] , [ColWidths]) as String

.ColumnName: exposes the column name in the current result set of a QueryResults object; object.**ColumnName**(OrdinalColumn)

.Columns: exposes the number of columns contained in the current result set of a QueryResults object; object.**Columns**

.ResultSets: counts the number of result sets returned in the QueryResults object; object.**ResultSets**

.CurrentResultSet: controls access to the result sets of a QueryResults object. The QueryResults object may contain more than one result set; object.**CurrentResultSet** [= value]

QueryResults2 Object

Extends the functionality of the QueryResults object.

.GetColumnSQLVARIANT: retrieves a **sql_variant** column as an array of bytes from a QueryResults2 object; object.**GetColumnSQLVARIANT**(Row , Column) as Byte

.GetColumnSQLVARIANTToString: converts a sql_variant column to a string and returns its value; object.**GetColumnSQLVARIANTToString**(Row , Column , ObjName) as String

NameList Object

The NameList object is a string container object returned by methods that enumerate SQL Server components by name.

.FindName: returns the ordinal position of a string within a NameList object; object.**FindName**(Name) as Long

.Count: indicates the number of items in the list; object.**Count**

Replication Object

The Replication object represents the entire replication system for an instance of SQL Server, and it is the root of all replication objects.

.Script: generates a Transact-SQL command batch that can be used to re-create the entire replication set-up; object.**Script**([ScriptType] , [ScriptFilePath]) as String

.Uninstall: removes replication from the server; object.**Uninstall**( )

Distributor Object

The Distributor object will send out your publications.

.DistributionDatabase: read-only; name of the distributor database (default distribution); object.**DistributionDatabase** [= value]

.DistributionServer: name of the server on which the distributor runs; object.**DistributionServer** [= value]

.DistributorAvailable: tells if you have the distributor available; object.**DistributorAvailable**

.DistributorInstalled: returns TRUE when SQL Server has been configured to use a Distributor; object.**DistributorInstalled**

.Install: installs the distributor; object.**Install**()

.UnInstall: uninstalls the distributor; object.**Uninstall**()

.Script: scripts out the properties and configuration for the distributor; object.**Script**([ScriptType] , [ScriptFilePath]) as String

DistributionDatabase Object

The DistributionDatabase represents a database located at the Distributor used to store replication information. A Distributor can have multiple distribution databases.

.HistoryRetention: how long history is kept in the distribution database (in hours); object.**HistoryRetention** [= value]

.Name: name of this distribution database; object.**Name** [= value]

.BeginAlter: starts a multiproperty Distribution Database alteration; object.**BeginAlter**()

.DoAlter: commits the alterations listed previously; object.**DoAlter**( )

.CancelAlter: rejects the alterations listed previously; object.**CancelAlter**( )

DistributionPublisher Object

The DistributionPublisher object represents a Publisher using this Distributor for replication.

.DistributionDatabase: name of the distribution database for this DistributionPublisher; object.**DistributionDatabase** [= value]

.DistributionPublications collection: The Distribution Publications for this publisher.

.DistributionWorkingDirectory: the working directory for this DistributionPublisher; object.**DistributionWorkingDirectory** [= value]

.Enabled: read-only - the enabled DistributionPublisher; object.**Enabled** [= value]

.Script: generates scripts for the referenced DistributionPublisher; object.**Script**([ScriptType] , [ScriptFilePath]) as String

.RegisteredSubscribers: a collection of registered subscribers for the referenced publisher.

DistributionPublication Object

The DistributionPublication object exposes the properties of a Distributor's image of a snapshot, transactional, or merge replication publication.

.DistributionSubscriptions: collection of subscriptions to this publication

.Name: name of the publication; object.**Name** [= value]

.PublicationType: what type of publication it is; returns one of four values. (2 = merge, 1 = Snapshot, 0 = Transactional and 1000 = Unknown); object.**PublicationType** [= value]

.DistributionArticles: collection of articles that make up the publication

.Remove: removes the publication; object.**Remove**( )

DistributionSubscription Object

The DistributionSubscription object exposes the properties of subscription to a publication maintained by a Distributor.

.Name: the name of the subscription; object.**Name** [= value]

.Remove: removes the subscriber; object.**Remove**( )

.Subscriber: the name of the subscription Server; object.**Subscriber** [= value]

.SubscriptionDB: the name of the Subscription database;
object.**SubscriptionDB** [= value]

.SubscriptionType: type of subscription (push/pull/anonymous);
returns object of SQLDMO_SUBSCRIPTION_TYPE;
object.**SubscriptionType** [= value]

.SyncType: synchronisation type (No sync, Automatic(default));
object.**SyncType** [= value]

DistributionArticle Object

The DistributionArticle object exposes the properties of a Distributor's image of
replicated article.

.Name: the name of the article; object.**Name** [= value]

.SourceObjectname: base object being published;
object.**SourceObjectName** [= value]

.SourceObjectOwner: owner of the base object;
object.**SourceObjectName** [= value]

RegisteredSubscriber Object

The RegisteredSubscriber object represents what information a Publisher has
about a Subscriber.

.Name: name of the subscriber; object.**Name** [= value]

.Script: scripts out the subscriber; object.**Script**([ScriptType] ,
[ScriptFilePath]) as String

.Type: what type of subscriber; returns one of the following:

   4 = SQLDMOSubInfo_ExchangeServer

   2 = SQLDMOSubInfo_Jet

   1 = SQLDMOSubInfo_ODBCDatasource

   3 = SQLDMOSubInfo_OLEDBDataSource

   0 = SQLDMOSubInfo_SQLServer

The SQL-DMO Object Model

Here is the much talked about object SQL-DMO object model. It is taken straight
from BOL and serves as an excellent reference for the internals of the model.

```
┌─────────────────────────────────┐
│      SQL-DMO Object Model        │
│   Source: Microsoft Corporation  │
└─────────────────────────────────┘
```

SQLServers
└ SQLServer
  ├ BackupDevices
  │ └ BackupDevice
  ├ Configuration
  │ └ ConfigValues
  │   └ ConfigValue
  ├ Databases
  │ └ Database
  │   ├ DatabaseRoles
  │   │ └ DatabaseRole
  │   ├ DBOption
  │   ├ Defaults
  │   │ └ Default
  │   ├ FileGroups
  │   │ └ FileGroup
  │   │   └ DBFiles
  │   │   └ DBFile
  │   ├ FullTextCatalogs
  │   │ └ FullTextCatalog
  │   ├ Rules
  │   │ └ Rule
  │   ├ StoredProcedures
  │   │ └ StoredProcedure
  │   ├ SystemDatatypes
  │   │ └ SystemDatatype
  │   └ Tables
  │   └ Table
  │   ├ Checks
  │   │ └ Check
  │   ├ ClusteredIndex
  │   ├ Columns
  │   │ └ Column
  │   │   └ DRIDefault
  │   ├ Indexes
  │   │ └ Index
  │   │   └ IndexedColumns
  │   ├ Keys
  │   │ └ Key
  │   │   └ KeyColumns
  │   │   └ ReferencedColumnf
  │   ├ PrimaryKey
  │   └ Triggers
  │   └ Trigger
  ├ FullTextService
  ├ IntegratedSecurity
  ├ JobServer
  │ ├ AlertCategories
  │ │ └ Category
  │ ├ Alerts
  │ │ └ Alert
  │ ├ AlertSystem
  │ ├ JobCategories
  │ │ └ Category
  │ ├ Job Filter
  │ ├ JobHistoryFilter
  │ ├ Jobs
  │ │ └ Job
  │ │   ├ JobSchedules
  │ │   │ └ JobSchedule
  │ │   │   └ Schedule
  │ │   └ JobSteps
  │ │   └ JobStep
  │ ├ OperatorCategories
  │ │ └ Category
  │ ├ Operators
  │ │ └ Operator
  │ ├ TargetServerGroups
  │ │ └ TargetServerGroup
  │ └ TargetServers
  │   └ TargetServer
  ├ Languages
  │ └ Language
  ├ LinkedServers
  │ └ LinkedServer
  ├ Logins
  │ └ Login
  ├ Registry
  ├ RemoteServers
  │ └ RemoteServer
  │   └ RemoteLogins
  │   └ RemoteLogin
  └ Replication
    ├ Distributor
    │ ├ DistributionDatabases
    │ │ └ DistributionDatabase
    │ ├ DistributionPublishers
    │ │ └ DistributionPublisher
    │ ├ DistributionPublications
    │ │ └ DistributionPublication
    │ │   ├ DistributionArticles
    │ │   │ └ DistributionArticle
    │ │   └ DistributionSubscriptions
    │ │   └ DistributionSubscription
    │ │   └ DistributionSchedule
    │ ├ PublisherSecurity
    │ ├ RegisteredSubscribers
    │ │ └ RegisteredSubscriber
    │ ├ DefaultDistributionSchedule
    │ ├ DefaultMergeSchedule
    │ └ ReplicationSecurity
    └ Publisher
      └ RegisteredSubscribers
```
```

```
            ┌ TransactionLog
            │  └ LogFiles
            │     └ LogFile
            ├ UserDefinedDatatypes
            │  └ UserDefinedDatatype
            ├ UserDefinedFunctions
            │  └ UserDefinedFunction
            ├ Users
            │  └ User
            └ Views
               └ View
                  └ Triggers
                     └ Trigger
```

```
  ┌ RegisteredSubscriber
  ├ ReplicationDatabases
  │  └ ReplicationDatabase
  ├ MergePublications
  │  └ MergePublication
  │     ┌ MergeArticles
  │     │  └ MergeArticle
  │     │     └ MergeSubsetFilters
  │     │        └ MergeSubsetFilter
  │     ├ MergeDynamicSnapshotJobs
  │     │  └ MergeDynamicSnapshotJob
  │     ├ MergeSubscriptions
  │     │  └ MergeSubscription
  │     ├ MergeSchedule
  │     ├ SnapshotSchedule
  │     ├ MergePullSubscriptions
  │     │  └ MergePullSubscription
  │     ├ DistributorSecurity
  │     ├ MergeSchedule
  │     └ PublisherSecurity
  ├ ReplicationStoredProcedures
  │  └ ReplicationStoredProcedure
  ├ ReplicationTables
  │  └ ReplicationTable
  │     ┌ Columns
  │     │  └ Column
  │     └ DRIDefault
  ├ TransPublications
  │  └ TransPublication
  │     ┌ SnapshotSchedule
  │     ├ TransArticles
  │     │  └ TransArticle
  │     ├ TransSubscriptions
  │     │  └ TransSubscription
  │     ├ TransSubscriptions
  │     │  └ TransSubscription
  │     ├ TransPullSubscriptions
  │     │  └ TransPullSubscription
  │     ├ DistributionSchedule
  │     ├ DistributionSecurity
  │     └ PublisherSecurity
  ├ Subscriber
  └ ServerRoles
     └ ServerRole
```

Knowledge-Base Articles and Other SQL-DMO Resources

SQL-DMO, LIKE ANY SOFTWARE, is by no means perfect. This appendix lists for you all the knowledge-base articles that Microsoft has on SQL-DMO up to SQL Server 2000 SP2. If you want to search the knowledge base, you can do so at http://search.microsoft.com/advanced_search.asp.

This appendix also includes some URLs to Web sites that we find useful.

Bugs

The following articles deal with SQL-DMO bugs.

- DOC: SQL Server 2000 Books Online OLE Automation Example May Leak Memory (Q320130)

- BUG: SQLDMO Transfer Operation Truncates Transaction Log of Destination Database (Q316213)

- BUG: DTS Copy Objects Task (DMO) Breaks Transaction Log Backup Chain by Switching Recovery Mode to Simple During Transfer (Q308267)

- BUG: WMI MSSQL_Table.ExportData Always Uses Standard Security (Q295021)

- BUG: ExecuteWithResultsAndMessages2 Does Not Return Results (Q279514)

- BUG: SQL-DMO Treats Shutdown Message from SQL Server as Error Condition After Shutdown Method Runs (Q272145)

- BUG: ListAvailableServers Method of the SQLDMO.Application Object Causes Error 0x800A000E (Q254759)

- BUG: DTS: Table Transfers Incorrectly if Using Char or Varchar Larger than 4000 Characters (Q244537)

- BUG: SQLDMO - Query Analyzer May Fail to Connect if SQL Server Is Started as Part of Connection Attempt (Q234736)

- BUG: SQL-DMO: ExportData Method of BulkCopy Object Causes VB Run-Time Error (Q238558)

- BUG: SQL Enterprise Manager Generates SQL-DMO Error for DBO Updating Permissions (Q229052)

- BUG: SQL 6.5 DMO GetItemByOrd and GetItemByName Causes 4K Leak in Private Bytes (Q216714)

 NOTE Q216714 is a bug in WMI, not SQL-DMO.

- BUG: DMO BCP Fails When Using Mixed Security and Trusted Connection (Q180711)

- BUG: DMO BulkCopy Leaves File Locks when Format File Is Missing (Q177207)

- BUG: SQL-DMO BulkCopy Object IncludeIdentityValues Property Fail (Q167867)

- BUG: SQL-DMO's::ImportData Method Does Not Function Properly (Q163450)

- BUG: SQL-DMO ::GetMemUsage Method Returns Empty String (Q152621)

- BUG: DMO Script() Method Generates GO Following CREATE INDEX (Q147391)

Fixes

The following articles list fixes for bugs not shown in the bugs section.

- FIX: SQL DMO's SQLBackup Method Fails with Error Message 3206 (Q308789)

- FIX: Objects May Fail to Retain Quoted Identifier Setting when You Use SQL-DMO to Create or Alter Objects (Q306334)

- FIX: The SQL-DMO Transfer Method Silently Fails to Copy All Data (Q300195)

- FIX: SQLDMO ExportData Method Fails If There Is a Space in the Database Name (Q308860)

- FIX: DMO BulkCopy Fails to Copy Data when Column Names Contain the Space Character (Q299865)

- FIX: Invoking SQL-DMO Methods by Using "By Reference" Parameters May Cause a Memory Leak (Q293636)

- FIX: SP_OA Procedures Leak Memory and Cause Various Errors (Q282229)

- FIX: SQLDMO GetProcessInputBuffer Returns Incorrect Result (Q281843)

- FIX: Script Generation Using SQL-DMO Results in Database Name that Is too Long (Q281137)

- FIX: DMO ExecuteWithResults Fails with Decimal Data (Q257515)

- FIX: DTS Object Transfer Does Not Transfer BLOB Data Greater than 64KB (Q257425)

- FIX: SQLDMO: DBFile.Shrink and LogFile.Shrink with SQLDMOShrink_EmptyFile Generates Invalid DBCC Command (Q247307)

- FIX: Generating Scripts to Multiple Files May Yield Error 20524 (Q247107)

- FIX: DMO Transfer Methods Does Not Do Code Page Conversion (Q236868)

- FIX: SQLDMO - . Login and .Password Properties are Ignored with .LoginSecure = FALSE (Q234268)

- FIX: SEM Generates SQL-DMO Error when Adding an ODBC Subscriber (Q231759)

- FIX: SpaceAvailableInMB Property Returns Used Space Instead of Available Space (Q229007)

- FIX: SQL-DMO Operations on SQL Server 7.0 Uses More Memory (Q225501)

- FIX: SQL-DMO::EnumQueuedTasks May Cause Memory Leak (Q193390)

Problems

The following are known problems with SQL-DMO that are not listed as bugs.

- PRB: Errors when You Redistribute SQL Server 2000 DMO Clients in SQL Server 7.0 Environment (Q295026)

- PRB: Differences Between DMO 7.0 and DMO 6.5 with ExecuteWithResults (Q238332)

Information and How-To's

Further information from Microsoft on how to do things not covered in Books Online.

- HOW TO: Use the SQL Distributed Management Objects Model to Programmatically Transfer SQL Server Stored Procedures (Q315505)

- HOWTO: Deploy SQL Distributed Management Objects with the Visual Basic Package and Deployment Wizard (Q258157)

- INF: Enabling SQL DMO Clients Without Installing the Client-Side Utilities (Q248241)

- INF: How to List the Results of a SELECT Query on a Table Using SQL-DMO (Q241246)

- INF: Changes to SQL-DMO Objects in SQL Server 7.0 (Q239794)

- HOWTO: Using SQL DMO to Print Date in Regional Format (Q220918)

- INF: How to Use the SQL Server DMO Objects from VBScript (Q214820)

- INF: How to Use ListIndexedColumns in SQL-DMO Using Visual Basic (Q194522)

- INF: Using Smart Pointers to Simplify SQL-DMO (Q164292)

- INF: How to Use Connectable Objects in SQL-DMO (Q156434)

- INF: Sample of SQL-DMO Connection Point Interface (Q156100)

- INF: Distribution of SQL-DMO (Distributed Database Objects) (Q151862)

Useful URLs

Here are some helpful sites for further reference.

- Microsoft's official SQL Server Web site: `http://www.microsoft.com/sql`

- Microsoft's TechNet site for SQL Server: `http://www.microsoft.com/technet/prodtechnol/sql/default.asp`

- An old but useful introduction to SQL-DMO from Microsoft: `http://msdn.microsoft.com/library/default.asp?url=/library/en-us/dnautoma/html/msdn_dmoovrvw.asp`

- SQL Server worldwide user group—a fantastic online community— and SQL Server articles: `http://www.sswug.org`

- Gert Drapers' new SQL Agent Job Manager is a utility that allows you access to all SQL Agent related functionality, without having to use SQL Enterprise Manager. However since it uses SQL-DMO and the SQL Namespace objects it does require these to be installed.

  It provides 3 basic views: jobs, operators or alerts. Views can be switched using the View menu option of Ctrl+Shift+A for Alerts, Ctrl-Shift-O for Operators and Ctrl-Shift-J for Jobs. `http://www.sqldev.net/sqlagent/SQLJobMan.htm`

- Great resource for SQL-DMO and other areas of SQL Server: `http://www.sqlservercentral.com/`

- Huge SQL Server resource: `http://vyaskn.tripod.com/`

- The best DTS resource on the internet: `http://www.sqldts.com`

- The best technical SQL Server journal money can buy:
  `http://www.pinpub.com/sql`

- A very good online SQL Server magazine: `http://www.sqlmag.com`

- Articles and discussion forums from us, the authors of this book:
  `http://www.allisonmitchell.com`

- The UK SQL Server users' group: `http://www.sql-server.co.uk`

- The Professional Association for SQL Server (PASS) Web site:
  `http://www.sqlpass.org`

- Fernando Guerrero's site: `http://www.callsql.com/en/index.htm`. Fernando is
  a SQL Server MVP and principal technologist for QA training in the UK.

- Kalen Delaney's site: `http://www.InsideSQLServer.com`. Kalen Delaney,
  MVP continued Ron Soukup's great work with Inside SQL Server 7 and
  Inside SQL Server 2000.

- Chip Andrews's site: `http://www.sqlsecurity.com`

- Bill Graziano and Sean Baird's site: `http://www.sqlteam.com`

- A great site that is edited by Tim DiChiara, founder of DatabaseCentral.com,
  which merged with searchdatabase.com: `http://www.searchdatabase.com`

Index

Symbols and Numbers

, (comma), meaning of, 89–90

" (double quotes), appearance in object creation application, 33–34

' (single quotes), appearance in object creation application, 33–34

[] (square brackets), using with e-mail addresses and operators, 184

| (pipe) delimiter, using with QALite application, 311

0 value

FrequencySubDay property, 236
FrequencyType, 234

1 value

DISABLE_DEF_CNST_CHK configuration for connections, 263
e-mail alert notification type, 245
frequency interval, 226
frequency relative interval, 227
frequency type, 225
FrequencyRelativeInterval property, 235
FrequencySubDay property, 236
FrequencySubDay type, 227
FrequencyType, 233

2 value

e-mail alert notification type, 245
frequency relative interval, 227
FrequencyRelativeInterval property, 235
IMPLICIT_TRANSACTIONS configuration for connections, 263

4 value

CURSOR_CLOSE_ON_COMMIT configuration for connections, 263
e-mail alert notification type, 245

frequency interval, 226
frequency relative interval, 227
frequency type, 225
FrequencyRelativeInterval property, 235
FrequencySubDay property, 236
FrequencySubDay type, 227
FrequencyType, 233

8 value

ANSI_WARNINGS configuration for connections, 263
frequency interval, 226
frequency relative interval, 227
frequency type, 225
FrequencyRelativeInterval property, 235
FrequencySubDay property, 236
FrequencySubDay type, 227
FrequencyType, 234

13 value for FrequencySubDay property, explanation of, 236

15-minute database checker, code for, 93–96

16 value

ANSI_PADDING configuration for connections, 263
frequency interval, 226
frequency relative interval, 227
frequency type, 225
FrequencyRelativeInterval property, 235
FrequencyType, 233

32 value

ANSI_NULLS configuration for connections, 263–265
frequency interval, 226
frequency type, 225
FrequencyType, 233

64 value

ARITHABORT configuration for
connections, 263

frequency interval, 226

frequency type, 225

FrequencyType, 233

128 value

ARITHIGNORE configuration for
connections, 263

frequency interval, 226

frequency type, 225

FrequencyType, 234

255 value for FrequencyType, explanation
of, 234

256 value of QUOTED_IDENTIFIER
configuration for connections,
explanation of, 264

512 value of NOCOUNT configuration for
connections, explanation of, 264

1024 value of ANSI_NULL_DFLT_ON
configuration for connections,
explanation of, 264

2048 value of ANSI_NULL_DFLT_OFF
configuration for connections,
explanation of, 264

4096 value of
CONCAT_NULL_YIELDS_NULL
configuration for connections,
explanation of, 264

8192 value of NUMERIC_ROUNDABOUT
configuration for connections,
explanation of, 264

16384 value of XACT_ABORT configuration
for connections, explanation of, 264

A

ActiveX script step within jobs, purpose
of, 180

Add User application

activating application roles with, 145

adding users to and removing users
from database roles, 137–141

adding users to databases with, 129–132

adding users to fixed server roles, 123

changing membership of roles, 126–129

creating new database roles, 141–145

determining roles, 124–125

login additions, 116–119

login removal, 119–123

purpose of, 115–116

removing users from databases with,
133–136

ADO Connection object properties, setting,
341–343

affinity mask configuration option in
Enterprise Manager, explanation of,
257–258

alerts

creating in Enterprise Manager, 243–244

creating in SQL-DMO, 245–246

creating in T-SQL, 244–245

definition of, 181

scripting, 332–333

ANSI_NULL_DFLT ON and OFF
configuration for connections,
descriptions of, 264

ANSI_NULLS configuration for
connections, description of, 263–265

ANSI_PADDING configuration for
connections, description of, 263

ANSI_WARNINGS configuration for
connections, description of, 263

application database roles

activating, 145

characteristics of, 141

creating with T-SQL, 144

specifying passwords for, 143

Apress Web site

    DBCC DBREINDEX() procedure, 176

    Scripter application, 325

    server-wide properties application, 273

    tables permission script, 339

ARITHABORT configuration for connections, description of, 263

ARITHIGNORE configuration for connections, description of, 263

articles

    adding in Enterprise Manager, 297–298

    adding to publication when installing merge replication with SQL-DMO, 286–287

    role in replication, 283

Audit level, querying, 261–262

Authors table, granting SELECT permissions on, 151

auto options, setting for databases, 17–18

Autostart Mail, SQL-DMO code and description for, 270

B

/b parameter, checking with scripting tables, 338

[/b] argument in Scripter application, function of, 326

backup application

    adding new locations for backups with, 67–68

    Backup object properties in, 66

    backup type for, 66

    calling backup procedure with, 70

    checking soundness of, 66–67

    designating location of backup with, 66

    determining database backup for, 66

    error number generated by, 67

    example of, 61–72

    initializing backup device with, 68

    initializing backup in, 65–69

    length of backup, 66

    locating backup to restore with, 69–71

    log backups, 71–72

    media initialization by, 66

    outputting database names to combo boxes in, 63–64

    prompting backup in, 64–65

    removal of devices from Devices list box with, 70

    Restore object usage by, 66

    restoring objects in, 65–69

    setting backup type with, 68

    supplying backup names with, 69

backup devices

    adding to combo box, 81

    checking after restore configurations, 88

    determining type of, 82

    versus files, 91

    looping through, 82–84

    scripting, 333

    using, 53–56

backup names, supplying with Enterprise Manager, 65

backup origin, specifying, 80–93

backup/restore time-out period option in SQL Server Properties dialog box, values for, 268

BACKUP_DEVICE backup option, explanation of, 57

BackupDevice collection, looping through, 64

backups. *See also* databases; recovery options; restore entries; source databases

    checking integrity of, 59

    choosing for restore operations, 84–85

    choosing methods of, 50–53

    of databases versus logs, 88

examining details of, 75

forcing over existing databases, 91

importance of, 45

initializing in backup application, 65–69

moving files during, 91

performing, 56–59

prompting in backup application, 64–65

scenarios and methods, 48–50

sending with SQL Server, 53

specifying file numbers for, 59

types of, 46–48, 91

batch files, using Scripter in, 327

BCP operation, initiating when scripting tables, 338

BEFORE trigger, explanation of, 27

bit mask properties, setting, 279–280

BLOCKSIZE backup option, explanation of, 58

boonInList variable, declaring in Add User application, 126–127

bugs, knowledge-base articles about, 371–372

Bulk-Logged Recovery option in SQL Server 2000, explanation of, 53

BulkCopy object, 362

declaring objects for use with SQL-DMO scripting options, 330

role in scripting tables, 338

using to export data to text files, 172

BulkLogged property versus SelectIntoBulkCopy, 15

C

CanWe variable, determining ability to delete logins with, 120–121

cboDatabases, populating with database list, 24–25

check boxes, populating when setting properties in registry, 274

checkmarks, placing next to user roles, 137

Checked property, examining in New Operator application, 186

checkpoints, role in transaction log backups, 48

column names and headers, outputting in QALite application, 318–319

column widths, resizing in QALite application, 319–320

Columns collection

Column object, 354–355

Column2 object, 355

LogFile object, 355

TransactionLog object, 355

Columns collection, looping through, 36

columns, inserting in tables, 36

combo boxes

in backup application example, 63–64

populating in QALite application, 313–320

comma (,), meaning of, 89–90

comma-delimited files versus to TABs, using when exporting data to text files, 173

CONCAT_NULL_YIELDS_NULL configuration for connections, description of, 264

Configuration object

displaying affinity mask information with, 258

persisting changes to, 278

Connect button in Query Analyzer, purpose of, 310–312

Connect method of SQLServer objects, using, 250

connections, determining, 263

Connections tab in SQL Server properties dialog box, options on, 262–265, 279

constants, setting for SQL-DMO scripting options, 329–340

CREATE DATABASE command, T-SQL syntax for, 4–5

CREATE TABLE permission, granting to users, 107–108

CREATE VIEW in indexed and nonindexed views, using, 41

cursor options, setting for databases, 19

CURSOR_CLOSE_ON_COMMIT configuration for connections, description of, 263

D

data, exporting to text files with OLE, 171–176

data files
    adding to collections, 164
    adding to database objects, 7
    creating, 6–7
    in databases, 3
    initializing and setting properties for, 163

database backups versus log backups, 88

database checker, code for, 93–96

database items, defining for transfer operations, 167

database lists, populating, 24–25

database names, outputting to combo box in backup application, 63–64

database objects
    adding data files and log files to, 7
    creating, 19–21
    scripting, 334–335

database references, searching when exporting data to text files, 173

database roles. *See* roles

database scripts, creating with OLE, 169–171

Database Settings tab in SQL Server Properties dialog box, options on, 267–270

database tables. *See* tables

database terminology
    database roles, 103–106
    fixed server roles, 100–103
    logins, 100
    users, 100

database users. *See* users

DATABASE_NAME backup option, explanation of, 57

DatabaseRoles collection
    DatabaseRole object, 349
    DBOption object, 349

databases. See *also* backup entries; recovery options; restore entries; source databases
    adding file groups to, 8–9
    adding users to, 129–132
    adding views to, 39
    advisory about creation of, 9
    advisory about leaving in standby state, 88
    choosing for publications, 295–296
    creating on servers, 3–9
    indicating for restore operations, 91
    leaving in read-only state, 88
    leaving in Standby mode, 92
    leaving nonoperational, 92
    locating for transfer operations, 166–167
    recovering after restore operations, 88
    removing users from, 133–136
    restoring, 72–74, 72–77
    restoring and recovering, 48–53

setting options for, 9–19

setting recovery options for, 91

showing with combo box in QALite application, 314

transferring with OLE automation, 161–165

Databases collection

adding databases to, 164–165

Database objects, 347–348

getting handle when exporting data to text files, 173

Databases object, properties of, 347–348

DataMirror third-party replication tool, description of, 323

datatypes

creating, 26–27

forms of, 25

populating, 25–26

DBAs (database administrators), primary tasks of, 45

DBCC DBREINDEX() procedure, example of, 176–178

DBCCs (Database Console Commands), running, 176–178

DBFiles collection

DBFile object, 350

FullTextService object, 350

DBOption versus DBOption2 object, 15

DDL generation, advisory about, 86

DDLs, generating, 90

default constraints, adding to object creation application, 33

defaults, scripting, 340

DENY object permission, using, 107–111

DESCRIPTION backup option, explanation of, 58

destination files, naming when exporting data to text files, 175

DIFFERENTIAL backup option, explanation of, 58

differential backups

dynamics of, 47

scenarios and methods, 49–50

Dim statement, role in scripting out configured and runtime values, 255

DISABLE_DEF_CNST_CHK configuration for connections, description of, 263

distributor, role in replication, 283

distributors

determining availability of, 284–285

selecting and configuring in Enterprise Manager, 290–291

DLLs, registering, 3

[/dnum_log_days] argument in Scripter application, function of, 326

double quotes ("), appearance in object creation application, 33–34

DoubleTake third-party replication tool, description of, 323

DTS packages, advisory about scripting of, 340–341

DTS transfer objects task, displaying, 168

DUMMY node, role in SQL-DMO jobs, 198, 210

E

e-mail alert notification type, value of, 245

e-mail levels for T-SQL jobs, list of, 220

Enterprise Manager. *See also* SQL Server Properties dialog box of Enterprise Manager

adding database roles with, 144–145

adding jobs to SQL Server in, 214–219

adding logins with, 118

adding operators to SQL Servers with, 181–190

adding users to and removing users from roles with, 141

backing up databases with, 59, 70–71

backup application, 62–72

backup device addition example, 54

columns displayed in, 23

creating alerts in, 243–244

creating tabs in, 270–272

database roles example, 103–104

Database User Properties screen in, 132

extracting server properties with, 249–250

finding product names when extracting server properties, 252–253

granting permissions with, 151–152

grouping servers in, 62–63

installing merge replication with, 288–305

investigating servers in, 248–249

notifying operators in, 183

querying server property information with T-SQL, 253–254

querying servers with, 251–252

refreshing advisory, 77

relationship to SQL-DMO, 2

removing users from databases with, 135–136

Restore database screen in, 75–76

setting recovery mode in, 14

supplying backup names with, 65

viewing jobs with, 190–193

EnumJobHistory results, list of, 212–213

error-checking procedure, checking when using OLE, 159

ExecuteWithResultsAndMessages, returning QueryResults object when using DBCC DBREINDEX() procedure, 178

exists = item, completing, 129

EXPIREDATE backup option, explanation of, 58

ExportData method of Table object, using, 176

exposure, role in backup methods, 48

Extras tab of SQL Server Properties dialog box, options on, 276–278

F

file group backups, dynamics of, 47–48

file groups, adding to databases, 8–9

FILE option, restoring databases and logs with, 74

FileGroups collection, FileGroup object in, 349

FileNumber, role in performing restore operations, 84–85

FillFactor, assigning in object creation application, 33

fixed server roles

    adding users to, 123

    explanation of, 100–103

fixes for bugs, knowledge-base articles about, 373–374

flags parameter, role in T-SQL jobs, 224

flex grids

    role in restore operations, 85

    using with backup devices, 83

For Each...Next construct, role in scripting logins, 332

foreign keys, explanation of, 19

FORMAT/NO FORMAT backup option, explanation of, 58

/foutput_path argument in Scripter application, function of, 326

frequency intervals in SQL-DMO, list of, 234

FrequencyRecurrenceFactor property, values and actions of, 235

FrequencyRelativeInterval property constants and values, descriptions of, 235

FrequencySubDay property constants and values, descriptions of, 236

FrequencyType constants and values, descriptions of, 233–234

full backups

dynamics of, 46–47

example of, 59–60

restoring databases from, 75–77

scenarios and methods, 48–50

Full Recovery option in SQL Server 2000, explanation of, 53

full-text service installation, checking when scripting tables, 338

FullTextCatalogs collection, FullTextCatalog object in, 351

G

General tab in SQL Server properties dialog box, options on, 250–254, 273

Generate SQL Script option in Enterprise Manager, using, 306–307

GenerateDBScripts procedure in Scripter application, purpose of, 328–329

GeneratedDTSPackages procedure in Scripter application, purpose of, 340–341

GetColumnString method of QueryResults object, role in extracting server properties, 253

GetRegisteredServers procedure, role in viewing server options, 249

GetServerGroupsInGroups procedure, role in viewing server options, 249

GetServerInfo procedure, extracting server properties with, 249–250

glb_Server global variable, using with QALite application, 313

GRANT object permission, using, 107–111, 151

grids, outputting QALite results to, 315, 318–319

groups, role in backup application, 62–63

H

Hand button in Query Analyzer, purpose of, 310

HouseKeepLogs procedure in Scripter application, purpose of, 344

I

IMPLICIT_TRANSACTIONS configuration for connections, description of, 263

indexed views

advisory about, 42

creating, 38–44

indexes, reindexing on database tables, 176–178

INIT/NOINIT backup option, explanation of, 58

INSERT command, using with triggers, 27

INSERT INTO versus SELECT INTO, role in point-in-time recovery, 52

instance_id column of EnumJobHistory history method, datatype and description of, 212

INSTEAD OF triggers, explanation of, 27

isqlw /? command, issuing from command prompt, 321

J

job details, showing with SQL-DMO, 200–201

job execution, determining with SQL-DMO, 202–209

job execution examples, 227–228

job history

outcomes for, 195

showing with SQL-DMO, 211–214

viewing with Enterprise Manager, 192–193

job outcomes, list of, 198

job schedules

adding, 224–225

adding in Enterprise Manager, 217–218

adding in SQL-DMO, 232–242

checking with SQL-DMO, 201–202

job steps

adding in Enterprise Manager, 215

adding with T-SQL, 221, 224

defining in Enterprise Manager, 216

defining with T-SQL, 230

determining flow control in Enterprise Manager, 217

showing command with SQL-DMO, 211

showing with SQL-DMO, 209–210

T-SQL constants for, 231

job_aspect, purpose of, 194

job_id column of EnumJobHistory history method, datatype and description of, 212

job_name column of EnumJobHistory history method, datatype and description of, 212

JobBuilder application, creating jobs with, 229–232

jobs. *See also* recurring scheduled jobs

adding in SQL-DMO, 229–242

adding in T-SQL, 219–228

adding to SQL Server in Enterprise Manager, 214–219

checking activities with SQL-DMO, 201

defining execution in Enterprise Manager, 217–218

defining in Enterprise Manager, 215

explanation of, 180

frequency types for, 225

populating trees with, 198–199

sample outcome of, 213–214

scheduling for execution with SQL Server Agent starts, 236–242

showing with SQL-DMO, 197

success and failure actions in T-SQL, 223

T-SQL subsystems for, 222

T-SQL tokens for, 222–223

viewing with Enterprise Manager, 190–193

viewing with SQL-DMO, 196–214

viewing with T-SQL, 193–196

Jobs collection, Job object in, 358–359

JobSchedules collection

JobSchedule object, 360

Schedule object, 360

JobServer object, role in scripting alerts and operators, 332

JobSteps collection, JobStep object in, 360

K

Key objects, defining in object creation application, 30

Keys collection, adding key to, 37

knowledge-base articles, searching, 371

L

Legato RepliStor third-party replication tool, description of, 323

Lightning Bolt button in Query Analyzer, purpose of, 310

ListAvailableSQLServers method of Application object, advisory about, 63

locks, explanation of, 16

log backups versus database backups, 88

log files

adding to collections, 164

adding to database objects, 7

advisory about, 4

creating, 6–7

initializing and setting properties for, 164

log shipping

definition of, 45

Web resources for, 324

Login object, creating for use with OLE, 158

login types, determining for use with OLE, 159

logins

adding to server roles in T-SQL, 128

adding with Add User application, 116–119

adding with OLE, 157–161

adding with T-SQL and Enterprise Manager, 118

assigning new passwords when using OLE, 160

checking association with users, 131–132

code for display of, 277

dragging into Users list box, 130–131

explanation of, 100

removing with Add User application, 119–123

scripting out SQL Server configuration options with, 331–332

testing existence with Add User application, 117

Logins collection

adding logins for Add User application to, 118

adding logins to, 160

BulkCopy object, 362

DistributionArticle object, 367

DistributionDatabase object, 365

DistributionPublication object, 366

DistributionPublisher object, 366

DistributionSubscription object, 366

Distributor object, 365

grabbing handle when using OLE, 160

Login object, 361

NameList object, 364

QueryResults object, 363

QueryResults2 object, 364

RegisteredSubscriber object, 367

Registry object, 362

Registry2 object, 362

SQLObjectList object, 363

logs

backing up, 57, 71–72

restoring, 73

LogScripting procedure in Scripter application, purpose of, 344

lstDatatypes list box, populating, 25–26

lstRoles list box, purpose of, 138

M

Mail password, SQL-DMO code and description for, 270

mail notification, setting for job outcome, 241

Main() procedure

role in Scripter application, 328–329

role in viewing server options, 248

master database path, SQL-DMO code and description for, 270

max server memory in Enterprise Manager, advisory about, 256

MEDIADESCRIPTION backup option, explanation of, 58

MEDIAPASSWORD backup option, explanation of, 58

memory options, scripting out using Enterprise Manager, 256

Memory tab in SQL Server properties dialog box, options on, 254–256

Merge Agent schedule, setting for subscriptions to publications, 303 merge replication, 180

    explanation of, 282, 296–297

    installing with Enterprise Manager, 288–305, 288–305

    installing with SQL-DMO, 284–288

    resolving conflicts in, 303–304

message column of EnumJobHistory history method, datatype and description of, 212

MOVE option, restoring databases and logs with, 74, 77

MyDMODatabase

    backing up with T-SQL, 59–60

    backup application for, 59–72

N

NAME backup option, explanation of, 58

Name server name, purpose of, 251

NameList object, using, 272

net send alert notification type, value of, 245

net send levels for T-SQL jobs, list of, 220

NetName server name, purpose of, 251

New columns, initializing in object creation application, 30

New Operator application, 182

    complete code for, 188–190

    determining existence of operators in, 186

    determining pager days in, 186–188

    purpose of, 185

NO_TRUNCATE and NO_LOG options, explanations of, 72

NOCOUNT configuration for connections, description of, 264

nodes

    checking prepopulation status of, 198

    populating with SQL-DMO jobs, 198–199

NORECOVERY/RECOVERY/STANDBY option, restoring databases and logs with, 74, 77

NOREWIND/REWIND option, explanation of, 58

Northwind database, accessing when exporting data to text files, 173–174

NOSKIP/SKIP option, explanation of, 58

Notifications tab of Backup Databases Properties screen in Enterprise Manager, contents of, 192

NOUNLOAD/UNLOAD option, explanation of, 59

NT event logging, SQL-DMO code and description for, 270

NT-SQL procedure, role in adding logins with Add User application, 117

NUMERIC_ROUNDABOUT configuration for connections, description of, 264

O

object creation application

    adding default constraints in, 33

    coding primary keys in, 32–33

    columns in, 21–22, 31–32, 31–32

    creating physical table for, 22–29

    dynamics of, 21–22

    exploring underlying code in, 29–34

    FillFactor assignment in, 33

    illustration of, 20

object permissions, using, 107–114

objects

    creating for database scripts, 169

    creating when exporting data to text files, 172

    restoring in backup application example, 65–69

OLE automation
adding logins and users with, 157–161
creating database scripts with, 169–171
exporting data to text files with, 171–176
and running DBCCs, 176–178
transferring databases with, 161–165
transferring source databases with, 165–168
using in T-SQL, 156–157

OLE stored procedures, list of, 156–157

oList variable, role in Permissions application, 147

OPENQUERY, purpose in determining roles, 125

operating system (CmdExec) step within jobs, purpose of, 180

operating system, determining when extracting server properties, 253

operator_emailed column of EnumJobHistory history method, datatype and description of, 212

operator_netsent column of EnumJobHistory history method, datatype and description of, 212

operator_paged column of EnumJobHistory history method, datatype and description of, 212

operators
adding to SQL Server, 181–190
adding with SQL-DMO, 184–188
determining existence in New Operator application, 186
notifying, 180–181
notifying in Enterprise Manager, 183
notifying of outcome in SQL-DMO, 240
scripting, 332–333
start and end time formats for, 184

Operators collection, Operator object in, 361

options, setting for databases, 9–19

P

page levels for T-SQL jobs, list of, 220

pager alert notification type, value of, 245

pager days
determining in New Operator application, 186–188
role in operators, 184

pager notification, setting for job outcome, 241–242

parsing, role in QALite application, 314, 317

PASSWORD backup option, explanation of, 58

passwords
specifying for application database roles, 143
SQL-DMO code and description for, 271
viewing for registered servers, 277

Perfmon mode, SQL-DMO code and description for, 270

permissions
checking existence of, 149–152
finding for Public role, 104–105
granting to users, 151
list of, 113–114
scripting for roles, 335–337

Permissions application
changing user permissions with, 148–149
checking for existing permissions with, 149–152
dynamics of, 146–147
purpose of, 145
showing table permissions with, 147–148

permissions for backup up and restoring databases, explanations of, 96

pipe (|) delimiter, using with QALite application, 311

point-in-time recovery, explanation of, 52

pointers, setting for database scripts, 170

[/ppassword] argument in Scripter application, function of, 326

Primary file group

adding data files to, 164

explanation of, 8

primary keys, coding in object creation application, 32–33

Processor tab

in SQL Server properties dialog box, 257–259

retrieval of, 259

product names, finding when querying servers with Enterprise Manager, 252–253

profiler traces, applying to servers, 259

properties

defining for log and data files, 6–7

setting in registry, 273–274

Provider property, setting in ADO connection objects, 342

Public role, finding permissions for, 104–105

publication type, selecting in Enterprise Manager, 297

publications

adding subscribers in Enterprise Manager, 300–302

adding when installing merge replication with SQL-DMO, 285–286

creating with Enterprise Manager, 295–299

displaying information about using Enterprise Manager, 292–294

reviewing details in Enterprise Manager, 300

role in replication, 283

selecting names and descriptions in Enterprise Manager, 299

publishers

adding when installing merge replication with SQL-DMO, 285

checking existence of, 284

displaying information about using Enterprise Manager, 292

role in replication, 283

Pubs database, granting CREATE TABLE permission in, 110

Push Subscription wizard, using, 301–305

Q

QA look-alike tools Web sites, 309

QALite application

code for, 311–312

combo box population, 313–320

delimiters for returning results in, 311

logon form, 312–313

purpose of, 309–311

resizing column widths in, 319–320

running queries in, 315–320

queries, executing and parsing in QALite application, 314–315

Query Analyzer tool

dynamics of, 309–310

instantiating from command line, 321

Query Pane, using in QALite application, 315–320

QueryResults object

assigning EnumFixedDatabaseRolePermission output to, 106

assigning results of EnumServerRolePermission to, 102

purpose in determining roles, 124

returning with ExecuteWithResultsAndMessages in DBCC DBREINDEX() procedure, 178

using with backup devices, 83

QUOTED_IDENTIFIER configuration for connections, description of, 264

R

RAID 10 arrays, using file group backups with, 47

READ ONLY option

using, 11

using with SQL options, 16–17

read-only properties error, displaying, 272

ReconfigureWithOverride property, using, 278

recovery options, setting for databases, 12–15

recurring scheduled jobs. *See also* job entries

recurring scheduled jobs, defining in Enterprise Manager, 218

registered owner, SQL-DMO code and description for, 270

registered servers, viewing passwords of, 277. *See also* servers; source servers

RegisteredServers collection of ServerGroup object

looping through, 62–63

using, 24

registry

advisory about making changes in, 274

setting properties in, 273–274

Registry2 object, setting properties with, 275

relationships, adding to tables, 34–37

Relgrid, explanation of, 37

Remarks in EnumJobHistory method, explanation of, 213

REPLACE option, restoring databases and logs with, 74

replication

scripting, 333–334

scripting with SQL-DMO, 308

types of, 281–283

replication distribution step within jobs, purpose of, 180

Replication menu, locating in Enterprise Manager, 288–289

replication scripting options, constants for, 330

replication scripts, generating with SQL-DMO, 306–307

replication tools, list of, 323

replication Web sites, 305

RESTART option, explanation of, 59

Restore application. *See also* backup entries; recovery options; source databases

DDL tab options for, 80

General tab options for, 78

Options tab options for, 79

RESTORE FILELISTONLY, equivalent of, 85, 89

RESTORE HEADERONLY, equivalent of, 82–83

restore operations

checking forcing over existing databases, 87

choosing backups for, 84–85

configuring, 85–88

example of, 91

restore procedure, calling, 86

restore statement, example of, 92

restore types, choosing, 88–93

restored files, changing physical locations of, 86

restoring databases, 72–77

with SQL-DMO, 77–80

with T-SQL, 72–73

RETAINDAYS backup option, explanation of, 58

retries_attempted column of
EnumJobHistory history method,
datatype and description of, 212

REVOKE object permission, using, 107–111

roles

adding, 143

adding users to and removing users
from, 137–141

creating, 141–145

changing membership of, 126–129

checking existence of, 142–143

determining, 124–125

explanation of, 103–106

scripting, 335–337

rules, scripting, 340

run_date column of EnumJobHistory
history method, datatype and
description of, 212

run_duration column of EnumJobHistory
history method, datatype and
description of, 212

run_status column of EnumJobHistory
history method, datatype and
description of, 212

run_time column of EnumJobHistory
history method, datatype and
description of, 212

S

SaveToStorageFile method of Package
object, using with ADO Connection
objects, 342

Schedules tab of Backup Databases
Properties screen in Enterprise
Manager, contents of, 192

Script method of Replication object,
using, 308

Script method of Table object, options
for, 330

Scripter application

connecting to SERVER1 with trusted
security, 327

connecting to SERVER2 with standard
SQL security, 327

Main() procedure in, 328–329

parameters for, 326–327

purpose of, 324–325

setting constants and connecting to
SQL Server with, 329–340

structure of, 328–329

using in batch files, 327

Security modes in Enterprise Manager

descriptions of, 260–262

querying, 261

Security tab in SQL Server properties dialog
box, options on, 260–262

select convert(), using with T-SQL to query
server names, 252

Select Into/Bulk Copy setting in SQL Server
7.0, explanation of, 51–52

SELECT INTO versus INSERT INTO, role in
point-in-time recovery, 52

SELECT permissions

denying on tables, 112

granting on tables, 111

granting to users, 151

revoking on tables, 112–114

SelectIntoBulkCopy property versus
BulkLogged, 15

server column of EnumJobHistory history
method, datatype and description
of, 212

server connections

establishing for database scripts, 170

establishing when exporting data to
text files, 173

Server drop-down box, populating in
object creation application, 23–24

server groups

explanation of, 24

iterating through using Enterprise Manager, 248

server names, querying with Enterprise Manager, 251–252

Server object, creating for use with OLE, 158

server options, viewing, 248–249

server properties, extracting with Enterprise Manager, 249–250

Server Role Properties screen, displaying, 102

server roles, using T-SQL to add logins to, 128

server settings, querying with Enterprise Manager, 266–267

Server Settings tab in SQL Server properties dialog box, options on, 265–267

server-wide options, setting, 272–280

ServerGroups collection, looping through, 62

servers. *See also* registered servers; source servers

adding backup devices to, 53–56

creating databases on, 3–9

grouping in Enterprise Manager, 62–63

identifying for SQL-DMO jobs, 197

locating for source databases, 165

logging on when installing merge replication using SQL-DMO, 284

logging onto, 5–6, 69

logging onto for backup application, 66

querying, 251–252

transferring databases between, 161–165

Windows authentication used with, 25–26

Servers combo box, populating in backup application, 62

servers in groups, iterating through using Enterprise Manager, 249

SET options, defaults for connections, 263–264

SIDs (security identifiers)

determining for logins with T-SQL, 122

role in scripting logins, 332

Simple Recovery option in SQL Server 2000, explanation of, 52

single quotes ('), appearance in object creation application, 33–34

snapshot replication, explanation of, 281, 296

snapshot replication step within jobs, purpose of, 180

source databases, transferring with OLE, 165–168. *See also* backup entries; recovery options; restore entries

source servers, logging onto, 166. *See also* registered servers; servers

sp_help_job, contents of, 194

sp_help_job_jobschedule, explanation } of, 195

SQL Agent jobs, scripting, 333

SQL-DMO bugs and fixes, knowledge-base articles about, 371–374

SQL-DMO (Distributed Management Objects)

adding job schedules in, 232–242

adding jobs in, 229–242

auto options example, 18

Autostart Mail code, 270

backup device addition example, 54–55

benefits of, 1

checking job schedules with, 201–202

creating alerts in, 245–246

cursor options example, 19

declaring variables in, 5

determining job execution with, 202–209

discovering sysadmin passwords with, 276

files needed for, 2

fixes, 101

frequency intervals, 234

generating replication scripts with, 306–307

granting CREATE TABLE permission with, 110

indexed view creation, 40

information and how-to's, 374–375

installing merge replication with, 284–288

login addition example, 116

mail password code, 270

master database path code, 270

NT event logging code, 270

obtaining, 2

operator addition example, 184–188

password code, 270

Perfmon mode code, 270

permissions example, 105–106

purpose of, 2

recovery option settings, 14–15

registered owner code, 270

relationship addition example, 35

restoring databases with, 77–80

scripting replication with, 308

setting server-wide options with, 272–280

showing all jobs with, 197

showing commands of job steps with, 211

showing job details with, 200–201

showing job history with, 211–214

showing job steps with, 209–210

SQL error log path code, 270

SQL options example, 16

state option settings, 12

stored procedure example, 43–44

syntax advisory, 17

trigger creation example, 28–29

view creation example, 38

viewing jobs with, 196–214

Web sites, 375–376

weekday constants, 188

SQL-DMO object model, 367–369

SQL-DMO problems, knowledge-base articles about, 374

SQL-DMO scripting options, setting constants for, 329–340

SQL error log path, SQL-DMO code and description for, 270

SQL Mail password, displaying with Registry object, 278

SQL options, setting for databases, 16–17

SQL Server 2000

database settings for backups, 52–53

granting permissions through Enterprise Manager, 151–152

SQL Server 7.0, database settings for backups, 51–52

SQL Server Agent start, scheduling jobs for execution at, 236–242

SQL Server Books Online, purpose of, 3

SQL Server logins, adding with Add User application, 117

SQL Server Logins tree, displaying, 161

SQL Server Properties dialog box of Enterprise Manager. *See also* Enterprise Manager

Connections tab, 262–265, 279

Database Settings tab options, 267–270

Extras tab, 276–278

General tab options, 250–254, 273

Memory tab options, 254–256

Processor tab options, 257–259

Security tab options, 260–262

Server Settings tab options, 265–267

SQL Servers

adding logins to, 157–158

adding operators to, 181–190

connecting to when extracting server properties, 250

grabbing names of, 24

logging onto, 87

logging onto with OLE, 158

looking for, 63

querying servers for instances of, 272

scripting out configuration options for, 255

sql_message_id column of EnumJobHistory history method, datatype and description of, 213

sql_severity column of EnumJobHistory history method, datatype and description of, 213

SQLAgentLogFile property, setting, 275

Sqldmo.dll, purpose of, 2

SQLDMOPriv_CreateFunction permission, advisory about, 114

SQLDMO.User object, declaring, 129–130

SQLObjectList, looking for permissions with, 148

SQLServer 2 object, role in extracting server properties, 253

SQLServer object

    connecting to when using SQL Server 2000 scripting options, 330

    properties of, 345–346

SQLServers collection

    Configuration object, 346

    ConfigValue object, 347

    IntegratedSecurity object, 347

    SQLServer 2 object, 346

    SQLServer object, 345–346

square brackets ([]), using with e-mail addresses and operators, 184

/sserver_name argument in Scripter application, function of, 326

standard database roles

    characteristics of, 141

    creating with T-SQL, 144

state options, setting for databases, 10–12

statement permissions, purpose of, 106

STATS = [percentage] option, explanation of, 59

step_id column of EnumJobHistory history method, datatype and description of, 213

step_name column of EnumJobHistory history method, datatype and description of, 213

Steps tab of Backup Databases Properties screen in Enterprise Manager, contents of, 191

STOPAT option, restoring databases and logs with, 74

STOPATMAR/STOPBEFOREMARK option, restoring databases and logs with, 74

stored procedures

    creating, 42–44

    in OLE, 156–157

    scripting, 340

StoredProcedures collection

    StoredProcedure object, 352

    SystemDataType object, 352

subgroups in groups, iterating through using Enterprise Manager, 249

subscriber type, specifying in Enterprise Manager, 297–298

subscribers

    adding to publications in Enterprise Manager, 300–302

    displaying information about using Enterprise Manager, 293–294

    initializing in Enterprise Manager, 304

    registering when installing merge replication with SQL-DMO, 287

    role in replication, 283

subscriptions, updating information in Enterprise Manager, 303

syntax advisory, 17

sysadmin passwords, discovering with SQL-DMO, 276

sysadmin role, advisory about, 103

system tables. *See also* table entries

   querying when setting ADO Connection object properties, 342

system tables, determining for use with DBCC DBREINDEX() procedure, 177

T

T-SQL

   adding jobs in, 219–228

   adding jobs steps with, 221

   adding logins to server roles with, 128

   adding logins with, 118

   adding operators to SQL Servers with, 181–190

   adding users to roles with, 141

   auto options example, 17–18

   backing up MyDMODatabase with, 59–60

   backup device addition example, 54

   backup example, 56

   checking READ ONLY status with, 11

   CREATE DATABASE command syntax, 4–5

   creating alerts in, 244–245

   cursor options example, 19

   database restoration example, 72–73

   database roles example, 103

   Database Settings tab code, 269

   defining jobs steps with, 230

   determining maximum concurrent user connections with, 263

   determining SID of logins with, 122

   extracting Enterprise Manager server property information with, 253–254

   fixed server roles example, 101

   granting CREATE TABLE permission with, 107

   indexed view creation example, 39

   information not found in Enterprise Manager, 271

   log backups, 71–72

   operator addition example, 183

   physical table creation, 22–23

   querying Audit level with, 262

   querying Security modes with, 261

   querying Server Settings tab with, 267

   querying servers with, 252

   recovery options example, 13

   relationship addition example, 34

   removing users from databases with, 135

   removing users from roles with, 141

   retrieving configuration information with, 258–259

   scripting out SQL Server configuration options with, 255

   SQL options example, 16

   standard and application database role creation, 144

   stored procedure example, 43

   subsystems for jobs, 222

   success and failure actions for jobs, 223

   tokens for jobs, 222–223

   trigger creation example, 27–28

   using OLE in, 156–157

   view creation example, 38

   viewing jobs with, 193–196

table counters

   increasing when exporting data to text files, 176

   indicating when exporting data to text files, 174

table names

   determining when exporting data to text files, 174–175

   referencing and setting, 37

Table objects, defining in object creation application, 30

table permissions

   scripting, 339

   showing with Permissions application, 147–148

table references, finding when exporting data to text files, 175

tables. *See also* system tables

   adding relationships to, 34–37

   creating triggers for, 27–29

   denying SELECT permissions on, 112

   granting SELECT permissions on, 111

   inserting columns in, 36

   looping when exporting data to text files, 174

   reindexing indexes on, 176–178

   revoking SELECT permissions on, 112

   scripting, 337–338

Tables collection

   looking for handle when exporting data to text files, 174

   looping through, 36

   Table object, 352–353

   Table2 object, 354

tabs, creating in Enterprise Manager, 270–272

TABs versus comma-delimited files, using when exporting data to text files, 173

text files, exporting data to, 171–176

TextMatrix property, purpose in object creation application, 31

tokens for jobs in T-SQL, list of, 222–223

transaction log backups

   dynamics of, 48

   restoring databases, 75–77

   scenarios and methods, 49–50

transaction logs

   advisory about, 51

   in databases, 3

   locating, 9

transactional replication, explanation of, 180, 282, 296

TransactSQL step within jobs, purpose of, 180

Transfer objects

   creating for use with source databases, 166

   using with database scripts, 170

   using with databases and DMO, 162–165

triggers

   advisories about, 28–29

   creating for tables, 27–29

   scripting, 339

Triggers collection

   Alerts collection, 358

   JobFilter object, 358

   JobServer object, 358

   Trigger object, 357

   Trigger2 object, 357

TrueName server name, querying, 251–252

Truncate Log on Checkpoint setting in SQL Server 7.0, explanation of, 51

TRUNCATE options for log backups, explanation of, 72

trusted authentication, using with OLE, 158, 162–163

Type Mismatch error, receiving, 159

U

[/ulogin] argument in Scripter application, function of, 326

user-defined functions, scripting, 340

user membership of databases, determining, 122, 126

user permissions, changing, 148–149

UserDefinedDatatype, mapping to base datatypes, 26–27

usernames

    checking existence of, 131–132

    displaying, 134

users

    adding to and removing from database roles, 137–141

    adding to databases, 129–132

    adding to fixed server roles, 123

    adding with OLE, 157–161

    explanation of, 100

    removing from databases, 133–136

    scripting, 335

    searching when using database roles, 139

Users collection, User object in, 356

Users list box, dragging logins into, 130–131

V

[/v] argument in Scripter application, function of, 326

values for placement of files in grids, comparing in restore operations, 89

variables

    declaring, 5

    declaring in object creation application, 30

View2 objects, declaring indexed views as, 40

views

    creating, 39–42

    scripting, 340

Views collection

    adding views to, 39, 41

    View and View2 objects in, 356–357

VLDBs (very large databases), using file group backups with, 47–48

W

/wait switch, using with Scripter application and batch files, 327

while loop, using when exporting data to text files, 174

Windows Authentication

    logging into servers with, 25–26

    setting when creating database scripts, 170

    setting when exporting data to text files, 172

WITH MOVE option, equivalent of, 86

WITH SCHEMEABINDING clause, appearance in views, 41

X

XACT_ABORT configuration for connections, description of, 264

xp_regwrite, using, 274

Apress Titles

ISBN	PRICE	AUTHOR	TITLE
1-893115-73-9	$34.95	Abbott	Voice Enabling Web Applications: VoiceXML and Beyond
1-59059-061-9	$34.95	Allen	Bug Patterns in Java
1-893115-01-1	$39.95	Appleman	Dan Appleman's Win32 API Puzzle Book and Tutorial for Visual Basic Programmers
1-893115-23-2	$29.95	Appleman	How Computer Programming Works
1-893115-97-6	$39.95	Appleman	Moving to VB .NET: Strategies, Concepts, and Code
1-59059-023-6	$39.95	Baker	Adobe Acrobat 5: The Professional User's Guide
1-59059-039-2	$49.95	Barnaby	Distributed .NET Programming in C#
1-59059-068-6	$49.95	Barnaby	Distributed .NET Programming in VB .NET
1-893115-09-7	$29.95	Baum	Dave Baum's Definitive Guide to LEGO MINDSTORMS
1-893115-84-4	$29.95	Baum/Gasperi/Hempel/Villa	Extreme MINDSTORMS: An Advanced Guide to LEGO MINDSTORMS
1-893115-82-8	$59.95	Ben-Gan/Moreau	Advanced Transact-SQL for SQL Server 2000
1-893115-91-7	$39.95	Birmingham/Perry	Software Development on a Leash
1-893115-48-8	$29.95	Bischof	The .NET Languages: A Quick Translation Guide
1-59059-041-4	$49.95	Bock	CIL Programming: Under the Hood™ of .NET
1-59059-053-8	$44.95	Bock/Stromquist/Fischer/Smith	.NET Security
1-893115-67-4	$49.95	Borge	Managing Enterprise Systems with the Windows Script Host
1-59059-019-8	$49.95	Cagle	SVG Programming: The Graphical Web
1-893115-28-3	$44.95	Challa/Laksberg	Essential Guide to Managed Extensions for C++
1-893115-39-9	$44.95	Chand	A Programmer's Guide to ADO.NET in C#
1-59059-015-5	$39.95	Clark	An Introduction to Object Oriented Programming with Visual Basic .NET
1-893115-44-5	$29.95	Cook	Robot Building for Beginners
1-893115-99-2	$39.95	Cornell/Morrison	Programming VB .NET: A Guide for Experienced Programmers
1-893115-72-0	$39.95	Curtin	Developing Trust: Online Privacy and Security
1-59059-014-7	$44.95	Drol	Object-Oriented Macromedia Flash MX
1-59059-008-2	$29.95	Duncan	The Career Programmer: Guerilla Tactics for an Imperfect World
1-893115-71-2	$39.95	Ferguson	Mobile .NET
1-893115-90-9	$49.95	Finsel	The Handbook for Reluctant Database Administrators
1-893115-42-9	$44.95	Foo/Lee	XML Programming Using the Microsoft XML Parser
1-59059-024-4	$49.95	Fraser	Real World ASP.NET: Building a Content Management System
1-893115-55-0	$34.95	Frenz	Visual Basic and Visual Basic .NET for Scientists and Engineers
1-59059-038-4	$49.95	Gibbons	.NET Development for Java Programmers
1-893115-85-2	$34.95	Gilmore	A Programmer's Introduction to PHP 4.0
1-893115-36-4	$34.95	Goodwill	Apache Jakarta-Tomcat
1-893115-17-8	$59.95	Gross	A Programmer's Introduction to Windows DNA

ISBN	PRICE	AUTHOR	TITLE
1-893115-62-3	$39.95	Gunnerson	A Programmer's Introduction to C#, Second Edition
1-59059-030-9	$49.95	Habibi/Patterson/Camerlengo	The Sun Certified Java Developer Exam with J2SE 1.4
1-893115-30-5	$49.95	Harkins/Reid	SQL: Access to SQL Server
1-59059-009-0	$49.95	Harris/Macdonald	Moving to ASP.NET: Web Development with VB .NET
1-59059-006-6	$39.95	Hetland	Practical Python
1-893115-10-0	$34.95	Holub	Taming Java Threads
1-893115-04-6	$34.95	Hyman/Vaddadi	Mike and Phani's Essential C++ Techniques
1-893115-96-8	$59.95	Jorelid	J2EE FrontEnd Technologies: A Programmer's Guide to Servlets, JavaServer Pages, and Enterprise JavaBeans
1-59059-029-5	$39.99	Kampa/Bell	Unix Storage Management
1-893115-49-6	$39.95	Kilburn	Palm Programming in Basic
1-893115-50-X	$34.95	Knudsen	Wireless Java: Developing with Java 2, Micro Edition
1-893115-79-8	$49.95	Kofler	Definitive Guide to Excel VBA
1-893115-57-7	$39.95	Kofler	MySQL
1-893115-87-9	$39.95	Kurata	Doing Web Development: Client-Side Techniques
1-893115-75-5	$44.95	Kurniawan	Internet Programming with Visual Basic
1-893115-38-0	$24.95	Lafler	Power AOL: A Survival Guide
1-59059-066-X	$39.95	Lafler	Power SAS: A Survival Guide
1-893115-46-1	$36.95	Lathrop	Linux in Small Business: A Practical User's Guide
1-59059-045-7	$49.95	MacDonald	User Interfaces in C#: Windows Forms and Custom Controls
1-893115-19-4	$49.95	Macdonald	Serious ADO: Universal Data Access with Visual Basic
1-59059-044-9	$49.95	MacDonald	User Interfaces in VB .NET: Windows Forms and Custom Controls
1-893115-06-2	$39.95	Marquis/Smith	A Visual Basic 6.0 Programmer's Toolkit
1-893115-22-4	$27.95	McCarter	David McCarter's VB Tips and Techniques
1-59059-040-6	$49.99	Mitchell/Allison	Real-World SQL-DMO for SQL Server
1-59059-021-X	$34.95	Moore	Karl Moore's Visual Basic .NET: The Tutorials
1-893115-27-5	$44.95	Morrill	Tuning and Customizing a Linux System
1-893115-76-3	$49.95	Morrison	C++ For VB Programmers
1-59059-003-1	$44.95	Nakhimovsky/Meyers	XML Programming: Web Applications and Web Services with JSP and ASP
1-893115-80-1	$39.95	Newmarch	A Programmer's Guide to Jini Technology
1-893115-58-5	$49.95	Oellermann	Architecting Web Services
1-59059-020-1	$44.95	Patzer	JSP Examples and Best Practices
1-893115-81-X	$39.95	Pike	SQL Server: Common Problems, Tested Solutions
1-59059-017-1	$34.95	Rainwater	Herding Cats: A Primer for Programmers Who Lead Programmers
1-59059-025-2	$49.95	Rammer	Advanced .NET Remoting (C# Edition)
1-59059-062-7	$49.95	Rammer	Advanced .NET Remoting in VB .NET
1-59059-028-7	$39.95	Rischpater	Wireless Web Development, Second Edition
1-893115-93-3	$34.95	Rischpater	Wireless Web Development with PHP and WAP
1-893115-89-5	$59.95	Shemitz	Kylix: The Professional Developer's Guide and Reference

ISBN	PRICE	AUTHOR	TITLE
1-893115-40-2	$39.95	Sill	The qmail Handbook
1-893115-24-0	$49.95	Sinclair	From Access to SQL Server
1-59059-026-0	$49.95	Smith	Writing Add-ins for Visual Studio .NET
1-893115-94-1	$29.95	Spolsky	User Interface Design for Programmers
1-893115-53-4	$44.95	Sweeney	Visual Basic for Testers
1-59059-035-X	$59.95	Symmonds	GDI+ Programming in C# and VB .NET
1-59059-002-3	$44.95	Symmonds	Internationalization and Localization Using Microsoft .NET
1-59059-010-4	$54.95	Thomsen	Database Programming with C#
1-59059-032-5	$59.95	Thomsen	Database Programming with Visual Basic .NET, Second Edition
1-893115-65-8	$39.95	Tiffany	Pocket PC Database Development with eMbedded Visual Basic
1-59059-027-9	$59.95	Torkelson/Petersen/Torkelson	Programming the Web with Visual Basic .NET
1-59059-018-X	$34.95	Tregar	Writing Perl Modules for CPAN
1-893115-59-3	$59.95	Troelsen	C# and the .NET Platform
1-59059-011-2	$59.95	Troelsen	COM and .NET Interoperability
1-893115-26-7	$59.95	Troelsen	Visual Basic .NET and the .NET Platform: An Advanced Guide
1-893115-54-2	$49.95	Trueblood/Lovett	Data Mining and Statistical Analysis Using SQL
1-893115-68-2	$54.95	Vaughn	ADO.NET and ADO Examples and Best Practices for VB Programmers, Second Edition
1-59059-012-0	$49.95	Vaughn/Blackburn	ADO.NET Examples and Best Practices for C# Programmers
1-893115-83-6	$44.95	Wells	Code Centric: T-SQL Programming with Stored Procedures and Triggers
1-893115-95-X	$49.95	Welschenbach	Cryptography in C and C++
1-893115-05-4	$39.95	Williamson	Writing Cross-Browser Dynamic HTML
1-59059-060-0	$39.95	Wright	ADO.NET: From Novice to Pro, Visual Basic .NET Edition
1-893115-78-X	$49.95	Zukowski	Definitive Guide to Swing for Java 2, Second Edition
1-893115-92-5	$49.95	Zukowski	Java Collections
1-893115-98-4	$54.95	Zukowski	Learn Java with JBuilder 6

Available at bookstores nationwide or from Springer Verlag New York, Inc. at 1-800-777-4643; fax 1-212-533-3503. Contact us for more information at sales@apress.com.

 **books for professionals by professionals™**

About Apress

Apress, located in Berkeley, CA, is a fast-growing, innovative publishing company devoted to meeting the needs of existing and potential programming professionals. Simply put, the "A" in Apress stands for *"The Author's Press™"* and its books have *"The Expert's Voice™."* Apress' unique approach to publishing grew out of conversations between its founders Gary Cornell and Dan Appleman, authors of numerous best-selling, highly regarded books for programming professionals. In 1998 they set out to create a publishing company that emphasized quality above all else. Gary and Dan's vision has resulted in the publication of over 50 titles by leading software professionals, all of which have *The Expert's Voice™*.

Do You Have What It Takes to Write for Apress?

Apress is rapidly expanding its publishing program. If you can write and refuse to compromise on the quality of your work, if you believe in doing more than rehashing existing documentation, and if you're looking for opportunities and rewards that go far beyond those offered by traditional publishing houses, we want to hear from you!

Consider these innovations that we offer all of our authors:

- **Top royalties with *no* hidden switch statements**
  Authors typically only receive half of their normal royalty rate on foreign sales. In contrast, Apress' royalty rate remains the same for both foreign and domestic sales.

- **A mechanism for authors to obtain equity in Apress**
  Unlike the software industry, where stock options are essential to motivate and retain software professionals, the publishing industry has adhered to an outdated compensation model based on royalties alone. In the spirit of most software companies, Apress reserves a significant portion of its equity for authors.

- **Serious treatment of the technical review process**
  Each Apress book has a technical reviewing team whose remuneration depends in part on the success of the book since they too receive royalties.

Moreover, through a partnership with Springer-Verlag, New York, Inc., one of the world's major publishing houses, Apress has significant venture capital behind it. Thus, we have the resources to produce the highest quality books *and* market them aggressively.

If you fit the model of the Apress author who can write a book that gives the "professional what he or she needs to know™," then please contact one of our Editorial Directors, Dan Appleman (dan_appleman@apress.com), Gary Cornell (gary_cornell@apress.com), Jason Gilmore (jason_gilmore@apress.com), Simon Hayes (simon_hayes@apress.com), Karen Watterson (karen_watterson@apress.com), or John Zukowski (john_zukowski@apress.com) for more information.